Place and Postcolonial Ecofeminism

Expanding Frontiers:

*Interdisciplinary Approaches
to Studies of Women,
Gender, and Sexuality*

SERIES EDITORS:

Karen J. Leong

Andrea Smith

Place and Postcolonial Ecofeminism

Pakistani Women's Literary and Cinematic Fictions

SHAZIA RAHMAN

University of Nebraska Press / Lincoln

An earlier version of chapter 1 was published as "Land, Water, and Food: Eco-cosmopolitan Feminist Praxis in Sabiha Sumar's *Khamosh Pani*" in *Environmental Communication: A Journal of Nature and Culture* 5, no. 2 (June 2011): 187–201. Used with permission.

An earlier version of chapter 4 was published as "Karachi, Turtles, and the Materiality of Place: Pakistani Eco-cosmopolitanism in Uzma Aslam Khan's *Trespassing*" in *ISLE: Interdisciplinary Studies in Literature and Environment* 18, no. 2 (Spring 2011): 261–82. Used with permission of Oxford University Press.

Library of Congress Cataloging-in-Publication Data
Names: Rahman, Shazia, author.
Title: Place and postcolonial ecofeminism: Pakistani women's literary and cinematic fictions / Shazia Rahman.
Description: Lincoln: University of Nebraska Press, 2019.
| Series: Expanding frontiers | Includes bibliographical references and index.
Identifiers: LCCN 2018042177
ISBN 9781496213419 (cloth: alk. paper)
ISBN 9781496215123 (pbk.: alk. paper)
ISBN 9781496216113 (epub)
ISBN 9781496216120 (mobi)
ISBN 9781496216137 (pdf)
Subjects: LCSH: Pakistani fiction (English)—Women authors—History and criticism. | Pakistani fiction—Women authors—History and criticism. | Pakistan—In literature.
| Women in literature. | Environmentalism in literature.
| Motion pictures—Pakistan—History and criticism. |
Pakistan—In motion pictures. | Women in motion pictures.
| Environmentalism in motion pictures.
Classification: LCC PR9540.4 R34 2019 |
DDC 823/.92099287095491—dc23
LC record available at https://lccn.loc.gov/2018042177

Set in Merope by Mikala R. Kolander.

To all my sisters, especially the women in Pakistan,
for their strength and determination.

To Ammi and Abbu,
for letting me be me.

To Shiraz,
for understanding the power of story.

maiñ miṭṭī merā janam miṭṭī   میں مٹی میرا جنم مٹی
maiñ miṭṭī ko kaise chhoṚūñ?   میں مٹی کو کیسے چھوڑوں

How can I, born of the soil,
Renounce it?

FAHMIDA RIAZ

I think we learn to be worldly from grappling with, rather
than generalizing from, the ordinary. I am a creature of the
mud, not the sky.

DONNA HARAWAY

Contents

Illustrations

Acknowledgments

I began this book seven years ago in conversation with my colleagues, students, friends, and family. While it would be impossible to name all the people who have supported me along the way, I do feel it necessary to name a few people without whom this project would not have been possible. I am grateful to my colleagues at Western Illinois University (WIU): Amy Patrick Mossman for teaching me to be an ecocritic, Janice Welsch for bringing out the film critic in me, Gloria Delany-Barmann for reminding me to write in my voice, Erika Wurth for believing that I could be creative, Rebekah Buchanan for inspiring me to write for change, Mark Mossman for his unflagging encouragement, Roberta Di Carmine for listening over many dinners, David Banash for pointing out that writing is fun, Marjorie Allison for believing that my work does make a difference, Greg Baldi for his commitment to intellectual exchange in the face of electoral disaster, Alisha White and Magdelyn Helwig for giving a damn about ekphrasis, and Christopher Morrow and Jose Fernandez for reading early drafts.

I also want to recognize the help of my institution for giving me the time and space to work through sabbaticals, a summer stipend, and a research carrel in the library. WIU has been an important part of the formation of my ideas, particularly through teaching both undergraduate and graduate students. In particular, I deeply appreciate all my WIU students who pushed and prodded me into conversations that made me rethink and reconsider. I especially want to thank the graduate students who worked with me in seminars while I wrote this book: Nicole Hagstrom-Schmidt, Rayvon Shelton, Ashley Jones, Brandon Mooney, Abby Tichler, Elena Moran-Cortes, Sheldon Gaskell, Klaira Strickland, Felicia Appell, Micah Joel Tuhy, Laura Winton, and Dan Holst. None of what we do would be possible without the teaching that grounds us.

I thank my friends: anupama jain for our phone calls filled with long analyses of injustice, Penelope Kelsey for believing I could write a book, Bradley Dilger for his direct and blunt style of guidance, Pallavi Rastogi for her crucial feedback on the final manuscript, Asad Ali Ahmed for seeing my work as "new," Salma Monani for first sowing the seeds of what became this book, Mushtaque Silat for his love of Urdu, and Anu Taranath for inspiring me with her great desire to think and travel ethically. When I met Joni Adamson on a whale-watching trip, I had no idea how much I would grow to appreciate her as a friend and mentor, as someone who was there for me during a very difficult time. Thanks, Joni, for your compassion, your guidance, and your advice on this book and on life.

I am grateful to Paul Lindholdt and Tom Lynch for leading the bioregionalism preconference seminar at the Association for the Study of Literature and Environment conference in 2015. The conversations we had there were key to my work, especially in the second chapter. This book, as a whole, is much better than it otherwise would be because of Vicki Chamlee, who truly freshened up my prose and asked all the right questions. At the University of Nebraska Press, I am grateful for the encouragement of Alicia Christensen, Tish Fobben, Annie Shahan, Sara Springsteen, and Abby Stryker; all shepherded me and my work through an unfamiliar process. Many thanks go to the anonymous reviewers who improved my work with their invaluable comments, important questions, and insightful suggestions. Any omissions or mistakes in this book are all mine.

Finally, I'd like to thank my entire family for their love. I especially thank my late father for patiently instilling in me the desire to learn, my mother for teaching me to be a feminist above and before all else, my sister for her fierce love and devotion, and my late great uncle Zahir Butt for imparting to me an enduring love of literature. The greatest thanks, however, goes to Rizwan Hamid, who believes in my profession, moved across the continent, and reinvented his own job so that I could pursue the career I love. Thank you, Rizwan, for enriching my life every day through chai and meals, travel and staycations, words and deeds.

Place and Postcolonial Ecofeminism

Introduction

The Place That Is Pakistan

I miss everything about Pakistan . . . from the rivers, the mountains, to even the dirty streets and the garbage outside our house.
MALALA YOUSAFZAI

While postcolonial theories have altered the broader intellectual landscape of literary and cultural studies for the better, postcolonial theories of nation, cosmopolitanism, and globalization have thus far been unable to fill all the gaps in providing a theoretical framework for the many quandaries and contradictions of present-day Pakistan. Take Malala Yousafzai, for instance. Shot by the Taliban in 2012 for speaking out against them, she survives in the United Kingdom and won a Nobel Peace Prize for her tireless work advocating for girls' education. But her tearful return to Pakistan in 2018, her first visit since the attack, was met with equal parts welcome and suspicion. As literary critic Shazia Sadaf (2017, 864) states, "Women are scapegoats in Pakistan's uneasy position as a U.S. ally in waging a war within its own boundaries, caught between global (liberal) and national (religious) interests. Due to the complexity of Pakistan's political situation, any external criticism of its patriarchal structures only results in extremism as a counter measure." No matter how much Malala states her sense of belonging to the land of Swat Valley in Pakistan, many see her as a representative of U.S. imperialism in the area, not as a woman who belongs but as an outsider. Sadaf (2017) highlights this aspect of her reception: "Irrespective of Malala's words, the general view in Pakistan is that Malala has not only given the United States a moral framework for bombing their perceived enemies, but has also provided a political justification of revenge" (866). Without the benefit of an environmental framework, postcolonial studies can only lay out this quandary that Malala's reception in Pakistan symbolizes: Religious nationalists see these global, liberal discourses as imperialist.

Perhaps this is part of the reason for the paucity of research on Pakistan in literary studies. A Modern Language Association database search for peer-reviewed sources on June 1, 2018, for the subjects "Pakistan" and "postcolonial" reveals only twenty-three essays and no books. "Pakistan" with "feminism" reveals only six essays, and "Pakistan" with "ecocriticism" or "environmental justice" or even "ecofeminism" renders no entries at all. In *Place and Postcolonial Ecofeminism*, I argue that ecofeminist theories must be combined with Pakistani postcolonial studies to excavate and explore the idea of belonging. The example of Malala portrays how Pakistani intellectuals feel about being caught between Pakistani religious nationalism and U.S. imperialism. How can they think about belonging given that these frameworks seem to be their only choices? The films and novels released in the 2000s that I discuss here suggest provocative answers for both postcolonial literary scholars and film scholars working on Pakistan who are interested in exploring different types of attachment to place, attachments that are aligned with the land, with the ocean, and with the nonhuman.[1] In this book, I analyze Pakistani women's novels and films ecocritically to shift the conversation about social and gender inequality toward anthropogenic environmental change.[2] This lens brings a new understanding of Pakistan that counters the idea of religion as the only, or at least the most important, way of belonging in Pakistan.[3]

That postcolonial studies of Pakistani literature often eschew environmental frameworks is not surprising given the state of South Asian studies in general. At a recent annual conference on South Asia in Madison, Wisconsin, where scholars from across the humanities and social sciences came together because of their overlapping interest in the various regions of South Asia, I was surprised to find that while social inequalities were discussed on many of the panels, environmental problems were explored in far fewer forums. As a scholar of the environmental humanities who believes that "to create a truly sustainable future, we must think about social inequalities as much as we think about environmental problems, and we must understand their interrelations" (Sturgeon 2009, 5), I was disappointed.[4] Interdisciplinary analytical work on social and environmental justice is sorely needed given the increasingly stark ecological risks faced by many, especially the most vulnerable—nonhuman animals, women, children, and minorities—in South Asia and around the world. In my previous works and in this book, I aim to redirect current scholarship on Pakistani women's literary and cinematic fictions through the lens of postcolonial ecofeminism and emerging insights from the environmental humanities.[5] When we foreground place and the environment in Pakistani women's texts, we find alternate discourses of belonging to the land that resist patriarchal religious nationalism.[6] Thus, my book, *Place and Postcolonial Ecofeminism*, challenges stereotypes of Pakistan as an Islamic fundamentalist state and of Pakistani women as mere victims of a patriarchal society.

Postcolonial theories that do not take ecofeminist analyses into consideration have not been as useful in discussions of Pakistan partly because metropolitan theory does not represent what scholars in area studies describe in the global south (Cheah 2008). And what Asian studies scholars do, according to postcolonial critic Pheng Cheah (2008, 59), is merely "information retrieval and not theoretical reflection and speculation that pertain to the whole of humanity." Another part of the problem is that Pakistan studies as a discipline has been distorted in Pakistani school textbooks for so long that vibrant and healthy educational institutions supporting scholarship and creativity in the field of Pakistan studies have not had a chance to develop in large numbers (Hoodbhoy and Nayyar 1985; Jalal 1995a; I. Ahmad 2004; Zaidi 2011). Reviewing the trajectory of postcolonial studies since the 1990s, some of the most important and fruitful recent work has occurred with the renewed interest in cosmopolitanism (Cheah and Robbins 1998; Breckenridge et al. 2002; Krishnaswamy and Hawley 2008; Go 2013) because we must, in the words of Cheah (2008, 65), "treat [the] experiences [of Asians] as universalizable, shareable with everyone else—in a word, as translatable." However, for the purposes of theorizing about Pakistan and, specifically, the problems of Pakistani intellectuals in dealing with non-nationalist attachments to place, we must employ ecocriticism so that we can study the relationship between literature and the environment.[7] And since ecocritics should not lose sight of gender discrimination, postcolonial ecofeminism should be the future of Pakistani literary studies.

Pakistani women's attachment to their environment and their environmental concerns and issues are often ignored because patriarchal discourses about Islam and religion are dominant in multiple realms. This dominance undercuts women's important relationships to land and food, hiding the fact that women are still the most concerned and most likely to act when faced with food and water insecurity. According to Climate Asia's report on Pakistan, even in the face of "limited decision-making power ... [which] constrains women's ability to act ..., they tend to respond more actively than men to lack of food and water" (Zaheer and Colom 2013, 4).[8] This is the case not only in Pakistan but also throughout South Asia more generally, where despite having limited land ownership, poor rural women put obtaining food for the family before anything else.[9] As a result, South Asian women tend to have greater knowledge of land, agriculture, and plant life and, according to economist Bina Agarwal (2002, 6), are "better informed than men about traditional seed varieties and the attributes of trees and grasses." Agarwal adds that if women "had greater control over land and farming, this knowledge could be put to better use" and benefit many more people (6).

Unfortunately, according to development consultant Nira Ramachandran (2007), women in Pakistan are even less likely to have their voices about their environment heard because they rarely own and control land. "Discriminatory patterns of land ownership extend right across the South Asian region. Pakistan and North West India are characterized by the severest gender-based inequities" (224). Inequities in land ownership are not only gender based but also part of a long history that has led to the consolidation of both economic and political power in the hands of landowners in Pakistan. Sociologist Hassan Javid (2011) writes that this history in Punjab reaches back to Mughal times: "Like the Mughals and Sikhs before them, the British administration relied upon the services of a chain of landholding intermediaries. Once implicated in the exercise of colonial governance, the different fractions of the landowning class benefitted tremendously from their association with the British. In turn, they provided the colonial government with recruits, revenue, and stability, using their position within kinship net-works, village-level informal institutions, and the state, to ensure the maintenance of order in the countryside" (353–54). Landownership laws in contemporary Pakistan continue to benefit the landed aristocracy not only economically but also politically because "whichever party came to power even in later elections, they always secured a sizeable number of seats" (Khurshid 1994, 55).

In the context of Pakistan, while landownership laws are advan-tageous to the most powerful, who are usually not women, we can-not ignore that climate change affects some places and people more than others. For instance, "less developed countries are generally more affected than industrialised countries" (Kreft, Eckstein, and Melchior 2016, 2). If we look at Pakistan in particular, according to the global "Human Development Report" by the United Nations Development Programme (UNDP 2015, 210), Pakistan ranks 147 out of 188 countries.[10] This has a direct effect on Pakistan's capacity to adequately address climate change. According to the University of Notre Dame's Global Adaptation Index (ND-GAIN 2018), Pakistan has a high score for vulner-ability to climate change and a low score for readiness.[11] Global social inequalities translate into different environmental issues in different parts of the world. Environmental justice is inextricably bound to social justice everywhere but especially in places such as Pakistan, where the effects of climate change are compounded by issues of patriarchy and the landowning class structure.

In an attempt to address many of these issues, *Place and Postcolonial Ecofeminism* expands and enriches the fast-emerging methodologi-cal field of environmental humanities through an analysis of Sabiha Sumar's film *Khamosh Pani* (2003), Mehreen Jabbar's film *Ramchand Pakistani* (2008), Sorayya Khan's novel *Noor* (2006), Uzma Aslam Khan's novel *Trespassing* (2003), and Kamila Shamsie's novel *Burnt Shadows* (2009). I provide a nuanced understanding of Pakistani women's lives, particularly in terms of how they engage with the land and their envi-ronment, and demonstrate the ways in which these women explore alternative, environmental ways of belonging that counter dominant discourses of religious nationalism and global Islam. I also offer a cri-tique of nationalism by documenting place-based identities and take seriously the well-being of the nonhuman environment and the animals of Pakistan. By addressing place-based identities as a vital concept in Pakistani culture, my book contributes to evolving understandings of Pakistani women in specific relation to their environment and to various discourses of nation and patriarchy. I agree with geographers Dianne Rocheleau and Padini Nirmal (2016) that even though culture was once understood as separate from nature, it is now no longer the case partly because of the important work of postcolonial feminists. "The decolonial turn validates both the precolonial existence of multiple nature-cultures and the possibilities that particular existing nature-cultures provide for decolonization. Building on these decolonial visions, we see culture as the habit-forming practices and politics of connection and disconnection that shape, and are shaped by, the dynamic experiences of being-in-relation-in-the-world(s)" (55). My reference to Pakistani culture, therefore, also includes these ever-changing nature-cultures.

Any attempt to theorize the quandaries Pakistanis face must be grounded in the intersections of a geographical and ecological frame as it meets with theories of postcolonial feminism. For instance, to date, scholarship on the war of 1971 briefly mentions the Bhola cyclone of 1970 but does not address its effects on the land and the people. However, the novel *Noor*, which I discuss in chapter 3, "Bengal: Vernacular Landscape," forces readers to ponder the combined effects of the cyclone, the war, the genocide, and the rapes. My reading of that time and place contributes to both Pakistan studies and ecocriticism, bridging a prominent gap. Similarly, literary critics Ananya Jahanara Kabir (2011) and Aroosa Kanwal (2015) use postcolonial criticism to analyze another novel titled *Trespassing* (2003), which I discuss in chapter 4, "Karachi: Pakistani Eco-cosmopolitanism." However, neither scholar uses ecocriticism in her readings even though the larger themes of the novel are environmental and linked to nonhuman animals.[12] Theorizing about Pakistanis' attachment to their ecosystem—the land, the sea, the plants, and the animals—is crucial. The postcolonial ecofeminism discussed in my book is an important answer to the dilemma of Pakistani intellectuals; instead of embracing religious nationalism or siding with U.S. imperialism, this scholarship emphasizes embracing our ecosystem and all the creatures in it while simultaneously resisting patriarchy.

Therefore, going forward, postcolonial theorists must wrestle with the contradictions of globalization, patriarchy, and environmental degradation in the context of countries such as Pakistan if postcolonial theory is to remain a relevant reading strategy. To this end, my book addresses a gap in postcolonial Pakistani literary studies that has not adequately considered environmentalism or ecofeminism. Ecocritical and ecofeminist analyses need to become much more widespread reading strategies than they are now. Similarly, very few environmental humanists have considered women in a global south, Muslim-majority country such as Pakistan. This book aims to help fill this gap.

Women between Nation and Religion

In the context of a Muslim homeland, critical work on Pakistan in the disciplines of political science, history, or sociology often emphasizes the creation of Pakistan as a Muslim state. These studies show how Islam, as a discourse, has shaped the nation, as in political scientist Farzana Shaikh's *Making Sense of Pakistan* (2009) and historian Faisal Devji's *Muslim Zion: Pakistan as a Political Idea* (2013). Others, especially leftists, focus on the economic realities of people's lives. Works such as historian Ayesha Jalal's *The Struggle for Pakistan: A Muslim Homeland and Global Politics* (2014) emphasize material realities rather than religion as the reason for the nation's creation, while other studies, such as sociologist Saadia Toor's *The State of Islam: Culture and Cold War Politics in Pakistan* (2011), illustrate the ways in which religious nationalism has decimated socialist politics in Pakistan. In all of these works, people's sense of belonging is documented in a nationalist ideology that is limited by its disregard for the physical setting or environment of that place. While Devji and Shaikh focus on religion, Jalal and Toor concentrate on economics to explain the nation, its birth, and how it functions, but none of them draw attention to the landscapes, seascapes, and nonhuman animals of Pakistan. Even most film criticism of Pakistani cinema likewise overlooks the importance of the films' physical settings.[13]

In the fourth chapter of her book *Partition's Post-Amnesias* (2013), literary critic Ananya Jahanara Kabir does provide an alternate reading of Pakistan. Kabir argues "that post-amnesia's impact on contemporary

Pakistan can be seen in the attempts, by a range of cultural producers, to extract a national narrative from Pakistan's pre-Islamic past, particularly through the evidence of archaeology, geology, and palaeontology" (31). Kabir's book is an important beginning to an alternate vision of the history and geography of the place that is Pakistan within the larger region of South Asia. My work too is rooted in an alternative vision within women's texts that intersects with their ideas of belonging. While both Kabir and I resist the dominant nationalist discourse about Pakistan, my book focuses less on postcolonial concerns and more on providing an alternate vision via ecofeminist critical frameworks, which Kabir eschews.

Pakistan's unique history as a country made for members of a religion often means that affiliations based on religion are strong, especially in the dominant discourse of nationalist rhetoric. However, a sense of belonging to the place supersedes the singular Muslim identity that is dominant in Pakistan because the place precedes the nation. Nationalism is a relatively recent phenomenon compared with the ways in which people feel a sense of belonging to their villages, their towns, or their bioregions.[14] Consequently, an ongoing relationship exists between place and nation—a relationship I explore in my discussions about Punjab, Thar, Bengal, and Karachi, as well as, finally, about displacement itself. The 1947 partition of British India and the birth of Pakistan created one engagement with place and Pakistan. Here, the older sense of belonging to the place was uprooted by a sense of belonging to the nation. Similarly, the 1971 partition of Pakistan and the birth of Bangladesh created another engagement with place and Pakistan.

Women have been the central sites where the question of place and Pakistan has been explored. Nationhood, and the borders it has drawn, has been explored in partition studies in relation to women and, specifically, women's bodies, which have suffered the worst consequences of mass rape and death. Regarding the groundbreaking work of Ritu Menon and Kamla Bhasin (1998) and Urvashi Butalia (2000) on how the 1947 partition affected women, journalist Rita Manchanda (2001, 29) writes, "Their analysis of the nationalist obsession with the recovery of the abducted women explores the politics of their bodies becoming subjugated territory across which national and community boundaries were marked." South Asian feminists have argued that new nations have been mapped on the bodies of women. After and during the rule of Gen. Muhammad Zia-ul-Haq (1977–88), feminist scholarly work on Pakistan either emphasizes and pursues women's formal equality under the law within a nation-state framework or considers the mobilization of Pakistani women by the religious right. Again, most feminist work views women through the lens of nation or religion or both. By focusing on Pakistani women's cinematic and literary fictions in terms of their engagements with the more-than-human environment, I build on this feminist line of inquiry and take it further via theories of ecocriticism.[15] Rather than analyzing Pakistan through a religious and nationalist framework, this research shifts the center of analysis to the place that is Pakistan instead. This place is one that includes landscapes cut by man-made borders and seascapes where humans and nonhumans struggle to survive.

The Muslim nationalism of Pakistan is cosmopolitan not only because the nation was created as a homeland for South Asia's Muslims of all ethnicities but also because the Muslim fundamentalism that has become increasingly widespread in Pakistan now operates globally. In his book *Globalised Islam*, political scientist Olivier Roy (2004, 65) finds that "in the cases of Pakistan and Saudi Arabia, Islamo-nationalism seems to have been superseded by radical Islamic transnationalism." While I find Roy's idea of radical Islamic transnationalism, or globalized Islam, to be inherently cosmopolitan, philosopher Kwame Anthony Appiah (2006) opposes that view. Appiah has declared that "global Muslim fundamentalists" are counter-cosmopolitans because they are not tolerant of the beliefs of non-Muslims (138). While this is true, and this movement's effects on Pakistan, through its influence on various governments, have been deleterious, Appiah's argument is unconvincing. Global Islam is open to people of all ethnicities around the world, and sorting the tolerant from the intolerant does not negate the notion of cosmopolitanism. The suppression of women and minorities in Pakistan due to this transnational movement is an example of negative cosmopolitanism, but it is cosmopolitanism nonetheless.

Roy's distinction between Islamo-nationalism and Islamic transnationalism helps to elucidate the workings of these movements in many countries. He finds that outside Pakistan and Saudi Arabia, almost all Muslim-majority countries have become more nationalist. Islamo-nationalism pays lip service to religion, but ultimately politics leads to negotiations and compromises between secular members of a nation-state and Islamist political movements. All of this political participation eventually leads to greater democracy except in Pakistan because, according to Roy (2004, 66), Pakistan (and Saudi Arabia) tries "to bypass a lack of national identity and roots by pretending to herald a transnational Muslim identity." Roy's use of the word "pretend" points to the fact that he considers a transnational Muslim identity an illusion. If so, then it is a powerfully dominant one, especially in terms of its effects on Pakistani women and minorities.

Roy describes Pakistan as a country whose lack of nationalism is a key weakness, and Farzana Shaikh (2009) also views Pakistanis as increasingly denationalized.[16] Even Faisal Devji (2013, 9) insists that Muslim nationalism excludes the local: "What concerns me especially is the abstract idea at the heart of Muslim nationalism, one created by the forcible exclusion of blood and soil in the making of a new homeland." According to Devji, this exclusion leads to a challenge to nationalism: "And so the task I have set myself is to describe the religious state . . . as one that challenges nationalism itself, if only by questioning its attachment to the territory that makes a common history and culture possible" (16). Thus, Roy, Devji, and Shaikh find that Pakistan is negatively cosmopolitan—meaning not nationalist enough—and Shaikh finds two types of cosmopolitanism: one looking toward India and the other looking toward Arab Muslims for identification. Roy, Devji, and Shaikh rightly claim that the dominant sense of identity—what I call cosmopolitan global Islam—is overpowering the national identity, which I consider to be patriarchal.[17] However, the dominance of this global Muslim identity over a nationalist identity does not mean that a third, place-based identity no longer influences Pakistani feminists' sense of belonging. In fact, finding and documenting such place-based discourses are the most important steps toward political environmentalism. Moreover, since cosmopolitanism is not place based, in this book I discuss eco-cosmopolitanism to ground the theory in the environment within the larger framework of postcolonial ecofeminism.[18]

While some would argue that Pakistan was created for Islam, Ayesha Jalal (2014, 40) argues that the "historical evidence militates against such certitude. The demand for Pakistan was intended to get an equitable, if not equal, share of power for Indian Muslims in an independent India." According to Jalal, Pakistan was not intended as an idyllic, separate nation-state; it was simply the result of a demand for power sharing within India. In keeping with Jalal, Saadia Toor (2011) argues that the history of leftist activism and literary production in Pakistan shows that from the birth of the nation onward, Pakistan's radical intellectuals were trying to provide a counter-discourse to the establishment's overreliance on Islam to define a Pakistani national identity.[19] While Farzana Shaikh's and Faisal Devji's arguments about Pakistan may be overly reliant on Islam in terms of defining Pakistani identity, Saadia Toor's book emphasizes the efforts of leftists to counter Islamist ideology and use regional ethnic and linguistic cultures to create an alternate definition of belonging to the nation.

Even though the work of Toor and Jalal is more materialist than that of Shaikh and Devji, all of these scholars who work on Pakistan do so within a nationalist ideology or nation-state framework. Since my work is about the place that is Pakistan, I cannot explore belonging by engaging with the nationalist project as an analytical object for two reasons. First, nationalist projects in South Asia have led to multiple partitions that have created national identities that conflict with the place-based identities I am interested in documenting. Moreover, nationalist projects treat place in terms of the nation's territorial borders, while I consider places such as Punjab and Thar that extend beyond the borders of the nation. I completely agree with historian Vazira Zamindar (2007, 239), who writes, "Nation-state bound histories not only naturalize the nation, but also naturalize national difference. . . . It is the categorical order of the nation that produces 'stateless Indian-Pakistanis,' and at the same time renders invisible other forms of belonging." Since my purpose is to make visible other place-based forms of belonging, my critical framework cannot be bound to the nation-state.

Nonetheless, even though my work privileges place, noting the effects on women of navigating both the nation and religion is important. As feminist sociologist Shahnaz Khan (2006, 7) points out in her book *Zina*,

Transnational Feminism, and the Moral Regulation of Pakistani Women, the military regime of General Zia enacted the Hudood Ordinances, which includes the Zina Ordinance, in 1979 as part of Islamizing Pakistan. As a result, "for the first time in Pakistan's history, fornication and adultery became a crime against the state as opposed to individual husbands, fathers, or other men" (S. Khan 2006, 8). Pakistani feminists' work, especially during this era and after it, has focused on the effects of this law within a religious and nationalist framework. Later scholars, such as feminist sociologist Amina Jamal (2005), emphasize the success of religion in mobilizing women in Pakistan for the religious right. She concludes, "The task for feminism is to convince ordinary Muslim women why feminist modernity may offer more satisfying modes of being women than the modernist reworking of Muslim womanhood by Islamists" (118). While Shahnaz Khan engages and privileges the nation-state and law in her analysis, Amina Jamal privileges religion and politics. In contrast, my work privileges place over nation and religion to help fill in important gaps in the scholarship.

Postcolonial Ecofeminism

Our capitalist economic model oppresses the environment, nonhuman life, and human life, especially women, globally. European colonialism went hand in hand with capitalism, as both came out of the Industrial Revolution, exploiting people and nature alike. Thus, the driving motor of my book is postcolonial ecofeminism. I completely agree with the editors of *Global Ecologies and the Environmental Humanities: Postcolonial Approaches* when they state, "The history of European empire constructed a gendered and racial hierarchy of embodied and disembodied subjects along the lines of nature/culture that relegated women, the indigenous, non-Europeans, and the poor to an objectified figure of nature as much as the white propertied heterosexual male was tied to rationality, subjectivity, and culture" (DeLoughrey, Didur, and Carrigan 2015, 11). Since the empire has had a hand in oppressing the poor, sexual and gender minorities, nonwhite people, women, other species, and the environment, postcolonial theory, ecocriticism, and feminism are each equally important to my project despite the fact that ecocritics and feminists have had disputes. Nonetheless, bringing feminist ecocriticism together with postcolonial theory provides a compelling framework for thinking about the place onto which Pakistan is mapped.

Many ecocritical theoretical frameworks came from feminists who refused to separate these linking strands of oppression; however, ecocriticism and feminism have not always coexisted in harmony. Ecofeminist Greta Gaard (2010) argues that ecocriticism's feminist roots are being ignored in recent introductions to the discipline.[20] Part of the problem for ecofeminist visibility in the larger field of ecocriticism and even feminism itself is the widespread idea that ecofeminist critical frameworks are always essentialist because in linking oppression of women with oppression of nature, ecofeminists disregard the heterogeneity of both women and nature. However, this is not always the case. Feminist theorists Stacy Alaimo and Susan Hekman (2008, 4) argue that mainstream feminism has also ignored ecofeminism: "The mainstream of feminist theory . . . has, more often than not, relegated ecofeminism to the backwoods, fearing that any alliance between feminism and environmentalism could only be founded upon a naïve, romantic account of reality." Of course, this is not a foregone conclusion, and Alaimo and Hekman are quick to insist "the more feminist theories distance themselves from 'nature,' the more that very 'nature' is implicitly or explicitly reconfirmed as the treacherous quicksand of misogyny" (4). The binary between nature and culture is oppressive to both women and nature.

Feminist ecocritic Noël Sturgeon (2009) explains that ecofeminism includes the diverse interests of both academics and activists. She writes,

Basically, ecofeminism claims that the oppression, inequality, and exploitation of certain groups (people of color, women, poor people, LGBT [lesbian, gay, bisexual, and transgender] people, Global South people, animals) are theoretically and structurally related to the degradation and overexploitation of the environment. . . . If nature is devalued, so are women, people of color, animals and so forth. Women and nature are also seen as structurally and materially intertwined, as women do most of the domestic work and agricultural work in the world, putting them in integral relation with environmental questions of health, food safety, and water quality. Because most of the world's environmental activists are women, examples of ecofeminist activism abound, although sometimes the label of "ecofeminism" is not one the activists themselves would choose. (9)

Sturgeon shows that ecofeminist critical frameworks for academics and activists are multiple and diverse. In Pakistan, as elsewhere, women and the environment are oppressed in similar ways due to similar structures; however, the charge of essentialism certainly cannot be leveled against *all* feminist ecocritical work given how diverse it is. Moreover, in terms of discourse, according to Alaimo and Hekman (2008, 4–5), this work is crucial to rethink nature itself: "Nature can no longer be imagined as a pliable resource for industrial production or social construction." Rather than homogenize and essentialize, ecofeminism can and does work at the level of discourse and activism to help us reconceptualize our relation to nature.

The history of ecofeminists being accused of essentialism might explain why its scholars do not receive due credit, despite their role in creating one of the earliest fields that merged feminist and environmental theory. Moreover, ecocritics with a feminist agenda often rename their research to distance themselves from ecofeminism. According to literary ecocritic Serpil Oppermann (2013, 23), "Because of the unease about the usage of the name ecofeminism for its alleged essentialist transgressions that have foreclosed its path, many former ecofeminists have disavowed any debt or allegiance to ecofeminism and moved their gendered focus to new discursive areas of feminist research without abandoning their commitment to ending gender oppression and environmental degradation." Ecofeminist work has been published since 1975 (Kolodny) but continues to be published under other names, such as feminist ecocriticism (Gaard 2010) and material feminisms (Alaimo and Hekman 2008). My ecocritical study of women's literary and cinematic fictions that emphasize the plight of women (chapters 1 and 3), land and water (chapters 1 and 4), animals (chapters 4 and 5), and farmers (chapter 2) has been guided by ecofeminism at every step because of the way in which I discuss women's relationship to their environment and to nonhuman animals.

My focus on the formerly colonized country of Pakistan, discussing the borders drawn by the British (chapters 1 and 2), reflects my equal debt to postcolonial theory, which has influenced the rhetoric of environmental justice.[21] According to Erika Cudworth (2005, 34), environmental justice and liberation ecology movements both emerged from the global south: "It is within academic debate and political activism around 'development' that liberation ecologism has emerged, and its insights have been applied more broadly in the political language of 'environmental justice.' Liberation ecologism suggests that struggles for intra-human justice are closely bound with those to prevent environmental exploitation. In theoretical terms, it brings the conceptual apparatus of postcolonialism to bear on debates around social difference and human-environment relations."

International feminist ecocriticism also incorporates postcolonial critical frameworks. As literary ecocritic Chiyo Crawford (2013, 88) writes, "The issue of colonialism . . . is arguably *the* central ecological and social problem for indigenous women around the globe" (italics in original). As a postcolonial scholar, I frame my ecofeminist work through British India's decolonization and the international borders that were drawn around and between independent Pakistan and India in 1947, including how those borders continue to have material effects on the lives of its people. Chapters 1 and 2 on Punjab and Thar, respectively, both discuss the material effects of Pakistan's eastern border with India on women.

Within the larger framework of postcolonial ecofeminism, which drives all of my analyses, chapter 1, "Punjab: Eco-cosmopolitan Feminism," and chapter 4 are indebted to eco-cosmopolitanism because they focus on issues of globalization such as the global economy and imperialism. Chapter 3 explores the idea of vernacular and official landscapes in my discussion of the historical circumstances of war and genocide.[22] While chapter 5, "Displacement: Animalization," is concerned with the animalization that comes from racism, chapter 2, "Thar: Bioregionalism," focuses on the bioregion of a desert. When I use each of these environmental studies' methods—eco-cosmopolitanism, bioregionalism, vernacular landscapes, and animal studies—I reframe them through postcolonial ecofeminism. As such, I bring a postcolonial and feminist lens to environmental studies.

Reading Fictions

I use the plural "fictions" to describe my primary sources, both the novels and the feature films, because I want to emphasize that the feature films I discuss are not documentaries but fictions, as are the novels. When I talk about the work of fictions, I refer to both feature films and novels because nonfiction books and documentary films are not imaginative in the way these fictions are. Rather than represent only what *is*, fictions represent what *can be*. Through fictions, women can represent both what is and what could be, the dangerous possibilities and the ideal. Fictions allow us to imagine suffering as well as joy. They help us feel empathy for others and imagine better ways to live and seek justice.

The way we read fictions also matters. Usually, we attend to a central theme, which is often one the author intends to showcase. If the author or film director is not an environmentalist, then we rarely emphasize the environment in our readings of their fictions. This is why I am calling for a change in reading practice. As ecocritics, we must attend to the environment in our readings regardless of the perceived environmentalism of the writers and filmmakers we study. Even though the fictions discussed here, both cinematic and literary, are not overtly environmental and activist, an ecocritical lens brings to light new readings that draw attention to environmental ways of belonging in Pakistan. To foreground the environment, this book delves expansively and against the grain of the featured authors and filmmakers. While this reading may seem counterintuitive to those who work in fields outside the humanities, I agree with literary ecocritic Robert Kern (2003, 260):

> Although it is clear that some texts are more . . . environmental than others . . . ecocriticism becomes most interesting and useful, it seems to me, when it aims to recover the environmental character or orientation of works whose conscious or foregrounded interests lie elsewhere. One object of ecocriticism, as I see it, is to read in such a way as to amplify the reality of the environment in or of a text, even if in doing so we resist the tendency of the text itself (or of our own conditioning as readers) to relegate the environment to the status of setting.

In keeping with Kern, this book coalesces postcolonial ecofeminist critical frameworks by amalgamating them to discover new and useful ways to amplify issues of social and environmental justice in the fictions of Pakistani women. Nationalist and religious identifications often overshadow Pakistani ideas of belonging, including in women's fictions, but reading through place-based identities makes it possible to critique nationalism and emphasize the nonhuman environment and animals of Pakistan. By reading Pakistani women's literary and cinematic fictions through postcolonial ecofeminist critical frameworks, we thus increase our awareness of social and environmental injustice.

This book includes synthesized analyses of different types of cultural texts; interrogations of relevant feminist, ecocritical, and postcolonial theories of belonging; and engagements with key moments in Pakistani history in terms of attachments to place. While chapters 1–4 emphasize local places with research on Punjab, Thar, Bengal, and Karachi, chapter 5 highlights global displacement with an analysis of two different types of animalization: one violent and the other nonviolent. The book transitions from local to national to global, combining ecocriticism with postcolonial and feminist theories of social justice.

Within the larger framework of postcolonial ecofeminism, the span of chapters 1 and 4 moves from a local feminist eco-cosmopolitanism to an alternative Pakistani eco-cosmopolitanism that makes geographical connections across the land and sea of present-day Pakistan through attachments to its nonhuman animals. Chapters 2 and 3 augment postcolonial ecofeminist analysis with bioregionalism and vernacular landscapes, respectively, because Thar is a desert and Bengal was a province that was exploited by its own official government. Chapter 5 examines what happens in the context of forced migrations due to war, violence, and imperialism. Here postcolonial ecofeminism must include the work of scholars of animal studies because postcolonial racism is depicted as animalization.

Chapter 1, "Punjab: Eco-cosmopolitan Feminism," addresses the 1947 partition of British India and its continuing consequences for women in Punjab via Zia-era Islamization policies. Punjab was a province of British India that was divided during the 1947 partition and simultaneous independence of the new nation-states of Pakistan and India.[23] The chapter addresses the violence against women in South Asia in terms of the environment by showing how Sabiha Sumar's film *Khamosh Pani* (2003) resists both religious nationalism and global capitalism. To discuss the global dimensions of these movements, I draw on and extend the work of literary ecocritic Ursula Heise (2008) to formulate a *feminist eco-cosmopolitanism* to analyze the film and ground it in a materiality of place signified by land, water, and food.[24] The chapter argues that violence against women results in violence toward the environment: When male family members forced women to commit suicide by jumping in their villages' wells to avoid rape, they simultaneously poisoned the well water as the men migrated across the border. While the term "honor killing" was not used in 1947 to describe such murders, they were inspired by a sense of "honor" nonetheless. Sumar's feminist film shows both Muslim and Sikh men behaving violently toward women during partition and emphasizes that such brutality was also violence against the waters of the Punjab.

Chapter 2, "Thar: Bioregionalism," builds on and extends border theory to provide the environmental specificity to focus on people—particularly, Hindu Dalits—who belong to the bioregion of the Thar Desert and struggle to eke out a living as farmers. The chapter's analysis of Mehreen Jabbar's film *Ramchand Pakistani* (2008) reveals that, in the Thar Desert, the concepts of place, belonging, and agrarianism must take into account the forces of desertification that are correlated with oppressive labor conditions and cannot be separated from the negative effects of caste discrimination and religious nationalism.[25] The film exposes the effects of these forces on one Pakistani Hindu Dalit woman and her son, rendering visible their plight in the desert borderlands.

Chapter 3, "Bengal: Vernacular Landscape," considers the 1970 floods and Bhola cyclone together with the 1971 genocide and rapes in East Pakistan that led to the partition of Pakistan and the independence of Bangladesh. In particular, I use Joni Adamson's (2001, 90) definitions of these two keywords: The "vernacular landscape is a folk landscape," while an "official landscape . . . is an extraction-oriented landscape, imposed by government." Using descriptions of landscape art, or ekphrasis, in Sorayya Khan's novel *Noor* (2006), the chapter examines West Pakistan's atrocities and the way in which they imposed their own official landscape on the Bengali people and disregarded their vernacular relation to their own land. Ananya Jahanara Kabir (2009) refers to the visual art described in the novel as embedded nonnarrative moments. I extend Kabir's analysis to read these moments of ekphrasis as descriptions of the Bengali vernacular landscape of East Pakistan. This feminist novel's eco-strategies draw our attention to both the extraction economy and the atrocities that the state of Pakistan committed against its own land and citizens, especially women. This chapter also sheds light on the ways in which history is repeating itself as the current state of Pakistan continues to impose an extraction economy on Balochistan today.

Chapter 4, "Karachi: Pakistani Eco-cosmopolitanism," discusses a uniquely *Pakistani* eco-cosmopolitanism that grounds Heise's global theory (2008) in the place that is Pakistan in order to answer Gaard's (2010, 655) questions: "How does this ecocosmopolitanism [*sic*] account for real material and economic power differences across race, class, gender, and species—communities that are central to ecofeminist and feminist ecocritical concerns? . . . Unlike global elites, non-dominant communities of human and nonhuman animals, along with their environments, experience the effects of globalization on the local level, and organize or suffer and die locally. How can these discussions of eco-cosmopolitanism [*sic*] and environmental justice be enriched by recuperating the history of feminist and ecofeminist perspectives on place, home, and bioregion?" This chapter's focus on turtles, feminists, and a poor, indigenous Sindhi in Karachi responds to Gaard's skepticism of Heise's theory by grounding it in Karachi, specifically, and in an alternative vision of the place that is Pakistan, more generally.[26]

The chapter then analyzes human and nonhuman characters in Uzma Aslam Khan's novel *Trespassing* (2003) to theorize both a local and a place-based national consciousness that cannot be equated with nationalism. The novel's depiction of nonhuman attachments is neither a simplistic extension nor a rejection of nationalism. Khan shows how the actions of large global institutions such as the International Monetary Fund impact ordinary people in Karachi, thus drawing attention to how the people across Pakistan suffer from the scarcity of electricity and water. This national consciousness is portrayed as a Pakistani eco-cosmopolitanism that is local in the context of the global economy and global environment. Khan's critiques of Pakistani, U.S., and Sindhi nationalism are inextricably linked to a sense of belonging in relation to nonhuman others instead.

Chapter 5, "Displacement: Animalization," explores the complexities of deterritorialization due to nationalist violence that can also lead to a global sense of place. In analyzing Kamila Shamsie's novel *Burnt Shadows* (2009), an ecocritical reading helps us grasp the ways in which its critique of nationalism among humans is embedded in and inseparable from its resistance to humanism. In this novel, human characters are associated with birds in a way that does not elevate humans; instead, as violent humans animalize others, actual birds lead the human character Sajjad to ponder nonviolence. In fact, the protagonist, Hiroko, has the images of birds burned onto her back during the bombing of Nagasaki, which continues to influence her until the attacks of September 11, 2001. This type of animalization or brutalization is similar to racism and lies in stark contrast to feminist theorist Donna Haraway's idea of companion species (2008) that helps to explain Sajjad's nonviolence. In this novel, birds represent both the perpetrators of nationalist violence and those who resist it through the animalization trope, which challenges both nationalist violence and the dominant discourse of humanism. In this way, the novel is a catalyst for social and environmental action within and beyond Pakistan.

The conclusion of the book argues that the ongoing effects of climate change make it vitally important to link environmental and social justice issues around gender in Pakistan. It examines how deep ecology is biased against the global south and should not be used to analyze Pakistan, climate change, and women. The move from deep ecology to environmental justice has led to an infusion of postcolonial theory into ecological thinking; thus, we can no longer think of social and environmental justice, humans and nonhumans, and the global north and the global south separately. The chapter also discusses the recurrent catastrophic floods in Pakistan, especially the one in 2010. Even though, generally, women's nongovernmental organizations (NGOs) and environmental NGOs in Pakistan do not overlap in their concerns and their work, part of linking social justice with environmental justice is to consider women's relationship with their environments.

Pakistani women's literary and cinematic fictions serve as an ideal vehicle for these discourses. As postcolonial feminists have argued, women have long been regarded as subjects that resist nationalist projects. *Place and Postcolonial Ecofeminism* shows that an exploration of women's everyday practices opens up place-based lines of inquiry. My interest lies not in the territorially bounded nation-state of Pakistan but in the people's sense of belonging to the place onto which Pakistan is mapped. The material reality of the place indicates the way in which people live with each other, deal with their environment and with animal others, and intuit their sense of place and relationship to the more than human. An ecocritical approach allows theories of space and place-based identities to ground my analysis in the environment and to provide a framework for thinking about both its degradation and people's attachment to it. The literary and cinematic fictions I discuss refer to the lands, the seas, and the nonhuman animals of various parts of Pakistan and explain the intersections between people and place.

To define women as inherently associated with nature—a perspective that is typically used to denigrate women—would be a mistake.[27] Just as ecofeminist Stacy Alaimo (2000, 8), I "do not wish to minimize the problems with some ecofeminist arguments, [but] I would like to warn against hasty dismissal." For instance, according to Greta Gaard (2016, 69), "ecofeminism is unique for bridging human justice, interspecies justice, and human-environmental justice, while other feminist environmental perspectives ignore the species question, or subordinate it (they also fail to challenge the culturally produced links among gender/race/sexuality/nation/nature, and often reinscribe them as a result)." Because of this valuable work, ecofeminism should not be so hastily dismissed. As with Alaimo's (2000, 13), the purpose of my readings, then, is to illustrate the way Pakistani women's novels and films "transform the gendered concepts—nature, culture . . . and others— that have been cultivated to denigrate and silence certain groups of humans as well as nonhuman life." Importantly, my book studies Pakistani women writers' and filmmakers' negotiations with and contestations of the dominant nationalist and religious discourses of belonging by avoiding essentialism and resisting the denigration of both women and the environment.

No book-length studies of Pakistani women novelists or filmmakers have been published to date. As of this writing, only five books of literary criticism on Pakistani Anglophone fiction have been published, and two books explore Pakistani film.[28] Since none of these books are written from an ecofeminist and environmentalist perspective, my book seeks to contribute substantially to feminist scholarship, postcolonial studies, film studies, and the environmental humanities. An ecocritical lens is crucial to all of these fields, and the women's literary and cinematic fictions I discuss illustrate why attention to landscapes, seascapes, and other nonhuman aspects of Pakistan that convey how people become attached to their geographical homeplaces is so important. These women's attachments to place or place-based identities forcefully counter many transnational state-supported discourses and the violence they enable. In fact, philosopher Martha Nussbaum's (2005, 173) famous capabilities theory not only mentions both *"relationship to the world of nature"* and *"control over environment"* as major capabilities necessary for everyone but also argues that "violence and the threat of violence, greatly influence a woman's ability . . . to control both land and movable property" (italics in original). By analyzing the cinematic and literary fictions that portray Pakistani women's engagements with violence, patriarchy, religious nationalism, and the more-than-human environment, *Place and Postcolonial Ecofeminism* helps bridge the gap between ecofeminist theories and postcolonial Pakistani literary and film studies.

1

Punjab

Eco-cosmopolitan Feminism

Shabbo: It's a strange world. Our children must also make their
way in it. They're not ours to call our own forever. Let him go.

Ayesha: Then whom can we call our own? What can we call our own?

KHAMOSH PANI

Punjab literally means "land of five waters," or the five rivers that make
the area in both Pakistan and India the breadbasket of each country.
During the tumultuous 1947 partition at the end of the British occupation, this province of British India was split between India and Pakistan.[1] Since the partitioning of Punjab coincided with the simultaneous
independence of India and Pakistan, it is hard to discuss Punjab without also talking about both the gendered violence and the damage to
the region's land and water that resulted. This chapter expands upon
literary ecocritic Ursula Heise's work (2008) and suggests that Sabiha
Sumar's first Punjabi-language feature film *Khamosh Pani* (Silent waters,
2003),[2] which focuses on land, water, and food to account for this violence, resists both religious nationalism and economic globalization.
The film's eco-cosmopolitan feminist stance is grounded in the environment and cognizant of both the pitfalls and the advantages of the
local and the global. The resulting narratives of belonging show that
we all should have land, water, and food to "call our own."

Due to partition's large-scale migrations and the displacement of
17.2 million people along religious lines, the current region of Pakistani Punjab is no longer religiously diverse (Schaeffer 1999, 99). The
two new nations were not equipped to deal with these massive migrations. Their chaotic and violent split led to the deaths of nearly 1 million

people, and 75,000 women were "raped, kidnapped, abducted, [and] forcibly impregnated by men of the 'other' religion" (Butalia 2000, 34–35). Women were also further disproportionately affected by the violence as Hindus and Sikhs moved to India and Muslims moved to Pakistan.[3] As anthropologist Veena Das (2000, 205) stated about the partition of 1947, "The violations inscribed on the female body (both literally and figuratively) and the discursive formations around these violations made visible the imagination of the nation as a *masculine* nation." The masculinity of India and Pakistan was evident in the ways in which women were violated. Such violations of the other have been described as a weapon of war. As feminist sociologist Shahnaz Khan (2009, 138) writes: "The rape of women by men from the other community sends a message to their men that they cannot protect their families. As protection is a fundamental component of masculinity, such men are symbolically emasculated. Thus rape is domination by men but also domination of men. It becomes a weapon against women but also against men of their communities. Raping and impregnating women of the other communities thus become a strategy of war—a way of destroying the opposing communities." While many women were violated by men from the other community, many women were murdered by their own family members as well.

Men worried that their sisters and daughters could be abducted and raped because this violence was considered to be dishonorable and emasculating. This fear of emasculation led many families to force their female family members to commit suicide by jumping into wells or setting fire to their own homes. Feminist partition studies scholars Urvashi Butalia (2000), Ritu Menon (2006), and Kamla Bhasin (with Menon 1998) were the first to describe the honor killings perpetrated by women's family members. While the term "honor killing" was not used in 1947 to describe such murders, they were inspired by a sense of "honor" nonetheless, and I refer to them using that term in my discussion of Sumar's film, which places partition in the context of Pakistan's history of Islamization.[4]

Khamosh Pani depicts two linked but different moments of crisis in Pakistani history—the partition of British India in 1947 and the beginning of Islamization policies under Gen. Muhammad Zia-ul-Haq's military dictatorship in 1979 — that affect the lives of its citizens, particularly its women, in debilitating ways.[5] Because partition led to displacement, Sumar's film explores its Pakistani and Indian characters' cross-border attachments to Punjab; their attachments could also be considered cosmopolitan since they extend beyond the nation. Since cosmopolitanism is often defined as thinking or acting beyond the local, cross-border attachments are considered cosmopolitan, global, and open to differences among people all over the world (Appiah 2006; Breckenridge et al. 2002; Brennan 1997; Cheah and Robbins 1998). The term has wide appeal among scholars who believe in global human rights. However, the fact that cosmopolitans are considered loyal to all of humanity rather than to one local community or nation has been seen as the most positive, as well as the most negative, aspect of cosmopolitanism. For instance, some environmentalists (Naess 1993) and nationalists consider cosmopolitans as rootless, or lacking in attachments to their environments and their people — that is, local community members as well as fellow citizens of a nation-state.[6] These critics insist that without a sense of attachment to local environmental and social communities, politically progressive work leading to greater sustainability and democracy is impossible. In addition, some scholars consider cosmopolitanism synonymous with global capitalism, economic globalization, and a type of Western imperialism because cosmopolitanism was and is associated with colonists' claiming to "civilize" the "heathens" of cultures different from their own (Brennan 1997). In the same vein, transnational feminists have argued that first world feminists behave in a cosmopolitan manner when they impose their own idea of feminism on women from developing countries (Kaplan 2001). Clearly, colonialism, capitalism, the oppression of women, environmental hazards, and the functioning of the nation-state have concrete, material effects on people and environments, particularly on local places. Taking a more global view can make us lose sight of those material realities. However, because each of these different critiques comes out of a similar discomfort with an abstract, seemingly rootless theory that is not grounded in a local place, a vision that does not see the local and the global as mutually exclusive has become necessary.

In Pakistan the local and the global overlap in other ways. For instance, because cosmopolitanism includes being open to other cultures beyond national borders, cosmopolitanism denotes resistance against the excesses of national Islamization policies that oppress women and minorities. However, Pakistan's religious nationalism, a perpetrator of much violence, can itself be considered cosmopolitan. The Muslim nationalism of Pakistan is considered cosmopolitan not only because the nation was created as a homeland for South Asia's Muslims of all ethnicities but also because the Muslim fundamentalism that has become increasingly widespread in Pakistan operates globally.[7] Pakistani nationalism draws on religion, which is, by definition, not limited to one nation.[8] That cosmopolitanism works as a descriptor of these two opposing ideas — religious nationalism and the resistance to it — suggests the complicated nuance as well as the pitfalls of the term. As a result, especially when we discuss Pakistan, it is necessary to move beyond just cosmopolitanism.

Ursula Heise (2008) coined the term "eco-cosmopolitanism" to couple cosmopolitanism with an attachment to the ecosystem of a certain place. She wants people to have both a sense of place and a sense of planet, as her book is titled. She insists that eco-cosmopolitanism "reaches toward what some environmental writers and philosophers have called the 'more-than-human world' — the realm of nonhuman species, but also that of connectedness with both animate and inanimate networks of influence and exchange" (61). Similarly, historian Wendy Harcourt (2016) theorizes about place within global movements. She writes, "Though intuitively place may seem inherently conservative, a reading of place as a site of progressive politics allows us to understand more concretely how environment is linked to culture through relations of power, agency, and responsibility to human and nonhuman environments" (161). My interpretation of eco-cosmopolitanism in the place of South Asia emphasizes people's connections with a land and a topography that were severed during partition. In the context of partition, eco-cosmopolitanism includes not only a connectedness with inanimate landscapes but also the effects of the global economy and global Islam on the lives of ordinary people and, more specifically, of women. Thus, Pakistanis are cosmopolitan because they are connected not only to global networks of influence, which include the global economy and global Islam, but also to global feminist organizations. However, the cosmopolitanism of some Pakistanis is also local because it continues to be grounded in local traditions, places, and religious practices. This confluence of the local and the global is an example of eco-cosmopolitanism.

Because I am interested in the intersection between social inequalities and their relationship with the environment, I extend Heise's eco-cosmopolitanism to an *eco-cosmopolitan feminism* because eco-cosmopolitanism without feminism is insufficient for discussing gender relations. A cosmopolitan feminist perspective that critiques patriarchy while taking multiple viewpoints into consideration is also not sufficient to oppose the local and place-based particularities of the violence displayed during partition that currently flourishes in Pakistan.[9] Neither eco-cosmopolitanism nor cosmopolitan feminism captures the attachment to the land *and* social justice that marks both the specific partition narrative that I discuss and partition narratives in general. Grounded in the materiality of a local place that balances the local and global, while overemphasizing neither, an eco-cosmopolitan feminist theory allows for a more nuanced discussion of gender relations, social inequality, and attachment to the land that is rooted, in the case of *Khamosh Pani*, in the historical context of Punjab in Pakistan.

The eco-cosmopolitan feminism of this film critiques patriarchy in the Punjab across the border with India and, simultaneously, remains locally grounded in that place with its local language, history, and religious practices. During partition, when fathers and brothers forced their female family members to commit suicide by jumping in the village wells, they simultaneously poisoned the well water as the men migrated across the border. Violence against women was thus also violence against the waters of the Punjab. In addressing the continued violence against women in South Asia while also keeping the environment in mind, an eco-cosmopolitan feminist stance with a focus on land, water, and food counters the religious fundamentalism of Pakistan and the global economy.[10]

Feminist Cinematic Fictions

Khamosh Pani provides viewers with a snapshot of Pakistan at the beginning of Islamization to illustrate people's contradictory attachments to a place, a religion, and a nation in the context of partition and growing fundamentalism. The film focuses on Veero, a Sikh woman who watched as her father in 1947 forced her mother and sister to commit suicide by making them jump into the village well. Veero escaped these forced suicides but was abducted by a group of Muslim men. While sexual violence is not shown in the film, it does show the physical violence of one attacker while another attacker defends her. Eventually she converts to Islam, changes her name to Ayesha, and marries the man who defended her. The film begins in 1979, with Ayesha living as a widow in the village of her birth and raising her only son alone. Two mullahs befriend her teenage son, and he becomes involved with the patriarchal and religious nationalism that is slowly spreading throughout Pakistan. Her son is later horrified to discover that his mother was once Sikh, and Ayesha eventually commits suicide in the same well in which her mother and sister died. Postcolonial film critic Priya Jaikumar (2007, 217) argues that Sumar is able to "call into existence an imaginative sympathy" with Veero/Ayesha as part of a larger feminist project.[11] By including flashbacks to 1947, Sumar also shows the patriarchal nature of religious fundamentalism and connects atrocities waged against women during the 1947 partition of British India with the Islamization policies that military dictator Zia-ul-Haq implemented in the late 1970s in Pakistan.

As *Khamosh Pani* illustrates, Pakistan's religious nationalism can be traced to its roots as a country for the Muslims of South Asia. Even though the state of Pakistan has steadily curtailed the rights of women and minorities, General Zia's regime, which lasted from the late 1970s to the late 1980s, is remembered as particularly disempowering for women and minorities because he formally initiated the process of Islamization as state policy in 1977 (Jamal 2005). These policies range from formal legislation to informal proscriptions regarding everyday interactions, such as how people dress and greet one another.[12] Ayesha Jalal (1995b, 239) argues that Zia's Islamization policies are closely connected with controlling women: "While the Pakistani economy largely escaped being overhauled along Islamic lines and the military regime gave short shrift to the egalitarian aspects of Islam, it was women who came to symbolize the regime's Islamization policies and Islamic commitment." This portrayal is accurate. If Zia's military regime was actually interested in benefiting the people, it would not have been as oppressive to women and would have instead overhauled the Pakistani economy along Islamic lines. This policy would probably have been helpful for keeping food prices affordable for ordinary people. However, Islamization policies were not aimed at the good of the public. Sumar's film critiques these policies by showing how people, specifically women, lived in 1979 and how both Pakistani men's and women's attitudes changed as the political climate of the country changed.

Sumar's focus on the particularities of certain Islamization policies in one village helps to avoid orientalizing Islam in general. Her strategy is in keeping with that of sociologist Amina Jamal (2005, 64), who suggests "that religion acquires various forms and is differently involved in the construction of subjectivities at various times." Rather than stereotypically demonizing Islam, Sumar's film illustrates how the religion was used as a tool for political purposes, diminishing the rights of Pakistani women and minorities.

Khamosh Pani provides an example of the politicized nature of Islamization legislation in a scene set in 1979. The barber Mehboob (whose name means "lover") is cutting hair while the mullahs Mazhar and Rasheed sit nearby. The radio is on, and everyone hears, "This is Radio Pakistan. It's 1:00 p.m. Atiya Zahid presents the news. The president has announced that Islamic laws will be introduced within six months." The images of the president—military dictator and general Zia-ul-Haq—are shown throughout the film. Mehboob is aware of the self-serving nature of Zia's legislative changes as he asks Rasheed, "What's happening in Lahore?" Rasheed responds, "People are accepting the changes. They feel General Zia represents people like you and me." But Mehboob can see through his rhetoric and states, "How can I be compared to you, sir? I'm a naive villager. And you are a man of the political world. So that brings us to the question: who does the general represent, you or me?" To the chagrin of Rasheed, Mehboob then tells a joke about how Zia's barber "keeps asking him about holding elections" because the word "elections" makes his hair "stand on end so the barber could clip it easily!" Mehboob knows that Zia is not interested in ordinary people, does not represent him, and does not want to hold elections. No matter what

Rasheed says, these Islamization policies are not what the people want. Given the meaning of Mehboob's name and that he sings and dances with women in an earlier scene shows where his sympathies lie—not only with ordinary people but also with women—while Zia's policies undermine ordinary people and especially women.

The will of the male state is made clear in *Khamosh Pani* when the two mullahs, Rasheed and Mazhar, befriend two of the village boys, Zubair and Saleem. When Ayesha's son, Saleem, is asked if he will come to a public meeting in Rawalpindi, he hesitates and implies that he'll have to ask his mother's permission. His friend Zubair laughs; for him, the idea that a male should ever ask a female for permission is ludicrous. When Saleem looks for a gift for his girlfriend, Zubeida, Zubair tells him that "this love-marriage business isn't part of our culture." Here a consensual relationship between two people is considered anti-patriarchal because it might lead to equality between the sexes. While Zubeida wants her relationship with Saleem to be one of equals, Saleem begins to claim that she wants to enslave him. Zubair's final test of Saleem is to ask his mother to prove publicly that she is a pure Muslim. Saleem tells Ayesha, "All they say is that you stand in a public square and declare that you are a Muslim . . . that you accept Islam and reject your false beliefs." Saleem's new friends convince him that he must either control the women in his life or distance himself from them. When Ayesha refuses to make this public declaration, the gulf between her and Saleem increases, as does the distance between Saleem and Zubeida.

These events of 1979 are contrasted with the events of 1947 that are presented as sepia-tinted flashbacks remembered by Ayesha. The second of these flashbacks begins when her friend Shabnam (who is nicknamed Shabbo) mentions that her husband Amin will not go anywhere because "it's the anniversary of his first wife's death." This conversation reminds Ayesha of partition because, as we find out later, Amin's first wife was one of the abducted Muslim women. Ayesha's adult voice is heard in the voice-over as we see the well in which her mother and sister were forced to jump; it is the site of violence against both women and water. As Ayesha narrates, the subtitles read, "Two countries were born. Men abducted women. Fathers killed daughters . . .

All in the name of honour. Some women died. Some survived. People moved like the sea, leaving everything behind . . . Broken memories, half-dreamt dreams, places of worship." As she notes that "people moved like the sea," humans are connected to the nonhuman water. In addition, the English subtitles do not capture all of the nuances of the Punjabi. Another translation of the last sentence could have been that "people left everything behind as they went to the house of God"; that is, people traveled for reasons of religion: Muslims to Pakistan, and Sikhs and Hindus to India. The countries became associated with religions, and women, along with well waters, were made to bear the biggest burdens of family honor when, to avoid their female family members' being abducted and raped by others, the men forced them to commit suicide and jump into the village wells.

Khamosh Pani presents a feminist critique of patriarchy from an eco-cosmopolitan perspective by examining both Muslim and Sikh communities. Ayesha resists the religious nationalism and exclusivity of both her father and her son as she remains grounded in that particular place, refusing to be displaced from the land of her birth and eventually choosing to plunge into it to her death. The significance of this land is established in the opening shot of the film, as the viewer is introduced to the space in an extreme long shot. The camera slowly moves from left to right over the land of the village, with rooftops in the foreground and mountains in the background. Ayesha knows that she has suffered at the hands of her father, her late husband, and her son because of the rhetoric of religious exclusivity. Later, when her brother, Jaswant, asks her to come to India and see her dying father one last time, she asks, "Why? So he can do now what he couldn't do then? Killing Ma and Jeeto wasn't enough for him?" When Jaswant responds, "The old man just wants to die in peace," Ayesha knows that her history is not as simple as Jaswant wishes. She says, "But he wanted to kill me for his peace. So what will he do when he sees me alive? Alive and a Muslim. How will he go to his Sikh Heaven? And which heaven is there for me? A Sikh Heaven or a Muslim Heaven?" She asks Jaswant to leave, having rejected the brand of religion that forced her mother and sister to commit suicide, just as she rejects her son's plea that she publicly swear her belief in Islam.

Even as she defies both discourses of male exclusivity, she remains in the village of her birth, refusing to be displaced. The land and village of the opening panoramic shot, as well as in many other scenes of the film, become the site and means of her resistance when she commits suicide. Ayesha's refusal to be displaced from her village shows the importance of the local; her suicide by entering the land emphasizes the global in that women are oppressed by religious exclusivity across borders. For instance, when Jaswant mentions to his fellow Sikh pilgrims that some Sikh women must still be alive, he is told that they could not have survived because their fathers and brothers shot them. Thus, both Muslim and Sikh men are depicted as behaving violently toward women.

In addition, the film illustrates the complex relationship between the local and the global through its depiction of land, water, and food. Most people miss land and mountains when they migrate, but in the film the significance of water is more ambiguous. Those who migrate poison the well waters of the land they leave behind, and the water becomes definitely associated with death. However, its continuing presence in the film, visually and aurally, is not completely negative, as water also has the power to comfort Saleem and to carry Ayesha's story. Without land and water, there also can be no food. In this film, food represents hospitality, which helps people overcome their differences when they reach out to others and feed them.[13] By the same token, the lack of food or increased food prices makes life difficult. The film shows that food connects people to the land and water, providing their sense of place and belonging. These ways of belonging directly contrast and, in fact, resist ideas of belonging through religious nationalism.

Land

Renouncing the land, even for religion, can have a devastating effect. The film shows its characters' attachment to the land through both dialogue and landscapes. We hear a Sikh pilgrim who came from India to visit Punja Sahib in Pakistan tell another, "My father passed away still longing for these mountains" (see fig. 1). Sumar uses a long shot of the two Sikh pilgrims walking along a mountain path and toward the camera to impress the mountain range upon the viewer, while also

My father passed away
still longing for these mountains.

1. Image from *Khamosh Pani* showing its Indian characters' attachment to the land from which they were displaced. Dir.: Sabiha Sumar.

showing the men and the mountains in a single frame. As the men walk closer to the camera, they pass out of the frame, and the camera tracks down to the village below. One tracking shot captures the mountains, the people, and the village in one motion, thus connecting them all.

Even in the suicide scene at the end of the film, the land fills the frame. However, instead of the camera panning across the landscape, in the suicide scene it is still, and the scene is shot in complete silence. The moving camera signifies ongoing, living connections between people and places, while the still camera and silence represent a more lethal connection. This most crucial scene in the film calls for an ecofeminist critical examination. In the protagonist's suicide, we see her attachment to the land. Sabiha Sumar uses a large depth of field and an extreme long shot to effectively illustrate the connection between the land of Punjab and its people. The shot at once emphasizes the vast land and the female protagonist who stands, at the bottom right of the screen, at the edge of a well. The extreme long shot makes her appear small as most of the screen is filled with the arid land in the dim light of early morning, but her presence is undeniable (see fig. 2). The absence of non-diegetic sound (such as music) or even diegetic sound (such as wind) reinforces the premonition of death that the shot evokes. And,

2. Image from *Khamosh Pani* of Ayesha before she commits suicide. The land fills the screen, and when she jumps into the well, it appears as if she is entering the land. Dir.: Sabiha Sumar.

after a few seconds, the woman jumps into the well, appearing to enter the land at the very moment she is committing suicide. This representation of suicide reflects religious intolerance at the time of partition and in Pakistan's subsequent history because her suicide is a choice that she makes only after her son, her friends, and her community all turn their backs on her because of her Sikh identity.

Ayesha is an eco-cosmopolitan because she chooses to stay in the same village her whole life (many Sikhs lived there when it was British India), and when she jumps in the well at the end, the extreme long shot makes it appear as if she is entering the land and joining her mother and sister in an act of eco-cosmopolitan feminist solidarity. This reading of the film is complicated by the many religious, nationalist, and patriarchal pressures on Ayesha, and her suicide is a devastating indictment of the predicament of women in Pakistan. Jaikumar (2007) describes a screening where audience members discussed the film's multiple readings and mentions that the actress who played Ayesha argues that her suicide is an act of resistance: "The actress Kirron Kher . . . defended the suicide as a positive act of disengagement; an abnegation of the restricted choices available to a woman betrayed by her national past and religious present. Several Americans and South Asians in the audience saw it as a defeat" (221). Multiple and contradictory readings of the film show that women are oppressed in Pakistan but still resist their oppression. While it is possible that Ayesha sacrifices herself for her son, it is also possible that she rejects him and devotes herself to place. The film counters the religious fundamentalism of Pakistan with an eco-cosmopolitan feminism that is cognizant of women's particular oppressions as well as their relationship with their physical environments.

These relationships between women and their physical environments are sometimes referred to metaphorically. As noted, Amin, the husband of Ayesha's friend Shabbo, lost his first wife during partition while Ayesha was also abducted. When Amin hears Pakistan's prime minister Zulfiqar Ali Bhutto has been hanged, he tells Ayesha that the hanging of a head of state is as unnatural as partition. When she asks what will happen, he responds, "Nature will take its revenge someday. Who knows that better than you and I?" The film implies that partition was unnatural because the land was divided, creating man-made borders and boundaries where none had previously existed.[14] Nature will take its revenge, metaphorically, not only because of the border but also because of the violence.

This border dividing the region of Punjab is portrayed as being insignificant, which adds to the film's cosmopolitanism. The people of Punjab are similar regardless of the border, and the people of Indian and Pakistani Punjab share the same language, folklore, literature, music, geography, and religious practices.[15] The many similarities in religious practices are the result of shared ethnicity. According to historian T. G. Fraser (1984), most Muslims in India are not descended from Muslims of foreign origins such as Turks, Persians, Arabs, or Afghans, even though many did come into the subcontinent as the result of conquests. Apparently, "they did not constitute more than a tiny, if prestigious, element in the overall Islamic population. Most Muslims were of indigenous Indian descent. . . . Although conversion to Islam had meant adherence to a new faith, it had by no means removed the influence of the Hindu caste system. In the Punjab, for example, it was not unusual to find Hindus, Sikhs or Muslims all claiming to be Jats or Rajputs" (12). Since ethnicity is linked to religious practice, the people of all the religions of the region engage in similar practices. In the film, these religious practices are associated with Ayesha and Zubeida, and are contrasted with the forces of Islamization represented by the two mullahs, Mazhar and Rasheed. Ayesha and Zubeida frequent a saint's shrine, while Mazhar and Rasheed's more global Islam frowns on saint veneration.[16] While historian Farina Mir (2012, 244) argues that saint veneration was practiced by "Punjabis from an array of religions and classes," the film's depiction of mostly women's devotion to saints links the practice to eco-cosmopolitan feminism.

Moreover, local religious practices are associated with local environments. In one scene, the camera pans across the village, emphasizing the trees, the mountains, and the rooftops. In the next scene, Ayesha is shown praying at a saint's tomb, which is out in the open with a large tree at the center. Devotees who want a saint's help to solve their personal problems tie a flag at the tomb and make a *manat*, or "solemn pledge." The tree has many flags denoting *manats* hanging from its branches. Ayesha has clearly been frequenting this tomb for years; as she tells Shabbo at the beginning of the film and per my translation of the Punjabi, Saleem's birth was the result of her many solemn pledges. The subtitles translate as "he took so many years, so many prayers coming," but the Punjabi specifically uses the word *manat*. This scene shows that Ayesha has been a devotee of the saint's for some time.

When Zubeida enters, she kisses the tomb, then ties a flag to the large tree's branch directly above the grave (see fig. 3). That the tree with its flags representing pledges is used in this common tradition, which relates to earlier indigenous relationships to the land, demonstrates how this religious practice is grounded in the local environment.[17] Given that three devotees, all of them women, are present and praying in the scene also shows that women often engage in this religious practice.

This scene then cuts to a loud, raucous gathering outside the village mosque, where Mazhar and Rasheed have aroused a crowd of men, all of whom are loudly chanting slogans (see fig. 4). According to Olivier Roy (2004, 259), "Neofundamentalists reject local Islams . . . and wage a relentless war on folk customs. . . . For instance, they oppose any cult of the 'saints' (*zyarat* in Central Asia and *moussem* in North Africa, a religious pilgrimage in which people come to pray to the local patron saint). .... They reject Sufism and mystical practices (*zikr*), and any form of artistic performance associated with a religious practice (*qawwali* music in Pakistan, for example)." The globalized Islam of Pakistan depicted in the film is in line with these neofundamentalists and rejects local religious practice.[18]

Mazhar has energized the crowd by stating in his speech, "Friends, you all know our nation is emerging from a long period of darkness. And in this hour of need, we look to all of you to join us, to become one, so that the voice of the sons of the soil will be heard. The voice of the true Muslim will be the voice that matters!" Even though Mazhar mentions the "sons of the soil," it is clear that he means only the "true" Muslims matter. This point can be seen in Saleem's complete lack of interest in farming, despite Ayesha's desire for him to pursue it. He tells her, "Fields don't interest me, Ma." Mazhar tries to combine religion with a nationalism that relies on the idea of "the sons of the soil," but as the film shows, it is an exclusive religious nationalism and not actually associated with the sense of place that the women share. Their sense of place, their eco-cosmopolitan feminism, is interested both in farming for nourishing their bodies and in saint veneration for nourishing their spirit outdoors in the presence of trees.

The contrast between the scenes of the men at the mosque and the women at the shrine gets at the heart of Ayesha and Zubeida's eco-cosmopolitan feminism. The local form of Islam is shown as more female centered than the globalized Islam the men follow in the mosque. Quietly, the women bond together on the land under a tree, sharing their love for Saleem and praying for the future, while the militant men display a threatening religious fervor at the man-made mosque. Local religious practice, symbolized by the tree bearing the pledges at the center, represents eco-cosmopolitan feminism in silent opposition to the raucous forces of Islamization.

Water

The title of the film means "silent waters," and water is clearly significant. The image of the well water is repeated throughout the film, reminding the viewer of what Ayesha has survived and what she is silent about. There is also something unnatural about the way in which

The voice of the true Muslim
will be the voice that matters!

3. (*top*) Zubeida tying a *manat* to a tree next to a saint's tomb in *Khamosh Pani*. We see only women praying here. Dir.: Sabiha Sumar.

4. (*bottom*) Image from *Khamosh Pani* of the men being introduced to the discourse of the "true Muslim." Dir.: Sabiha Sumar.

water, which farmers often consider life giving in times of drought, is used to kill women. Because Ayesha has witnessed her mother and sister jumping into the village well in 1947, she is unable to go to the well and fetch water. Her friend Allabi brings her water for years afterward; however, close to the end of the film, when Ayesha's Sikh background becomes public knowledge, Allabi's husband forbids Allabi to get water for Ayesha.

The silent waters represent not only Ayesha's silence but also that of the villagers. No one speaks of the women who were forced to jump into the well, and the water cannot speak. But when the villagers do not defend Ayesha, their silence again equates to complicity with the forces of religious nationalism in Pakistan. As film scholar Pavitra Sundar (2010, 282) writes, "By shrouding the past in (discursive) silence and not speaking out against the forces of communalism that threaten Veero/Ayesha (in 1947 and then again in 1979), the villagers are complicit in the violence directed at her." In this sense, silence and silent waters really do mean death for Ayesha and many others.

Refusing Ayesha water is also a type of cowardly violence, much less a lack of hospitality, especially since these villagers know why Ayesha does not go to the well. Philosopher Jacques Derrida (2001) defines hospitality as culture and ethics. He writes, "Hospitality is culture itself and not simply one ethic amongst others. Insofar as it has to do with the *ethos*, that is, the residence, one's home, the familiar place of dwelling, inasmuch as it is a manner of being there, the manner in which we relate to ourselves and to others, to others as our own or as foreigner, *ethics is hospitality*; ethics is so thoroughly coextensive with the experience of hospitality" (16–17). In this way, the manner in which the villagers live at home is not hospitable and not ethical. Allabi will not bring Ayesha water from the well, and her best friends, Shabbo and Amin, will not allow her to attend their daughter's wedding. The film shows that Mehboob, Ayesha, and later Zubeida are much more inclusive toward others and are therefore very different from their inhospitable fellow villagers. Mehboob's hospitality is evident in his attitude and behavior toward the Sikh pilgrims. For instance, he offers Ayesha's brother tea despite the discomfort of others at the tea stall and challenges the mullahs when they are cruel to another villager. Zubeida stands by Ayesha when no one else in the village will, and Ayesha sends sweets to the Sikh shrine.

According to Sundar (2010), the silence of the water in the well, signifying the villagers' and Ayesha's silence, does not have to be read negatively. Ayesha's silence about the trauma she has endured might simply be necessary for her to move forward. Even Zubeida is quiet at the end of the film when Saleem appears on television to discuss the relationship between Islam and democracy. Sundar argues that all of these silences, including Zubeida's, are not passive: "Silence— manifest here as an absence of words spoken out loud—does not necessarily imply a lack of voice or of critique" (283). Sundar's reading of silence in the film, when extended to the silent waters of the well, shape another less negative reading of the film: The waters are silent because they need to be.

The still, silent, deathly water of the well is contrasted with the flowing water of the stream, where Saleem sits and thinks about how to deal with the news about his mother's past. In one scene, he throws his fundamentalist flyers in the stream and then shoots them with his gun. His violence shows his frustration. What can he do if her past stands between him and his future? The flowing stream is where he comes to think, and he has a lot to consider. Part of his reason for following Zubair, Rasheed, and Mazhar is that he needs to make a financially viable living. As Shahnaz Khan (2009, 139–40) states, "In Zia's Pakistan, minorities and women were legally and institutionally excluded from full citizenship. By such logic, as a Muslim male, Salim [sic] ought to have a fully realized future. Class is working against him, however. Denied a future by years of state corruption, underdevelopment, and mis-development as well as overspending on the military, in joining a politicized religious group Salim [sic] is offered a window of opportunity." This opportunity is jeopardized by the revelation of Ayesha's past. Saleem betrays his conflicted feelings by shooting Mazhar and Rasheed's propaganda flyers floating in the stream. Unlike the well water, which is a place of silence and death, the flowing water of the stream is a place of contemplation for Saleem.

After his mother's suicide, Saleem takes a box containing her belongings to the same flowing stream because he cannot have a viable future identity in Pakistan post-Islamization without shedding the remnants of his mother's past. When Saleem first opens the box, he sees that it contains women's clothing; a steel glass for drinking water; two books written in Gurmukhi, the script the Sikhs use to write Punjabi; and an old pair of glasses, possibly belonging to Ayesha's father. Saleem adds to the box her eyeliner, her comb, a photo of himself when he was younger, her fan, and, on top of everything, her Quran. These belongings signify her life from beginning to end. Saleem puts the box into the loud, flowing stream and pushes it. Then he sits and watches it float away. Again, the loud flowing stream is shown as a place of contemplation and conflict for Saleem and the site of his conflict with himself. Here he has actively rejected his mother yet then shot the flyers that told him to reject her. While the water in the well is still and silent because no one spoke of the women who were forced to jump into it, the flowing stream, as with the film itself, carries Ayesha's story in the box with all of her possessions, old and new. In a way, the water of the flowing stream is not silent; it speaks by carrying Ayesha's story in her box of belongings. However, even as her past life lives on in Saleem and in her box of belongings, it is simultaneously discarded by Saleem. The complexity of how water is depicted in this film represents the complexity of an eco-cosmopolitan feminist stance.

The film shows that partition and fundamentalism have marred people's relationships with each other and with water, with the latter being poisoned by suicides and carrying the painful stories of women. Water is often present in the film, either visually or aurally, and the non-diegetic sound of water produces an offscreen space that links important shots together. For instance, two shots before his mother's suicide, Saleem sits on the stairs with his head against a wall as water burbles in the background. He is thinking and can hear the flowing stream even though he cannot see it. In the next shot, we see into the well full of water but hear nothing. It is silent. In the next soundless shot, Ayesha jumps into the well. Both the images and sounds of the well water and the water in the flowing stream produce a complex and contradictory eco-cosmopolitan feminism that is grounded in a sense of place but shows how women are oppressed across national boundaries regardless of religious differences.

The importance of the land and the water is palpable when the film's audience is made aware of the border partitioning Punjab. Indian Punjabis long for the mountains that are now in Pakistan, but the film implies that those same men who long for this place had also poisoned its wells with the bodies of their female family members. Ayesha's father once encouraged her, as well as her mother and sister, to jump in the well, but later his son tells Ayesha that their father just wants to die in peace. The water links feminist and environmental issues and functions as a symbol of a local resource with global implications that was once poisoned by the migrating men but continues to flow and carry stories such as Ayesha's.

Food

During partition, people were separated from their ancestral homes, their lands, their cities, and the environments that nurtured them and that they nurtured in turn—all on the basis of religion.[19] As American photographer Margaret Bourke-White (1949) notes, these separations affected the agriculture of Punjab. She writes that in Lyallpur in Pakistan's Punjab after the area's Sikhs departed "it would take some time before the incoming refugees, who had grown up in another type of agriculture, would develop comparable skill in handling the irrigation channels and spillways. Already the cycle of harvest and planting had been disrupted throughout the entire area where populations were being exchanged. Delay in the next crop would intensify the coming food shortage, inevitable with the ever growing flood of refugees" (10–11). Colonialism, partition, and religious nationalism had negative consequences not only for individuals but also for their relationships with their environments and for their knowledge of and ability to obtain food.

More recently, one reason for the food insecurity problem is water scarcity. Economists Munir Hanjra and Ejaz Qureshi (2010, 366) write that "global demand for water has tripled since the 1950s, but the supply of freshwater has been declining." Since agriculture is the largest user of water, water scarcity leads to food insecurity. "Some of the most densely populated regions of the world, such as the Mediterranean, the Middle East, India, China, and Pakistan are predicted to face severe water shortages in the coming decades" (Hanjra and Qureshi 2010,

366). These dense populations, especially in South Asia, are becoming more food insecure not only because of a shortage of water but also because of corporate greed.

According to environmental activist Vandana Shiva (2000), religious conflicts, patriarchy, and economic liberalization have interrupted the local ability to achieve food democracy. For instance, the few corporations that control the commercial seed market also control the global pesticide market and actively shape international trade agreements. In India in 1991, "as part of a World Bank/International Monetary Fund (IMF) structural adjustment package," cash crops such as cotton "started to displace food crops" (Shiva 2000, 10). Eventually, after aggressive marketing that appealed to religion in Indian Punjab, corporate hybrid seeds, which were more vulnerable to pests and therefore required more pesticides, began to replace local varieties. The corporations stood to gain much from the poor and appealed to their religion in their marketing efforts. Shiva writes that even "gods, goddesses, and saints were not spared," because in Indian Punjab "Monsanto sells its products using the image of Guru Nanak, the founder of the Sikh religion" (10). As food crops are replaced by cash crops whose seeds and pesticides are controlled by corporations, farmers have less and less power to provide food and make a living. When the crops failed, many farmers committed suicide. Decolonization has not ended the global forces that keep food from the poor, and hunger and malnutrition remain a problem.

Food is represented in *Khamosh Pani* in many interesting ways, not just as sustenance but also as a global economic marker. When food prices become intertwined with religion and nationalism, these ideologies serve to divert attention from the global economy. *Khamosh Pani* shows how the global is imbricated in the local, and the film, having been endorsed by Human Rights Watch, is in keeping with cosmopolitan discourses of global human rights. While these global discourses appear to be benign for the most part, according to literary theorist Pheng Cheah (2006), we must always ask "whether or not the . . . contemporary international division of labor, with its stratification and polarization of the world . . . , as well as the historical legacies of colonialism and anti-imperialist struggle . . . indelibly compromises, circumscribes, and mars the face of global human solidarities and belongings staged by new cosmopolitanist and human rights discourses" (3). Cheah forces us to see cosmopolitan discourses of global human rights in the context of imperialism. He asks an important question, given the global inequalities and histories of injustice that are often associated with cosmopolitanism. However, even while the film is enmeshed in these cosmopolitan human rights discourses, it is simultaneously grounded in the local effects of the global economy, as represented by food prices and by hospitality through sharing food. The film holds a promise that in valuing the local, perhaps we might avoid the problems associated with the global.

An example of Ayesha's eco-cosmopolitan openness and hospitality can be seen when she teaches the Qur'an to some small children in her home. One child asks her, "Chachi, will nonbelievers also go to Heaven?" Ayesha's response leads to some raised eyebrows between the mullahs and her son, who are listening at the door. She says, "No, children! All those who are good go to Heaven. Allah is most generous." Ayesha's religion is not exclusive. While the mullah-influenced boys tell derogatory jokes about the Sikh pilgrims, Ayesha, in a moment of hospitality, sends sweets to the Sikh shrine. When Saleem confronts her for sending the sweets, she asks, "What has happened to you? These people were our brothers once." Saleem responds by violently destroying the food, but Ayesha stands firm. She may not wish to return to her dying father in India, but she also does not want to submit to the forces of Islamization in Pakistan. The destroyed food that lies between Ayesha and Saleem is a symbol of her eco-cosmopolitan hospitality and her son's refusal of this kind of openness, compassion, and generosity. The film also shows the importance of offering food and hospitality to others when Ayesha is abducted and offered food by her soon-to-be husband. While she is clearly traumatized by her abduction, the moment when she is offered food is when she finally breaks down and cries, possibly because she is finally viewed with compassion. Last, food also shows how the underlying causes of such enmities are often economic because when religious nationalism is at its peak in the film, characters twice ask how it all relates to the price of food. In doing so, the film critiques the global economy, as well as religious nationalism, in terms of its negative consequences for the poor and women.[20]

These negative consequences should be at the center of our attention; however, two points in *Khamosh Pani* remind us that nationalist Islamization policies divert attention from more pressing economic considerations that have material consequences for the lives of ordinary people. When the two mullahs, Rasheed and Mazhar, along with various other male villagers watch television together at a restaurant, a mullah on television says, "Muslims and Hindus constitute two separate nations." This kind of nationalist rhetoric emphasizing basic differences between the peoples of India and Pakistan is often called the two-nation theory and is quite common. (This rhetoric has become more disturbing as the two countries have become nuclear powers.) In the film, Rasheed responds by saying, "Well said!" But one of the villagers asks, "What does it have to do with us? We have Pakistan. Then why do they harp on the same tune. Talk about the price of wheat for a change" (see fig. 5). Instead of Pakistani religious nationalism, the villager wants to talk about the price of wheat; he is interested in food and land. Rasheed responds, "People have sacrificed blood for this country . . . and all you can think of is eating? You'll be stuffing your face, while they take our women." Rasheed combines nationalism with patriarchy to convince the villagers not to focus on food, but the film is sympathetic toward the villagers, especially when Rasheed menaces and taunts them by insisting, "Eat, eat. Have some more."

Cheah (2006, 102) argues that movements such as Pakistan's Islamization of the 1980s are deeply imbricated in economic globalization because "political elites may . . . draw on 'tradition' or 'intrinsic cultural values' to maintain hegemony and justify their actions, sometimes over-emphasizing cultural issues such as religion, morality, cultural imperialism, and women's appearance to divert attention from economic failures and social inequality." The film shows Rasheed and Mazhar drawing on tradition, religion, morality, and patriarchy to convince the villagers of their cause and to distract them from the high price of food. The extreme emphasis on religion in Pakistan since 1979 can partly be attributed to such diversionary tactics. Interestingly, the same processes of globalization that lead to uneven development and unequal distribution of wealth also lead to the anti-corporate globalization effort that supports the widespread discussion of women's rights and

Talk about the price of wheat
for a change.

5. A villager wants to talk about the price of wheat instead of Pakistani religious nationalism in *Khamosh Pani*. Dir.: Sabiha Sumar.

democracy.[21] The film makes sense of these two contradictory sides of globalization—the former, imperial; the latter, progressive—by focusing on food, globalization, and women to bring together all the concerns of an eco-cosmopolitan feminism.

In a similar vein, according to Vandana Shiva (2000), the primary target for change should be the high price global corporations set for food to maximize profits rather than the misguided attempts to protect women in the name of God and country. She argues that democratic "control over food requires the reining in of the unaccountable power of corporations" and creating "an ecological and just system of food production and distribution, in which the earth is protected, farmers are protected, and consumers are protected" (117). Rhetoric emphasizing differences between people merely diverts attention from what Shiva calls the "food dictatorship" that is all around us because of economic globalization (117).

This food dictatorship, which leads to the high price of food, is visible in the film's third scene as Ayesha haggles over the price of onions. She tells the vegetable seller, "Make it six rupees, and I'll take 2 kilos." He responds, "It's summer. Honestly, I can't." Ayesha asks him, "Summer's only for you, is it? The rest of us should die . . . Six and a half rupees,

Does it change the price of onions?

6. Image from *Khamosh Pani* with the film's second reference to the price of food. Dir.: Sabiha Sumar.

then." But this counteroffer, too, doesn't work, and the seller responds, "I swear by my children. I can't. 7 is my price. Now, don't haggle and don't say no." At first blush, this scene seems intended only to demonstrate how everyone lives. But after two later scenes in which characters discuss the high price of food, this earlier scene carries new meaning. The vegetable seller is forced to swear by his children to show that he cannot afford to lower the price *and* cannot afford to lose Ayesha as a customer. These times are tough for everyone. Even Zubeida, at the end of the film, draws attention to the economic situation. As she looks at herself wearing Ayesha's pendant in the mirror, she says in voice-over, "I remember Ayesha very well. But what's the point of remembering her? Does it change the price of onions?" (See fig. 6.) If there were no point in remembering her, however, then Zubeida would not continue wearing the pendant. Both wearing the pendant and pondering the price of food show the importance of an eco-cosmopolitan feminist stance that emphasizes food security and addresses the patriarchy and the global economy.

One reason for tough times in poor, debt-laden countries is the pressure to pay their debts; thus, they increase the price of food, resulting in inflation. Inequalities rose in the time of Zia-ul-Haq, but he told the Pakistani people that their problems could be solved if they followed Islam and became true Muslims. Shahnaz Khan (2009, 134–35) states, "Poverty, labor strife, and rising indebtedness, in the General's view, had little to do with internal and external structural conditions generating inequality. Instead, a lack of individual and societal morals was responsible for social woes. The solution to these ills, Zia believed, was a program of Islamization called *Nizam-e-Mustafa* (Governance inspired by the Prophet)." In the film, Rasheed and Mazhar, the two fundamentalists who represent this ideology, are more than aware of the social inequalities plaguing the country. Rasheed even refers to the landlord and his family as hypocrites: "Look at the size of this house and the hole he has put us in." Because Rasheed is a true believer, he just wants to sleep at the mosque, but Mazhar is crafty enough to realize about the landlord, "What we do with his support in a week, we can't do alone in a year. Once we get going, nothing will stop us. Eat something. You'll feel better." Gaining the landlord's support means an introduction to the villagers and, of course, food. After all, everyone needs food.

Despite Mazhar and Rasheed's understanding of economic inequalities, their desire for justice does not involve fighting for women and minority rights, and we are reminded that in addition to its pernicious patriarchal effects, religious nationalism also diverts attention from fighting for food democracy. Mazhar and Rasheed will eat the landlord's food, but they are not interested in securing food for everyone. Rather than espousing a simplistic anti-nationalist cosmopolitanism, however, the film succeeds in troubling our ideas about religious fundamentalists by showing us that they too want to fight against inequality and injustice. Mazhar and Rasheed are not sympathetic characters, but they are not flat and stereotypical either. Their influence on Zubair and Saleem is actually understandable because the young boys need a higher purpose and a career. The film ends with a television interview, showing that Saleem has, in fact, gained the career he sought.

However, through the eco-cosmopolitan feminist stance of the film, we see that Saleem's victory is juxtaposed against many other losses. He gained a profession but lost his mother. The loving way in which he sets her things in her box of belongings shows that he has lost not only her but also a part of himself. Recalling Ayesha, Zubeida states, "We did not want her to leave . . . Sometimes I dream of her. I preserve each dream and try not to let it go." The film demonstrates that these losses to the integrity of the community are the result of religious and patriarchal nationalism, which can and has destroyed the lives of so many. But in making this critique alongside the critique of economic globalization, the film is careful to show that this violence is not only a local problem that can be blamed on a "primitive" religion in a distant part of the world. Feminist literary critic Kumkum Sangari (2008) has critiqued culturalism as a way of blaming gendered violence on the culture of countries in the global south. She writes, "Culturalism works as a code for tradition and religion, conflates religion and patriarchies with 'culture,' and turns acts of violence into religion-driven third world pathologies or customary/sacred traditions. This complicates feminist attempts to critique violent practices, especially since culturalist accounts also tend to spectacularise and decontextualise violent acts. As 'sati' is to India, so clitorodectomy is to North Africa, and 'honour' killings to so-called Islamic countries. Culturalist accounts are unable to explain similar practices among different religious groups" (2).

The film shows Sikhs committing honor killings even though these murders are often associated with Muslims. Yet because the film portrays Muslims committing gendered violence as well, it helps keep its audience from resorting to a decontextualized culturalist account for gendered violence. What we see is not merely religion-driven pathology; patriarchy across religions and the references to food prices remind us of that. Gendered violence, uneven development, and rising food prices are not simply a local problem. When it comes to countries such as Pakistan, local authoritarian regimes, and global institutions such as the World Bank and the IMF all have a hand in outcomes. Because of the film's eco-cosmopolitan feminist perspective, the viewer sees the local consequences of Zia's regime as well as the critique of food prices that provides a global view and shows the importance of making both types of critiques—against religious and patriarchal nationalism and against uneven development—together.

As Sumar explores people's relationship with land, water, and food in the context of religious fundamentalism, she links partition with Pakistan's contemporary history and current crisis with the Taliban, and she inserts discussions of the local and the global to show that they are not mutually exclusive. Here the global can be understood only in terms of the local, and cosmopolitanism can be understood only in terms of the materiality of a particular place—that is, through an eco-cosmopolitanism. The film's eco-cosmopolitan feminist stance establishes that people's bonds with their homeplace environments, such as Punjab, can be understood only within larger contexts of patriarchal oppression, religious nationalism, and the effects of the global economy.

As we live through the effects of climate change on a global level, we must consider the situation in South Asia. The 2010 flood in Pakistan was among the largest humanitarian disasters the world had ever seen. It revealed the ways in which an environmental crisis, relating to land, water, and food, in a country such as Pakistan can take its toll on women and children. One-fifth of the country was under water, and women trying to access aid in displacement camps faced harassment and violence. According to the United Nations Development Fund for Women, "In many cases, local men would even hinder aid workers in approaching women" (UNIFEM 2010). An eco-cosmopolitan feminist approach can keep us focused on such a disaster's global as well as local impact, especially on women, given that flooding continues year after year. In directing this film, Sumar works as an eco-cosmopolitan feminist based in the local but not necessarily in the national environment, crossing borders without losing sight of the materiality of a specific, local geography and directly confronting the problems of partition and its severing of ourselves from each other, our land, water, and food. In times such as these, we all also need to embrace an eco-cosmopolitan feminism that resists both religious nationalism and global north exploitation through a materiality of place that engages the local and the global.

Chapter 2 focuses on the film *Ramchand Pakistani*, which is set in rural Sindh. Given the country's lower levels of literacy, particularly in English, both *Khamosh Pani* and *Ramchand Pakistani* are widely accessible in Pakistan because the dialogue in both films is in local, indigenous languages.[22] These films open a window into the lives of ordinary rural Pakistanis in Punjab and Sindh whose existence and livelihoods are dependent on their environment. Thus, they represent the majority of Pakistanis as seen through the lens of women directors. My readings of these films draw attention to the plight of women and religious minorities in the context of environmental degradation as they resist religious nationalism in Pakistan.

2

Thar

Bioregionalism

> Borders suggest both containment and safety, and women often pay a
> price for daring to claim the integrity, security, and safety of our bodies
> and our living spaces. I choose "feminism without borders," then,
> to stress that our most expansive and inclusive visions of feminism
> need to be attentive to borders while learning to transcend them.
> CHANDRA TALPADE MOHANTY

The Thar Desert, as with the province of Punjab, is a place where environmental issues having to do with the growth of deserts and social justice issues around gender, caste, and poverty are inseparable. Part of the reason for this is that Thar too has an international border cutting across the region that serves to oppress women, as Chandra Mohanty (2003) points out. Mehreen Jabbar's film *Ramchand Pakistani* (2008) engages all these issues by portraying the plight of a Hindu Dalit woman in Pakistan after her son and husband mistakenly cross the border into India and end up in jail. The film reveals that in the Thar Desert, ecological issues such as agrarianism and desertification are correlated with social issues such as oppressive labor conditions, caste discrimination, and patriarchal religious nationalism. Thus, when we think about Thar, we must theorize about the concepts of place and belonging in such a way that we think about environmental and social justice together.[1]

Pakistan's continuing struggles with religious fundamentalism, particularly since the late 1970s, have made its dominant hegemonic discourse of nationalism not only more patriarchal but also Muslim centered. Chapter 1 discusses *Khamosh Pani*, a film by an independent Pakistani woman director, Sabiha Sumar, who resisted both aspects of this discourse by making a film about a non-Muslim Pakistani woman.

This chapter examines how Jabbar in *Ramchand Pakistani* draws attention to Pakistan's Hindu religious minority and reminds Pakistanis of minority rights. Both Sumar's and Jabbar's films can be compared to earlier Indian films that emphasized similar themes about integrating minorities. According to South Asianist Rachel Dwyer (2006, 8), Indian films after independence included a popular historical genre that shows "a national integration of minorities, notably Muslims, mostly through presenting images of syncretic Mughal culture." In Pakistan both Jabbar's and Sumar's films encourage a similar integration of Sikhs and Hindus through images of syncretic religious practices. Moreover, these films' integration of religious minorities does not end at the territorial border of the nation-state. In Sumar's film, Punjab extends beyond the border, and in Jabbar's film, the Thar Desert likewise continues into India. Both films also emphasize the similarity of Pakistan's people, culture, language, and landscape with those of India. In reflecting this chapter's epigraph by postcolonial feminist Chandra Talpade Mohanty (2003, 2), these films work to be "attentive to borders while learning to transcend them." The relationship of women to borders, which serve to protect and oppress them simultaneously, is fraught at best.

One major difference between the two films is that while *Khamosh Pani* is grounded in Punjab, which includes more than one bioregion, *Ramchand Pakistani* is clearly grounded in the life place of the Thar Desert. The Thar Desert lies near the southern part of the 1,800-mile border between India and Pakistan, and is home to the Kohli people of Sindh (in Pakistan) and Gujarat (in India).[2] Unlike Punjab, the Thar Desert, on both sides of the border, is its own bioregion. The Kohlis find these desert borderlands difficult to live in not only because their livelihoods depend on a very limited amount of rainfall but also because they are Hindu Dalits. According to the International Dalit Solidarity Network (2014, 2), "'Untouchables'—known in South Asia as Dalits—are often . . . assigned the most . . . menial and hazardous jobs, and many are subjected to forced and bonded labour. Due to exclusion practiced by both state and non-state actors, they have limited access to resources . . . , keeping most Dalits in severe poverty." Pakistan has its own branch of the Dalit Solidarity Network, and its annual report provides concrete evidence of caste discrimination there. In addition, because Pakistan is predominantly Muslim, Dalits face further discrimination as a religious minority. Jabbar's film effectively conveys the plight of these desert people as they struggle to make ends meet and to navigate the border between two nations that simultaneously exclude them despite their having a sense of belonging to the bioregion that defies such exclusions.

Bioregionalism comes out of the idea that bioregions have their own internal workings and that paying attention to one's own bioregion prompts a sense of place that results in better decisions about how to live sustainably with others, human and nonhuman. Literary ecocritic Paul Lindholdt (2003, 244) defines bioregionalism as "the process of rediscovering human connections to the land." This broad definition includes the more-than-human animals, plants, and mountains. However, postcolonial critics are apprehensive about the ways in which connections to the land can become insular and xenophobic. While I agree on this point, these tensions do not merit abandoning one approach for the other.

Rob Nixon (2011) explains that bioregionalism can exclude both indigenous peoples as well as immigrants through nationalism. "There is much to be said for a bioregional approach: it can help instill in us an awareness of our impact on our immediate environment, help ground our sense of environmental responsibility. However, from a postcolonial perspective, a bioregional ethic poses certain problems, for the concentric rings of the bioregionalists more often open out into transcendentalism than into transnationalism. All too frequently, we are left with an environmental vision that remains inside a spiritualized and naturalized national frame" (238).

Bioregionalists can end up as nationalists who erase the history of indigenous peoples and belittle new immigrants. As Ursula Heise (2008, 47–48) has written, "The political consequences of encouraging people to develop a sense of place . . . are far from straightforward and predictable, and environmentalists need to be aware that place awareness can be deployed in the service of political ideals they may not judge desirable." Heise points out that her own suspicion of bioregionalism and other place-based environmentalisms stems from her German heritage. She writes, "Since National Socialism had appropriated many of the Romantic symbols of connection to soil, place, and region in the 1930s and 1940s, localism has not played the same central role in German environmental rhetoric as in the United States" (9). While I agree with both Nixon and Heise about the possible disadvantages of having a sense of place, a superior methodology for understanding Pakistan entails a perspective that is both place based and postcolonial.

Moreover, one can see that Heise's critique of bioregionalism is quite nuanced even as she appears to prefer the global over the local. On the one hand, she argues that "the challenge for environmentalist thinking . . . is to shift the core of its cultural imagination from a sense of place to a less territorial and more systemic sense of planet" (Heise 2008, 56). Heise also insists that "ties to local places" are not, and perhaps should not, always be the primary basis for ecological advocacy and that a sense of planet or eco-cosmopolitanism can also be just as important to environmental justice (10). On the other hand, this critique is not a complete rejection of a sense of place. As Tom Lynch, Cheryll Glotfelty, and Karla Armbruster, editors of the important anthology *The Bioregional Imagination* (2012, 9), have argued, "The shift from place-based bioregionalism to eco-cosmopolitanism is not an either/or proposition, but a matter of emphasis. Heise clearly does not advocate abandoning a sense of place, but rather warns that the cultivation of such a sense is no panacea and that we must add a much greater degree of global awareness to local and bioregional understandings than has typically been done, especially in the United States." This important point cannot be stressed enough in light of other bioregionalist critiques of Heise and global thinking.

Landscape architect Robert Thayer Jr. (2003, 3) defines a bioregion as "literally and etymologically a 'life-place'—a unique region definable by natural (rather than political) boundaries with a geographic, climatic, hydrological, and ecological character capable of supporting unique human and non-human living communities." Punjab's bioregions include subtropical moist forests and subtropical thorn woodland, as well as a small part of the Thar Desert. The female directors of the films discussed here represent a Sikh woman and a Hindu family, respectively, to draw attention to the plight of those whose belonging to Pakistan is fragile and precarious. They ground their sense of belong-

7. Ramchand inadvertently crossing the border in the Thar Desert in *Ramchand Pakistani*. Dir.: Mehreen Jabbar.

ing in the landscape and environment of each homeplace[3]—that is, landscapes that cross the border with India. While Sumar never physically shows the border cutting through Punjab, by contrast, *Ramchand Pakistani* includes a number of important scenes that draw attention to the border in the desert by focusing on its being marked only by white concrete markers (see fig. 7). This emphasizes in a much more material and concrete way that the border is man-made and arbitrary, cutting through the bioregion rather than following a geographical boundary. Because *Ramchand Pakistani* portrays a sense of belonging in the bioregion of the Thar Desert, it counters Pakistan's and India's nationalist ideologies of exclusion that emphasize and naturalize the place of the border cutting through Thar.

Bioregionalism does not only focus on nature. Lynch and his coeditors of *The Bioregional Imagination* (2012, 11) argue that "bioregionalism is about creating place-based communities, or, cultures-in-place, yet, curiously, it is exactly the *cultural* dimension of bioregionalism that has been undertheorized and only minimally explored." One way to ponder the questions that bioregionalists raise is through emphasizing this cultural dimension. The Hindu culture of the film's main protagonists is clearly linked to their natural environment, partly because they engage in small-scale subsistence farming and partly because their rituals and customs make use of the land, soil, and mud of the desert. Unfortunately, according to the World Food Programme (2014, 2), this region is one of twelve districts in Pakistan with "alarming food insecurity and acute malnutrition due to the impact of drought-like conditions on livelihood, water and sanitation, and health conditions." Within the larger umbrella of ecocriticism, a bioregional approach to this film enhances our perception of the ways in which the people's culture and religion are tied to their environment and of the conditions under which they must eke out a living. The film represents the complex relationship of a woman farmer to her physical environment in the context of extreme poverty and patriarchy.[4]

At first glance, *Ramchand Pakistani* does not appear to be a feminist film. In fact, Jabbar has stated that stories, rather than social issues, drive her filmmaking. Nonetheless, the film clearly directs our attention to feminist issues such as gendered oppression. As with Sumar's film, Jabbar shows non-Muslim Pakistani characters, and especially women, as oppressed not only by the local patriarchy and the nation-state of Pakistan but also by the border between India and Pakistan. Both films share a larger "feminism without borders" agenda, which reflects Mohanty's (2003) insightful words about physical colonial borders and metaphorical borders. While Sumar's film expresses a more explicit feminist and anti-capitalist critique as part of its eco-cosmopolitan feminism, Jabbar's is more centered on the effects of the man-made border in the bioregion and on the effects of other borders between men and women, Muslims and Hindus, people of different castes, farmers and landowners, and Pakistanis and Indians. It is a more local film than Sumar's but contains a much harsher critique of borders; as the Thar Desert is one bioregion, the border running through it has a greater impact, both visually and ideologically. *Ramchand Pakistani* conveys the ways in which its main Hindu characters, a woman and her child, uphold a place-based identity that resists easy interpellation by nationalist discourses as well as more traditional notions of agrarianism. The film shows that social and ecological justice are inseparable because of the deep ties of belonging that people have with their bioregion.

Set in 2002 during the standoff between Pakistan and India,[5] *Ramchand Pakistani* is about an eight-year-old Hindu Pakistani boy named Ramchand who inadvertently crosses the border in the Thar Desert from Sindh, Pakistan, into Rajasthan, India. Consequently, he suffers, along with his father, Shankar, a five-year-long ordeal in a Gujarati Indian jail. The film also follows the experiences of Ramchand's mother, Champa, as she tries to live without any news of her child and husband and eventually becomes convinced that they are dead since she is unable to get word of their whereabouts. The film questions the border in the desert by highlighting the similar topographical features of the environment. Even though the film seems to uphold the border as an important protector of national identity, it clearly advocates for a more place-based identity rather than a nationalist or religious one. Ramchand and his father consistently refer to Bhimra, their village in the desert, as their home, and at no point do they state any kind of allegiance to their country or even their religion. Nonetheless, officials from Pakistan and India are deeply suspicious of them on the basis of both religion and nationality. Their ordeal at the hands of state officials, combined with their desire to return home to the desert, emphasizes the politics of place-based belonging without and beyond borders.

Jabbar's film opens up a new discursive space at the intersection of bioregionalism, border studies, and ecofeminist scholarship. Its protagonists are a farming family with goats and a bull; they live off the land in the desert but are displaced from the bioregion to which they belong. Jabbar shows that their sense of belonging comes not so much from an allegiance to the nation-state as to their village of Bhimra. These characters are dislodged from both their local environment and their local secular and religious cultures. These narrative aspects are illustrated visually, in part, through changes in imagery to depict dreams and hallucinations, and variations of color, texture, lighting, angles, and focus emphasize the ephemeral, interior states of mind of the main characters, a woman and her child. Their sense of belonging to the desert and of their displacement from their community is presented in a way that critiques local patriarchy, caste discrimination on both sides of the border in that bioregion, and colonial cartography.

Postcolonial feminist Ambreen Hai (2000, 382) writes, "Because inequity tends to build upon Manichean dichotomies, a feminist or liberationist strategy seeks border spaces, the in-between that challenges the very structure of those oppositions." However, the border spaces we seek are not always easy to find and not always worthy of celebration. While Hai warns against "an automatic, ipso facto resonance of laudability" (383), she and other border theorists tend to emphasize border spaces through regions where people's cultures and languages are similar on both sides.[6] My analysis builds on and extends border theory to provide the environmental specificity that focuses on people who belong to a particular bioregion.

For instance, the international border that cuts through the Thar Desert clearly hinders social and ecological sustainability. While both India and Pakistan are continuing efforts to alleviate poverty and environmental degradation in their own parts of the Thar Desert, they are not working together, and the problems are enormous. In Pakistan, according to journalist Zofeen Ebrahim (2015, para. 3), the Tharparkar district "lies in the south-east of Sindh province. With a population of about 1.2 million, it is one of the poorest of Pakistan's 120 districts, with the lowest Human Development Index." The bioregion's environmental difficulties are the same on both sides of the border, but the governments of Pakistan and India do not cooperate in resolving them. Research analyst Sreya Panuganti (2012, para. 9), writing for the Stimson Center, insists that "Indian and Pakistani policy makers could both benefit from discussing best practices regarding how to contain shifting sands, achieve balanced soil fertility management, and manage the area's scarce surface- and groundwater supplies. Taking up such a dialogue could allow both countries the opportunity to open up a rare unified front in tackling a pressing transboundary issue" (Panuganti 2012). *Ramchand Pakistani* contributes to a bioregional agenda by highlighting the place-based belonging of these people of the desert, especially Champa, whose struggles are depicted through an ecofeminist stance. She and others are clearly attached to their homeplace, but women are treated similar to cattle and have to fight to make decisions for themselves.

In *Ramchand Pakistani*, the border cutting through the desert biore-gion causes a great deal of trauma for two of the characters, Ramchand and Shankar, because they end up in an Indian jail for five years for crossing it. This border is the result of what bioregionalist Gene Marshall (1993) calls a superimposed map. Marshall argues that mapping should be considered in a personal, rather than a political, way. He writes, "We cannot turn our mapping task to some professional geographer. Maps which are super-imposed upon us from 'higher authorities' or 'scien-tific theorists' mean nothing to us personally unless data from such sources resonate with our personally felt sense of place" (53). *Ramchand Pakistani* depicts a kind of a map that includes a personally felt sense of place for the characters. The film shows how a personally felt sense of place might ignore or deny such a political boundary, especially in the Thar Desert, where the economic and environmental struggle to grow food might supersede nationalism.

According to philosopher Jim Cheney (1989), the concept of place can help us think ethically, especially through narrative. He writes, "What I propose is that we extend these notions of context and narra-tive outward so as to include not just the human community, but also the land, one's community in the larger sense. Bioregions provide a way of grounding narrative without essentializing the idea of self, a way of mitigating the need for 'constant recontextualization' to undercut the oppressive and distorting overlays of cultural institutions" (128). In *Ramchand Pakistani* the oppressive and distorting cultural institutions are represented by the physical and political border and its associated discourses, which other not only Indians and Hindus in Pakistan but also Muslims and Pakistanis in India. However, the medium of film grounds this narrative in the landscape of Thar, a region whose geog-raphy undercuts religious nationalism.

As with other borders created by colonial powers around the world, the border between Pakistan and India does not take the local people or their environment into consideration. According to historian Lucy Chester (2009, 21), the Indo-Pakistan border was created using Brit-ish Survey of India maps rather than new surveys produced for non-colonial purposes. Non-colonial surveys would have included aspects of the land and its people that did not matter to the British. Chester writes that the British survey maps

> were invaluable as tools to help the British control British India as they understood it, but they did not display the kinds of information that would allow the division of India with the minimum disruption — or, perhaps, demonstrate that a minimally invasive procedure was not possible. Even on local revenue survey maps, the villages that were home to the vast majority of South Asians appeared only as blank space, outlined by administrative boundaries. The voices of those living in those villages, voices that might have argued for a different boundary line, were stilled by this cartographic silence. (22)

Chester's excellent work points to one reason why the border between India and Pakistan is fraught with tension: British survey maps made it appear that the partition would not be overly disruptive and invasive, but newer survey maps may have led to a contestation of the boundary line and perhaps of partition itself.

The border functions to demarcate the self from the other. According to sociologist Navtej Purewal (2003, 547), the border divides "the provinces/regions of Sindh, Rajasthan, Gujrat, Kashmir and Punjab . . . [and] not only signifies where the nation-states of India and Pakistan begin and end, but . . . also territorializes and nationalizes local populations and identities." On the one hand, the population is nationalized as either Indian or Pakistani depending on which side of the border the people call home. On the other hand, by simply looking across the border one can see the land and region are the same on both sides. Film critic Adrian Athique (2008, 475) points to the "obvious anomaly (and hence semiotic instability) of a border that has no established historical precedent, follows for the most part no obvious geographic feature, and which represents no clear cultural or linguistic disjuncture." Thus, the border's ability to nationalize local populations is simultaneously questioned and resisted by historical, cultural, linguistic, and geographical similarity.

Political scientist Sankaran Krishna (1994) argues that the border produces cartographic anxiety, which Athique (2008, 474–75) glosses as "an obsession with territorial fragmentation caused by the trauma of Partition" experienced by both India and Pakistan. Krishna points out that part of the reason for the anxiety is that the British drew the line arbitrarily before they left without even mapping the entire border. In fact, regarding the Siachen Glacier, Krishna (1994, 511) writes, "interestingly, this part of the Indo-Pakistan border was left unmapped at Partition because the cartographer considered definition to be unnecessary: the terrain was so inhospitable and the details so sketchy that it was not anticipated the area would become a matter of contention." Despite the inhospitable terrain, it has been "dubbed the world's highest battlefield" (BBC News 2014). Battle, however, is not what is killing the men who are posted there; instead, "more soldiers have died from harsh weather on the glacier than in combat since India seized control of it in 1984" (BBC News 2014). The perceived need for this border's violence comes out of Indian and Pakistani nationalism. Krishna (1994, 512) reports, "One in two soldiers posted to Siachen will die, and at any moment in time, over two thousand men are stationed at Siachen. On average, soldiers who return alive have lost from 7–12 kilograms in weight during their three-month stint. . . . The Indo-Pakistan border, here as elsewhere, is literally being drawn in blood." Krishna recommends "denationalizing the narratives that embody space and time" (518), and, to a large extent, that is exactly what both *Khamosh Pani* and *Ramchand Pakistani* are doing.

Place and Politics

The opening shot of *Ramchand Pakistani* establishes the significance of the land as the viewer is introduced to the place in an extreme long shot of the bioregion. While the credits appear, goats walk across the screen from left to right followed by eight-year-old Ramchand. The next shot is a close-up of a single goat, which Ramchand hurries along until it joins the other goats. In the next scene, Ramchand tries to use a whistle while a young boy on his way to school yells at him, "Ramchand! Your mother wants you to go to school." Ramchand scoffs and ignores him. The film then cuts to a farming scene in which Ramchand's parents, Shankar and Champa, are working the land (see fig. 8). Champa tells Shankar, "Go! You'll be late." As Shankar leaves for his job as a teacher at

LYRICS
Anwar Maqsood

8. Image from the beginning of *Ramchand Pakistani* that establishes the family's livelihood by showing Champa and Shankar farming in the desert. Dir.: Mehreen Jabbar.

the local elementary school, Champa continues farming. These scenes show Ramchand's skill as a goat herder and Champa's skill as a farmer, as well as the importance that she and Shankar place on education. Both the goat herding and the farming scenes occur before the credits end, establishing early on the family's ownership of farm animals and attachment to the land based on agriculture.

Due to the family's poverty, this attachment is extremely precarious. Later, when the Border Security Force in India questions Shankar, he reveals that he does not own any land. And the little property that he and Champa do own—the goats and a bull—is difficult to keep because of their debt. Director Jabbar focuses on the effects of this poverty on Champa. Ownership of the bull is important to her; after Shankar and Ramchand disappear and Champa is pressured to pay back their loan to the landlord Ghulam Rasool, she initially resists selling it.[7] When Rasool refuses to forgive the interest on the loan, Champa is given two options: She can either work for five years to pay back the loan or sell the bull to pay off the interest and only work for three years. She reluctantly chooses to sell the bull, and her dire straits are articulated by her sister-in-law when she states, "At least you'll get food for three years."

Between their lack of land and their loans for survival, the family has no possibility of advancement.

The film emphasizes the consequences for a poor woman. As Mohanty (2003, 243) has written, "Poor women and girls are the hardest hit by the degradation of environmental conditions, wars, famines, privatization of services and deregulation of governments, the dismantling of welfare states, the restructuring of paid and unpaid work, increasing surveillance and incarceration in prisons, and so on. And this is why a feminism without and beyond borders is necessary to address the injustices of global capitalism." By grounding the film in a subsistence farming community, showing its economic difficulties, and then highlighting its effects on a poor woman, Jabbar exposes the results of extreme poverty and critiques the gendered effects of global capitalism.

The landlord's manager tries to trick Champa into bonded labor when she attempts to settle her account with him. First, he refuses to acknowledge her, saying that he'll talk to Suresh, Shankar's brother. Even though Suresh has become her male guardian, Champa responds, "I'm the one who worked on the farm. So you settle with me." She continues, "I've spent a full 3 years on this land." The manager counters her claim: "There are still 4 months left. Get back to work." But she insists, "There are no more months left." She tells him that she remembers "the dates and the crops" and that she has "harvested 3 wheat crops and 2 sugar cane crops." She leaves him, saying, "Go and tell the landlord . . . Shankar's debt has been re-paid in full," and storms away (see fig. 9). Her insistence and aggressiveness lead to his silence, and the viewer is shown how easily all of these workers can slip into a cycle of bonded labor. According to Matthew Green of Reuters (2013, para. 10), "bonded laborer" is a "term used in Pakistan for an illegal but widely prevalent form of contemporary serfdom in which entire families toil for years to pay often spurious debts." Sometimes bonded laborers are referred to as indentured workers, but it is unquestionably a type of slavery. According to Owais Tohid (2003, para. 6) of the *Christian Science Monitor*, in Sindh, "indentured workers are mostly inhabitants of Pakistan's Thar Desert, bordering India's Rajasthan arid zone. They entered this cyclical trap when they needed money to survive during their seasonal migration from the drought-hit desert." Champa is able

9. Champa is not tricked into providing more labor for the landlord in *Ramchand Pakistani*. Dir.: Mehreen Jabbar.

to avoid this contemporary form of slavery, but many others do not. Even though many poor women end up becoming bonded laborers, this cinematic representation of Champa's fighting back shows viewers that resistance is possible.

One reason for such oppression is that Champa and others must migrate to farm for the landlord, who can then take advantage of their desperation. Ecological philosopher Mitchell Thomashow (1999) states that our sense of place must include those who simply cannot remain rooted and have to migrate. He writes that "in the twenty-first century, having a homeland will represent a profound privilege" (123). The film shows this with the family's treatment by both Pakistani and Indian state officials, and with the fact that Champa and her family must travel to find work because the Thar Desert region does not have the rainfall to sustain year-round farming practices. In the opening scenes, they are farming close to their huts in the desert, but later they must move with all their belongings and animals to live in quarters that the landlord provides to work his fields near the barrage areas. Journalist Salam Dharejo (2014, para. 7) writes, "Usually, every winter, the shortage of food and fodder leads to a mass migration of the residents of

Thar. Thousands of families, mainly the Dalits belonging to the Bheel and Kohli castes, make their way to the barrage areas where they work on farms. Most of the migrant workers, however, are paid poorly by the landlords." Champa and her family are not nomads but farmers working in conditions that do not allow them to remain at home to farm throughout the year. They farm for landowners to survive but can easily be exploited by them.

After Ramchand and Shankar have disappeared, Champa resists migrating in the same way that she resists selling the bull. Just as her animals are important to her, so is the place where she lives. When Shankar's brother Suresh tries to move her goats, Champa shouts, "My animals stay here!" Suresh is surprised because she risks starvation, but Champa states, "I told you I won't go." Suresh says, "Have you lost your mind? Are we supposed to leave you alone here? The Rangers said that border-crossers don't come back so quickly." Champa insists, "They will come back!" Suresh responds, "So we'll return next year." Champa repeats, "You go if you want to, I won't!" At this point, Suresh raises his hand to slap her but stops himself. Then he tells his wife, "Talk some sense into her or I will tie her up and take her anyway!" This threat of violence against Champa displays the film's ecofeminist stance; it parallels his treatment of the animals and shows the extent to which women are treated as if they are cattle and property in this patriarchal society.

Despite the threats of violence and starvation, Champa refuses to leave. She hides for three days and nights in an abandoned old building while Suresh and others search for her. At one point, one of the men in the search party says, "It's been three days. She must have crossed the border. Let's go back, Suresh. Come on." In the morning, she sees a caravan of people and animals leaving without her. When she returns to her hut, unlocks the door, and goes inside, she finds food has been left behind for her probably by Suresh's wife, who has tried to comfort Champa throughout her ordeal. Champa stays alone in her home for a year before finally agreeing to migrate. She does not have a choice, just as she did not have a choice but to sell the bull. Poverty, rather than a lack of attachment to the land and homeplace, is what drives these decisions. However, that Champa would have migrated if Shankar and Ramchand were present does not detract from the powerful representation of a religious-minority rural woman who, in the face of tremendous adversity, refuses to leave the place she calls home. In depicting religious-minority women with such deep attachments to the land of Pakistan, both *Khamosh Pani* and *Ramchand Pakistani* encourage audiences to be more inclusive and tolerant of difference.

Ramchand returns at the end of the film and reunites with his mother, who is living in the same hut in Bhimra, near the small-scale subsistence farm that provides her livelihood. The winter migration is obviously temporary, and this final scene of the film shows both mother and son's bond with what they consider their home. Ramchand waits at the hut as Champa arrives with firewood, showing that she continues to work and live off the land. Interestingly, at the film's conclusion, as we see Ramchand and his mother reunited at their hut, Shankar is absent. This is not how we expect the film to end; Shankar has suffered a great deal, and a final reunion scene with his wife and son might seem more appropriate. But by including only Champa and Ramchand, Jabbar not only refuses to present a stereotypical romanticized ending but also emphasizes the characters' sense of belonging to the place. When they are apart, both Champa and Ramchand are the ones shown worrying about and being traumatized by displacement. Literary critic Humaira Saeed (2009, 487) points out that a "shift in the film's visuality is . . . used in *Ramchand Pakistani* to represent a dream sequence of Ramchand's as well as a hallucination of Champa's. These moments . . . use shifts in filmic portrayal to disrupt the viewing experience." These two shifts and disruptions in lighting and color are associated with Champa and Ramchand but not with Shankar. Even though we see Shankar being tortured and traumatized, his role is secondary to those of Champa and Ramchand. We never see his dreams, hear his interior thoughts, or experience his trauma from within. He is there simply to protect and care for them. The shifts to interior life via visuals show that the woman director is more focused on the main woman character and her child.

When Ramchand is in jail, he falls asleep and dreams of running through the landscape of the desert to a saint's tomb and looking for his mother there. When he says, "Mother!" a bat flies down from the ceiling, and Ramchand runs out of the tomb in a flash of light and wakes up in jail. The same saint's shrine is shown when Champa goes there to pray for Ramchand and Shankar's safe return. Ramchand thus dreams of an actual place that his mother frequents. In his dream, Ramchand imagines the place he calls home, and part of that place is his mother. The sequence demonstrates that the boy has been traumatized by the loss of both his homeplace and his mother. Interestingly, he never sees his mother in his dream but only calls out to her. The bat might not be what he was looking for, but the tomb and landscape represent an idea of home. Also in his dream, he rolls a tire with a stick as he runs through the desert. This desire for mobility is shown as positive for Ramchand as he crosses other borders by climbing into someone's truck and pretending to drive it early in the film.

The second shift in visuality occurs when Champa hallucinates about the ways in which her local community might reject her if she is a widow. At first, she is convinced that Shankar and Ramchand are alive, but on one of her daily visits to the police for news, she overhears one of them say, "I doubt they're even alive." She then takes off some of her bangles in ritual recognition of her widowhood but puts them on again when she realizes the seriousness of being a widow in her patriarchal Hindu community, where the presence of a widow at a religious ceremony is considered inauspicious. Throughout the film, Champa engages in Hindu ceremonies including a marriage, Holi, and other festivals, as well as two scenes of prayer for the safe return of Shankar and Ramchand. The film's postcolonial ecofeminism illustrates that all of these religious ceremonies ground Champa in her environment, the land, and her culture. She is shown making idols out of the desert soil and sand, and she is present as musicians play, dance, and sing. When Champa realizes that she might be cut off from all of these ceremonies, she cries even more. She has lost her family but cannot admit that Shankar might be dead because her status as a widow would come at a high social cost.

At night she lies awake and hallucinates that everyone she knows, even Suresh's wife, turns away from her. The villagers stand around the desert huts, but the colors have changed; the scene lacks the warmth of the other scenes shot near the huts. The villagers' faces become slightly distorted as they stare, and Champa, terrified, behaves as if they are coming after her. She is awoken by a worried Abdullah, who says he had not seen her for three days and has brought her food and her son's whistle. Champa is suffering a kind of homelessness that is similar to what Ramchand experiences in his dream when he finds a bat instead of his mother. Both scenes show the important ways in which Ramchand and his mother have been displaced while also linking them on another level, rendering their reunion at the end even more significant.

The family engages in subsistence farming throughout the year until the winter when they are forced to move. They are clearly not nomads or people who have no permanent home, because their home, where they farm for themselves, is in Bhimra. They are not hunter-gatherers, and they do not travel to find pasture for their livestock. They are farmers who cannot farm at home all year long and must farm on other land-owners' farms to survive the winter. This mass migration of thousands of mainly Dalit families unsettles traditional ideas about agrarianism that emphasize belonging to the land and farming where one lives; these ideas do not include migration.[8] Writing in a North American context, ecocritic Janet Fiskio (2012) theorizes and explains these ideas. She writes, "The concept of place in ecocriticism and the New Agrarianism is complicated and intensified by the experiences of transient communities" (320). The transient communities of Thar complicate the idea of place.[9] Moreover, Fiskio states, "the question then becomes whether the concept of place can be reformulated in ways that are inclusive of communities who travel the borders of the food system and compelling to contemporary ecocriticism. An agrarianism of the margins unsettles the fundamental assumptions of traditional agrarianism and ecocriticism" (302). Fiskio's "agrarianism of the margins" is inclusive of this Dalit community, which is both agrarian and migrant. As noted, Ramchand's parents farm together where they live but they cannot make enough money to stay in one place all year round and must migrate every winter to Rasool's farm. The film draws attention to the plight of these people and reminds viewers of all the economic migrants of the world, displaced from their homeplaces and shunned wherever they go.

Denationalizing Official Narratives

Sumar's and Jabbar's films denationalize the narratives of space-time by countering state-supported national and religious narratives. These official nationalist narratives of Pakistan center on Muslims and marginalize Hindus, Sikhs, and other religious minorities, including Ahmadi and Shia Muslims. Sumar and Jabbar focus their narratives on religious minorities and depict religious practices that Muslims, Hindus, and Sikhs alike share. This dismantles the center/periphery binary that marginalizes these people. The films resist Pakistan's increasing overemphasis on global Islam by showing its damaging effects not only on women and non-Muslims but also on local, indigenous religious practices such as visiting saints' tombs and making pledges, or *manats*. While Sumar's film questions Pakistan's Islamization policies from an overtly feminist perspective, Jabbar's simply portrays the religious customs and practices of Pakistan's Hindus while showing how they are discriminated against in both Pakistan (for being Hindu) and India (for being Pakistani). Jabbar's critique is subtler than Sumar's, but it still takes an implicitly feminist stance.

In *Ramchand Pakistani*, we see a Muslim Pakistani named Abdullah arrive at and take part in the Hindu festival of Holi. The scene shows friendly relations between people of different religions. In addition, both films present Muslim and Hindu women engaging in the same indigenous religious practices, such as tying a *manat* to a tree next to a saint's shrine. In *Khamosh Pani*, Muslim and Sikh women are shown praying at a tomb and tying a flag (see fig. 3), while in *Ramchand Pakistani* Champa, a Hindu woman, engages in the same practice (see fig. 10), praying for her husband and son's return. That both female directors show women tying flags to trees at shrines regardless of religion emphasizes the value of these practices, especially for women who feel powerless. Moreover, especially in *Khamosh Pani*, these practices are set in direct opposition to the negative cosmopolitanism of globalized Islam, which frowns upon such customs and is represented by men. Sumar follows the scene with women praying at a saint's tomb—a multireligious practice—with one featuring men at the mosque talking about "the true Muslim" (see fig. 4). Thus, both films show that the religious syncretism of South Asia is alive and well in Pakistan, especially among rural women. They present women—Muslim, Sikh, and Hindu—engaging in an indigenous religious practice that global Islam blatantly condemns. These women, Ayesha and Champa, both refuse to leave their homeplaces.

10. Champa tying a *manat* to a tree next to a saint's tomb in *Ramchand Pakistani*. Dir.: Mehreen Jabbar.

The narrative of religious difference is denationalized here, and the Pakistani nationalist narrative that states caste discrimination only happens in India is also questioned. In Jabbar's film, the family is not only poor but also Hindu Dalit. As a result, when Ramchand is first introduced to Kamla, the Indian prison officer responsible for his education, she is horrified at having touched him and reprimands him for not telling her sooner that he is Dalit (see fig. 11). Eventually she grows to care for him, but she needs to be reminded by Deepak, a fellow officer, that everyone is equal in prison. Similarly, in Pakistan, having heard no news of her husband and son, Champa assumes that they are dead and becomes interested in Abdullah, a Muslim man. The landlord's manager quickly reprimands him and states, "You are betraying your religion . . . and you will destroy your life for a low-caste woman of another faith. Shame on you." This shaming tactic works, and Abdullah immediately stops seeing Champa. The shame is based on her faith but also, and possibly more important, her status as a low-caste woman; it would not have been stated if it was not significant. The film demonstrates caste discrimination is prevalent on both sides of the border, regardless of nation or religion, with Pakistani Muslims portrayed as prejudiced as Indian Hindus.

11. Image from *Ramchand Pakistani* showing caste discrimination in India. Dir.: Mehreen Jabbar.

Despite this prejudice, the film shows ways in which bias can be overcome. In his article "From *Padosi* to *My Name is Khan*: The Portrayal of Hindu-Muslim Relations in South Asian Films," religious studies scholar Pankaj Jain (2011, 349) states that *Ramchand Pakistani* "present[s] human relationships that . . . succeed in transcending the religious barriers, though unfortunately [it] fail[s] to cross the political boundaries created in the mid-20th century." This argument is understandable; Muslims and Hindus do overcome differences to work together and stand by each other in this film, especially in Ramchand and Shankar's prison cell. The friendship and camaraderie that develop in the prison cell among all the inmates, Muslim and Hindu alike, are generally positive.[10] Religious barriers are transcended, but political ones are not as the Muslims and Hindus come together but still adhere to their national boundaries. At one moment in the film, it seems as though borders are being defended when the prisoners are all talking together in their cell. Since many of them are in prison for crossing the border, one of them says, "Bloody borders!" Another responds, "There's no need to curse borders. If there were no borders, you wouldn't be a Bangladeshi . . . he wouldn't be an Indian, and I wouldn't be a Pakistani. Let's keep the borders, they're not such a bad thing." The implication is that without the borders, these men would have no sense of identity, and their national identity matters most. This scene is probably what leads Jain to believe that while religious barriers can be transcended, political boundaries cannot.

However, Ramchand and Shankar never refer to their home in nationalist terms, thus completely undercutting this conversation. When Ramchand first crosses the border into India and an Indian border guard asks him why he has come to the border and where he lives, Ramchand points to his village to show the guard where his home is. The guard asks, "Where? In India?" (see fig. 12). Ramchand never responds because as far as he is concerned, his home is his village, not his country. Similarly, during the interrogation scene, Shankar and Ramchand only name their village as their home. Humaira Saeed (2009, 490) writes, "Each time, it takes insistence by national security figures to confirm the national identity of the places being called home by Ramchand and his father." Later in the film, when Ramchand thinks he is being released, he tells Kamla, the female prison guard who has been responsible for his education, that he is leaving. She asks, "Where are you going?" When he responds, "Home," she asks, "Meaning Pakistan?" The film implies that people who are primarily in a governmental position can only think in terms of the national home, but Ramchand and Shankar reject those terms. Thus, Ramchand remains silent when asked about Pakistan. For him, his home is not related to the nation.

In another moment toward the end of the film, when prisoners are exchanged at the border and Ramchand and two of his cellmates—Vishesh and Latif—are released, the specter of nationalism looms over the narrative. But this moment of nationalism is undercut first by Ramchand's father telling him to go straight to Bhimra and then by the song playing in the background. The characters seem lost and uncertain after crossing the border into Pakistan. The border scenes are shot to look grainy, similar to news footage, and as people cross the border, they kiss the ground once they have been garlanded by state officials. However, we do not hear a nationalist song in the background. Instead, throughout these scenes and those depicting Ramchand's return to his village, we hear a song repeating the phrase "Known—or unknown, . . . this is my home—my Nagar." The film's subtitles don't translate

12. The border guard asks Ramchand which nation-state is his home in *Ramchand Pakistani*. Dir.: Mehreen Jabbar.

nagar, which actually means "town." Thus, the phrase can be translated as "my home is that town." The song makes the entire border scene less about the nation-state of Pakistan and more about belonging to the land or a town. In a less concrete way, it could also mean belonging to an idea of home because the song refers to it as "known or unknown."

Even though Ramchand, Vishesh, and Latif are garlanded upon crossing the border into Pakistan after spending years in jail in India, in the subsequent scene they sit on the side of a road looking lost and purposeless, not at all at home (see fig. 13). The film thus implies that in a postcolonial context, one's sense of belonging is place based, not nation based. The aforementioned song continues as we then see a long shot of a bus traveling through a dry, arid land. Following is a close-up of Ramchand, on the bus, looking at a ball in his hand that has been signed by all his Indian, Pakistani, and Bangladeshi cellmates. As he takes the bus from the border to his home, he thinks about the friends with whom he has formed a bond over five years. The song's lyrics become more meaningful once he is shown on the bus, traveling through the desert he knows. Interestingly, the rest of the song's lyrics are not subtitled and therefore not translated in the film. We hear, "This is not a story that I will tell, not a life that I will give up or lose" (my translation). After he

13. (*top*) Image from *Ramchand Pakistani* in which, after crossing the border into Pakistan, Ramchand and his cellmates look lost. Dir.: Mehreen Jabbar.

14. (*bottom*) Ramchand strides confidently from the paved road into the desert in *Ramchand Pakistani*. Dir.: Mehreen Jabbar.

gets off the bus, he walks with more determination and more certainty as the song lyrics also become more purposeful. In fact, we only see his legs walking as he leaves the paved road and continues through the sand in the desert (see fig. 14). In the background, the song lyrics state, "If a wall comes up now, I'll tear it down. Again, those paths known or unknown, my home is that town" (my translation). The final scenes of the film reinforce what Ramchand and Shankar have said all along: They are from Bhimra, a village in the desert, a desert that defies the border because it is on both sides.

The film critiques religious nationalism by depicting Pakistani Hindus and their place-based identities but also illustrates the negative effects of imprisonment for the "crime" of crossing the border. Saeed (2009, 487) argues that "the main project of the film [involves] drawing attention to the effects of the border." The film strongly questions the border by showing a child first inadvertently crossing that border in a terrain that does not change and then spending five years in prison for his error. As noted, the border between India and Pakistan in the Thar Desert bioregion is marked only with white cement markers. And as his father, Shankar, points out during his interrogation, no one was present to stop the boy from wandering across it. The punishment of five years in prison for the eight-year-old and his father, who follows him, is presented as unfair and overly severe, and the film powerfully demands that the viewer question the existence of the border.

This border also creates a discourse of otherness that leads figures of authority in both countries to be suspicious of Ramchand and his father. After Ramchand and Shankar disappear, a Pakistan Ranger tells his superior, Captain Saleem, "Shankar could be an Indian agent." The Pakistani officials suspect that Shankar simply went to India to file a report and share news. In the next scene, which is set in India, a Border Security Force officer tells Shankar, "You look like a Pakistani agent to me." During a later interrogation scene, he is asked, "How long have you been spying for Pakistan?"

The resulting distress exists both in a child's and his father's imprisonment and in a woman's trauma. The mother, Champa, is not given any word of what happens to Shankar and Ramchand. She waits and prays and tries to move on but is constrained by the patriarchal values of her society. When she realizes they must be dead, she considers committing suicide by jumping into the village well. Even though she does not go through with it, this scene is reminiscent of the many suicides women committed during the 1947 partition of British India. Saeed (2009) has argued that Jabbar's film deals with and evokes the 1947 partition of British India because of its focus on the trauma associated with the border. She writes, "The persistence of the Partition insists it has not been resolved, questioning whether the nation and the gendered subjectivities within it can be anything other than unsettled when such a turbulent past continues to repeat on and within cultural production" (497). As mentioned in chapter 1, this was a common result of men's fear of dishonor, which was associated with violence against women during partition. The gendered trauma of partition is also evoked in *Ramchand Pakistani* when the Indian Border Security Forces insist that Ramchand and Shankar be checked to see if they are Muslims or Hindus. In the end, having this information makes no difference to their suspicions against the Pakistanis. The child does not realize immediately that this means he will be stripped, and the father is angry yet helpless to stop the officials from inspecting their bodies to determine whether they had been circumcised. Conducting such examinations was also standard during the mass killings of 1947, as religion was used to decide one's fate. The image of the woman at the edge of a village well and that of men being physically inspected both evoke gendered partition violence and serve to question the discourses of otherness based on religion and on citizenship associated with the creation of the border. In questioning these discourses, the film questions the border itself.

Ethnically, Ramchand and his parents are Kohli people who are similar to the Kohli people in India both linguistically and culturally. When the Pakistanis speak to the Indians in the jail, they speak Urdu while the Indians speak Hindi. Linguistically, they are dialects of the same language and mutually comprehensible. Thus, the film highlights the similarity of both the land and the people on either side of the border.

The oppression of Ramchand's family is the direct result of a number of related and intersecting factors. The Thar Desert's shortage of rainfall forces poverty-stricken farmers to move and work for landowners who take advantage of them and discriminate against them. This situation is not entirely different in India. The film reveals that in the Thar Desert, the concepts of place, belonging, and agrarianism must take into account the forces of desertification that are correlated with oppressive labor conditions, which in turn cannot be separated from the negative effects of caste discrimination, patriarchy, and religious nationalism. The film requires us to see the effects of these forces, rendering visible the plight of a Hindu Dalit woman and her child.

In both the Thar Desert of *Ramchand Pakistani* and the homeplace of Punjab in *Khamosh Pani*, the rural Sikh and Hindu religious-minority women refuse to leave and emigrate from their homeplaces, demonstrating not only their attachment to place beyond nation but also their striving for a feminism without and beyond borders. Both films explicitly and implicitly link the gendered violence they depict to the violence of the first partition in 1947. Chapter 3 discusses a region of Pakistan that became Bangladesh after 1971, the second partition. While the first two chapters rely on films to show the attachments of Pakistan's religious minorities to place, the third chapter uses a novel to show the attachment to place of one ethnic minority group in Pakistan, the Bengalis. The landscape of this region is slowly recovered by a woman character who was displaced from it.

Bengal

Vernacular Landscape

> Our officers were very corrupt. But the Bengalis were loyal to their
> land. Even when we took their families hostage and shot them,
> some of them died crying *Joi Bangla* (Victory to Bangla). How
> can anyone conquer a people who love their land so much?
> WEST PAKISTANI SOLDIER IN INTERVIEW WITH YASMIN SAIKIA

This chapter explores the vernacular landscape of East Bengal, a place
that was East Pakistan between 1947 and 1971.[1] As historian Yasmin
Saikia (2010) and the West Pakistani soldiers discovered, the people of
Bengal love their land. The Bangladesh Liberation War of 1971 occurred
shortly after a huge environmental disaster, the Bhola cyclone, which
also killed many and devastated the region. Even though other critics
have not tied these two events together, separating the cyclone from
the war is as impossible as learning about that time without learning
about that place. For instance, reasons for the war include not only
social issues, such as discrimination against Bengali people, but also
environmental issues such as resource extraction of East Pakistan's jute
for the economic benefit of West Pakistan. In this chapter, I show that
a place-based postcolonial ecofeminist approach is crucial if we are to
understand and heal from the trauma of that time.

In keeping with this emphasis on place, Sorayya Khan's novel *Noor*
(2006) engages with the cyclone, the war, the genocide, and the rapes
by describing at length the drawings and paintings of its eponymous
character. Literary critic Ananya Jahanara Kabir (2009) argues that these
descriptions of art are nonnarrative moments within the narrative of
the novel. I agree with Kabir and extend her analysis to emphasize that
the descriptions are of mostly visual landscape art that depicts East

Pakistan in 1970, during the cyclone, and in 1971 during the war. These nonnarrative moments in the novel that describe visual landscape art (ekphrasis) draw attention to the space of what is now Bangladesh, where once-bloody rivers exist alongside mud pits that are actually mass graves. Reading the novel through a postcolonial ecofeminist perspective, we see that the violation of the land was commensurate with the violation of people, especially women, and true healing will only come about with that acknowledgement. Not only does the novel show how inseparable the environmental issues are from the social issues through the art but it also provides a blueprint for the possibility of healing from trauma as a result of engaging with visual landscape art.

The story of Bengal is the story of multiple partitions. While Lord Curzon was unable to partition Bengal in 1905,[2] when Punjab was partitioned in 1947 amid mass killings and rapes by Muslims, Hindus, and Sikhs against each other on the basis of religion, Bengal too was divided. According to historian Joya Chatterji (2007, 1), "Roughly two-thirds of the territory of Bengal was carved out to create the province of East Bengal in Pakistan." Calcutta and many Hindu Bengalis went to West Bengal in India, while Dhaka and Muslim Bengalis went to East Bengal in Pakistan. Feminist sociologist Shelley Feldman (1999, 168) finds that 1947 in Bengal was "less violent" than in Punjab.

However, even though in 1947 the violence in Punjab was greater, in Bengal in 1971, the violence was much more one sided and similar to ethnic cleansing and genocide because of the ethnic and linguistic differences between Bengalis and non-Bengalis. I define genocide as political scientist Bina D'Costa (2011, 12) does: "the systematic extermination of a human community because of its ethnicity, nationality or religion." In 1947 all sides in the conflict were equally to blame for the violence. As D'Costa (2011, 13) writes, "During the 1947 Partition of India, both Muslims and Hindus were the victims and agents of ethnic cleansing and murder." However, in 1971 in Bengal, members of the Pakistan Army killed and raped "in a strategic attempt to target Bengali ethnic identity" (19). According to anthropologist Nayanika Mookherjee (2015), when the East Pakistani leader, Sheikh Mujibur Rehman of the Awami League, won the 1970 elections and the West

Pakistani government refused to transfer power, East Pakistan broke out in protests. In response,

> the Pakistani army, under the command of Tikka Khan, attacked the movement in "Operation Searchlight," starting on the night of March 25, 1971. This crackdown involved setting fire to student hostels, killing various academics and attacking the civilian population. . . . Over the period of nine months and with the assistance of collaborators . . . the Pakistani army raped women and killed Bangladeshi men and women from all walks of life and all social classes, including intellectuals, journalists, students, workers, and villagers (the official but contested numbers are from 300,000 to 3 million dead and 200,000 women raped). Recent scholarship has also highlighted how the non-Bengali "Bihari" communities (who are considered to be collaborators) were killed, and Bihari women were raped by liberation fighters during and after the war. (34–35)

In 1971 the violence was based on not only religious identity but also ethnic and linguistic identity. And not all parties were equally guilty. Despite the killing and raping of Bihari women by East Pakistani Bengalis, for the most part, non-Bengali Muslims from West Pakistan killed and raped Bengali Muslims from East Pakistan on the basis of a long history of discrimination based on ethnicity. According to journalist Tariq Ali (1983, 91), "The soldiery had been told that the Bengalis were an inferior race. . . . Fascist talk of this character gave the green light for the mass rapes suffered by Bengali women regardless of class or creed."

The enormous statistical difference between the estimated death toll of Operation Searchlight—ranging between 300,000 and 3 million—is due in part to Pakistan's desire to downplay its crimes and in part because a massive environmental disaster, the Bhola cyclone, happened just before the war. According to Srinath Raghavan (2013, 12), "The crisis and war occurred in the immediate aftermath of the worst natural disaster to strike the Bengal delta in the twentieth century. Disentangling the numbers of fatalities caused by these natural and man-made crises is likely to be impossible." In keeping with Doreen Massey and an ecofeminist critical framework, I contend that this impossibility reflects an inability to disentangle the history of that time from the particularities of that place, or that vernacular landscape. Most scholarly work on the war of 1971 makes brief mentions about the cyclone but does not engage with its effects on the land and the people. The human and nonhuman are treated separately in the scholarship just as they are in our imaginations.[3] Massey (1994) encourages us not to separate history from geography. As she has pointed out in a different context, "One way of thinking about all this is to say that the spatial is integral to the production of history, and thus to the possibility of politics, just as the temporal is to geography. Another way is to insist on the inseparability of time and space" (269). Massey proposes that a particular place cannot be considered without also considering its moment in time and vice versa. To Massey's idea of space-time, I add Joni Adamson's (2001) vernacular landscape to take into account the people's relationship to the land. Together, both of these concepts allow us to be honest about what happened at that time to the people of that land, to understand what we can learn from it, and to determine how we should react in the future, because not only are we thinking of space and time together but we are also emphasizing people's relationship to that land. Read through this critical framework, *Noor* implies that attention to space-time and vernacular landscape can lead to understanding and healing from the trauma of war and violence.

Massey (2005) argues that when we think in terms of space-time, we cannot romanticize the past. In the case of East Pakistan, we cannot assume, as many West Pakistanis do, that what happened was inevitable because East Pakistan was geographically too far away from West Pakistan or because East Pakistani demands could not be accommodated. Alaska is geographically far from the rest of the continental United States, Canada has two official languages, and many countries function and thrive despite and because of ethnic differences. As Massey (2005, 141) writes, "There can be no assumption of pre-given coherence, or of community or collective identity. Rather the throwntogetherness of place demands negotiation." This negotiation then becomes the basis of our politics. What could we have done and what shall we do now? How could we have lived with those we were thrown together with then, and how shall we live with those we are thrown together with now?

Massey writes, "In sharp contrast to the view of place as settled and pre-given, with a coherence only to be disturbed by 'external' forces, places as presented here in a sense necessitate invention; they pose a challenge" (141). Massey's view is particularly apt for places in Pakistan pre- and post-1971 because Bengal was neither "settled and pre-given" nor coherent; it had already been divided between India and Pakistan. In 1971 East Pakistan or Pakistani Bengal necessitated "invention" and posed a "challenge" to think about how to live together.

Following Massey's important work, this chapter discusses 1971 as inseparable from space and place to open up the possibility of a politics of interrogation. When we envision East Pakistan in 1971, we must challenge ourselves to consider the possibility that East Pakistan's becoming Bangladesh was not inevitable but instead was the result of the genocide that the Pakistani military committed against its own Bengali population. Last, we must interrogate what happened in that space-time to see the parallels between Bengal 1971 and Balochistan today. In discussing the authors of narratives of social suffering, literary critic Ramu Nagappan (2005, 15) argues that they are "engaged in the pedagogical task of teaching audiences to see and reinterpret recent South Asian history from outside the confines of familiar discourses about the nation and national unity. . . . The text seeks to propel its audience back into the social realm where human intervention can have tangible effects."

In Bangladesh the violence of 1971 has been depicted in film, literature, and even sculpture.[4] As with 1947, most critics focus on trauma and the gendered nature of the violence, with feminist critics giving more attention to the sexual assaults.[5] Mookherjee (2012) writes that West Pakistani (read: mostly Punjabi because the majority ethnicity in the military is Punjabi) men not only raped Bengali women but also sexually assaulted Bengali men. "The issue of male rape, however, remains undocumented in the history of the Bangladesh war" (1600). These violent crimes against humanity were committed on what is now Bangladeshi soil, and Bangla-language narratives of this history persist as part of a Bangladeshi nationalist agenda in which West Pakistani soldiers are always perpetrators and East Pakistani women are always victims.[6] But in Pakistan, few narratives deal with this war, the violence, and the rapes.[7] Moreover, literary critics have not used ecocriticism to foreground the environment in the literary works they study. The focus on space-time and vernacular landscape rather than on nationalism has the potential to help deal with the trauma of 1971. This work is crucial after 1947, since the nationalism of all the countries of South Asia leads them to blame each other for past and continuing violence. As Saikia (2011, 4) has pointed out: "The tendency of national histories in Bangladesh, India, and Pakistan is to partition the memories of 1971, allowing for blame to be relegated to the Other." Ecocritical readings help us move away from othering while simultaneously encouraging us to process and learn from past crimes in Bengal and to imagine a different future for Balochistan.

Pakistani writer Sorayya Khan's novel *Noor* deals with the 1971 partition of Pakistan by using what Kabir (2013) calls embedded nonnarrative moments to better interrogate that time and space, as well as Pakistan's current political trajectory. Kabir argues that partitions are so traumatic that narratives, which often provide closure, cannot (only) be used to represent them. She argues "for the coexistence, and dialectic relationship, between two basic impulses: one, which we may term the 'narrative impulse,' which moves forward in time, and the other, then, the 'lyric impulse,' which lingers over moments and demands that we linger with it" (19). She contends that the lyric impulse of nonnarrative forms of art is better suited to representing partition because they steer away from closure. Her work on nonnarrative forms of art to represent partition trauma is particularly useful in discussing *Noor*, which contains ekphrasis, or descriptions of landscape art, that helps the characters confront their past and ultimately helps them heal. As noted, the novel's nonnarrative moments are descriptions of the drawings and paintings of the eponymous character. These works of visual art mostly depict the vernacular landscape of East Pakistan in 1971 and include important places that trigger memories of the other characters in the novel. These places include the mud pit where two of the characters first meet, the road where one adopts the other, a tree after the Bhola cyclone, and a river that flows with blood. When the novel's characters see these drawings of that landscape, their thoughts return to the place and time of East Pakistan in 1971 as their memories come rushing back to them. As a result, the landscape art is crucial to the characters' process of healing and moving forward by coming to terms with their past.

History, Politics, and Landscape

Bangladesh became independent from Pakistan partly because of Pakistan's violence against its own Bengali population. This violence was rooted in the decision of West Pakistani elites not to share power with East Pakistan. Historian Ian Talbot (2005, 183) writes, "The key to [united] Pakistan's survival lay not in maintaining a strong centre." Nonetheless, West Pakistani military and civilian elites insisted on establishing that strong center. East Pakistanis (now Bangladeshis) wanted both language rights and more political and economic power. According to historians Ayesha Jalal and Sugata Bose (2011, 182), "The Bengalis formed just over 50 per cent of the population of undivided Pakistan, but were poorly represented in the two main non-elected institutions of the state—the military and the civil bureaucracy." The war was precipitated by the 1970 election of a Bengali, Sheikh Mujibur Rehman. Saikia (2010, 182) writes, "The possibility of a Bengali becoming the Prime Minister of Pakistan created panic among the political elite in West Pakistan and the ruling military junta reacted by deploying the national army to frighten the Bengalis into giving up their claim to state power." This claim to state power would not have meant calling for a separate nation-state but simply installing a Bengali prime minister of an undivided Pakistan. Since even this was not acceptable to the West Pakistani elite and military, one reason for the Bengalis' desire for independence and a separate nation-state was very similar to the Muslims' desire for independence in 1947—power-sharing (Jalal 2014). In both cases, both sides were unable to agree on how to share power, and partition was the result.

Not only were Bengalis not represented in elected and nonelected institutions of power but also West Pakistan had a very extraction-oriented relation to East Pakistan's natural resources. West Pakistan was reaping the economic benefits from East Pakistan's jute, a vegetable fiber used to make burlap or gunny cloth. Political scientist Donald Beachler (2007, 472) writes, "While a significant portion of the country's foreign exchange was derived from jute grown in East Pakistan, it received just 35 per cent of the money spent on development projects. The Bengalis believed that they were an economic colony of West Pakistan." A postcolonial ecocritical reading of this situation shows that the ensuing civil war resulted from West Pakistan's extraction-oriented economic policies and its refusal to allow political participation to the majority of the country due to a fascist ethnocentrism that denigrated Bengalis, especially Bengali Hindus, and the Bangla language itself.

In light of these economic inequalities and East and West Pakistan's relations to the space and landscape of East Pakistan, John Brinckerhoff Jackson's (1984) distinction between the vernacular landscape and the official landscape is particularly apt. Joni Adamson (2001) finds in Jackson's work a useful referent to peoples' differing relations to landscapes. Adamson writes that the "vernacular landscape is a folk landscape in which people are attuned to the contours of home and place," whereas the "official landscape . . . is an extraction-oriented landscape, imposed by government and corporation on local geographies without regard for local peoples, cultures, or environment" (90). I use Adamson's definitions of both of these keywords in the context of Pakistan. In my reading, the government of Pakistan imposed an official landscape on East Pakistan because it extracted jute from Bengal without regard for the locals, who did not reap the economic benefit. More tellingly, West Pakistan was very slow to provide aid when the August 1970 floods were followed three months later by the Bhola cyclone, which was considered "the deadliest tropical cyclone in recorded history" (P. Ghosh 2011). In so doing, Pakistan imposed an official landscape on East Pakistan without regard for the local peoples or their environment, and this was part of the reason the East broke away.

While Adamson's discussion of these relations to landscapes appeared in her 2001 book *American Indian Literature, Environmental Justice, and Ecocriticism*, Rob Nixon uses her ideas in his 2011 book *Slow Violence*. He writes, "In the global resource wars, the environmentalism of the poor is frequently triggered when an official landscape is forcibly imposed on a vernacular one. A vernacular landscape is shaped by the affective, historically textured maps that communities have devised over generations. . . . By contrast, an official landscape . . . is typically oblivious to such earlier maps" (17). East Pakistan considered itself to be a colony of West Pakistan because its resources were being exploited. East Pakistan was also being forced to submit to a map that was oblivious to its own charting of space. This may not have led to an environmentalism of the poor, but it did lead to an international war in which India fought on the side of the Bengalis and, eventually, to the creation of the new nation-state of Bangladesh.

The differing mappings of the local Bengalis and the West Pakistanis were both spatial and ideological. Political scientist Philip Oldenburg (1985) argues that East and West Pakistanis had two different ideas about the promise of Pakistan. He writes that West Pakistan failed "to recognize what the meaning of Pakistan was for the Bengalis" (712) and that East Pakistani demands—"for Bengali as a state language, for representation in proportion to their numbers, for a state in which Hindus and Muslims would be politically equal—were aimed at *preserving* Pakistan" (731, italics in original). However, West Pakistanis saw Bengali demands as demands for secession long before they actually became attempts to separate. East Pakistani agitation for more power eventually led the Pakistan Army to launch Operation Searchlight on March 25, 1971. Most call the operation genocide (Mascarenhas 1971; Akmam 2002; Chaudhuri 1972; Jahan 1997; Beachler 2007, 467), and others call it a crime against humanity (Sisson and Rose 1990; Bose 2011, 412). Its goal was to stop the Bengalis from demanding equal rights and equal political power. According to Beachler (2007, 467), "The campaign of murder, rape and pillage that continued until December 1971 caused between one and three million deaths. By some accounts, 200,000 Bengali women were raped."

Amazingly, as Saadia Toor (2011, 116) points out, "There was a virtual silence in West Pakistan over this army action." Part of this silence was due to media censorship, but it was not completely impossible to find out what really happened. According to women's studies scholar Elora Halim Chowdhury (2015, 764), "The Bangladesh War of Liberation is . . . erased as a shameful past . . . in Pakistan"; thus, the silence continues in Pakistan after the truth came out. This silence, however, cannot continue if we are to deal with Pakistan's present and future.

Ali's Atonement

Writing in 1983, literary critic Muhammad Umar Memon was sorely disappointed to find that Pakistani creative writing in the national language, Urdu, did not discuss the disintegration of the nation or the reasons for it and its effects. He writes, "A few diaries, two to three dozen short stories, and a handful of elegiac poems pretty much sum up the corpus of Urdu creative writing on the theme of national disintegration" (Memon 1983, 108). The handful of elegiac poems include Faiz Ahmed Faiz's (1995, 87) "On My Return from Dhaka (Bangladesh III)," which is still one of the most memorable and beautifully haunting Urdu poems ever written on the separation of East Pakistan from the West. However, Memon analyzes a few works of short fiction in Urdu rather than Faiz's magnificent poetry, probably because he had at least two dozen short stories to choose from. Memon finds only one Pakistani fiction writer, Intizar Husain, whose short story "The Turtles" came out in 1981, who "attributes Pakistan's failure in national integration to [a] lack of analysis and self-criticism" (Memon 1983, 125). The story does not appear to be widely read because, as Memon notes, "few [Pakistanis] are willing—or able—to pursue Intizar Husain in his solitary concerns" (125). Thus, he concludes, "Urdu creative writing on the theme of national disintegration is surprisingly small in quantity and quite poor" (124).

This situation has certainly changed. By 2011 literary critic Cara Cilano had found a number of Urdu- and English-language fictional narratives that discuss the events of 1971 for her book of literary criticism *National Identities in Pakistan: The 1971 War in Contemporary Pakistani Fiction*. Cilano (2011, 2) argues that—given the censorship of the media at that time and the fact that the formal after-action Hamoodur Rahman Commission Report was not made public until 2000—these literary narratives are crucial to understanding the 1971 war because "a narrative vacuum emerged at the national level." Part of the reason for this vacuum is that there simply are not any materials to study. According to Raghavan (2013, 11), "Archives in Pakistan remain firmly shut on this controversial episode in the country's history. And there are no official archives relating to 1971 remaining in Bangladesh, as most of the documents were destroyed by the Pakistanis before they surrendered to the Indian forces." Among the narratives Cilano (2006) writes about, Sorayya Khan's *Noor* is the only Pakistani English-language novel to depict the events of 1971 through a "Bengali perspective" (223) and, more important, to force Pakistani readers to face what they owe their Bengali former-compatriots: trials of perpetrators, financial compensation, and an apology. None of these appear to be forthcoming from the state of Pakistan.

In 2002 on an official visit to Bangladesh, Pervez Musharraf, then the military dictator and president of Pakistan, left a hand-written note at a war memorial. While he expressed regret about the bloodshed, he did not actually apologize. Instead, he wrote, "Your brothers and sisters in Pakistan share the pain of the events in 1971. . . . The excesses committed during the unfortunate period are regretted" (Blair 2002, para. 5). The second sentence is constructed passively to allow Musharraf to express regret while completely disassociating himself. Moreover, the pain certainly is not shared equally between East Pakistan and West Pakistan. Musharraf's comments at a banquet later in the day are less passively constructed but still do not convey a direct apology. He said, "I wish to express to the Bangladeshi people sincere regrets for the tragic events, which have left deep wounds on both our nations" (BBC News 2002, para. 15). Musharraf expresses personal regret while refusing to take ownership of the tragedy, implying that it occurred without any instigation from state actors nor from generals, officers, and soldiers in the Pakistan Army.

The Hamoodur Rahman Commission Report, which was completed by three Pakistani judges and submitted to the Pakistani government in 1971 but not made public until 2000, recommended "trials of those who indulged in these atrocities, . . . and alienated the sympathies of the local population by their acts of wanton cruelty and immorality against our own people. The composition of the Court of Inquiry, if not its proceedings, should be publicly announced so as to satisfy national conscience and international opinion" (H. Rahman 2013, 37). This report recommended justice in the 1970s, but to date no legal measures have been taken. The Bangladesh government had found 195 Pakistan Army officers "against whom irrefutable evidence had been collected" (Raghavan 2013, 269). However, as Cilano (2011) writes, "it is important to note that no member of the Pakistani armed forces was ever prosecuted for the 'excesses' of the war, as the *Report* recommended. Nor were their names 'officially' released until the *Report* itself was leaked a generation and a half *after* the war" (25, italics in original). Because Bangladeshi courts cannot try Pakistani citizens, political scientists Jalal Alamgir and Bina D'Costa (2011, 39) maintain that an international war crimes tribunal is necessary, as both Pakistan and India "ratified the [United Nations] Genocide Convention that stipulated action against . . . genocide, conspiracy to commit genocide . . . [and] complicity in genocide." However, Bangladesh's current trials involve only local collaborators,[8] and no Pakistani citizens have ever been brought to trial. Moreover, Musharraf's expressed regret without a full apology inspires little confidence that the state, or even its military forces, will assume any responsibility or consider punishment. Leaders of the opposition in Bangladesh were quick to point out that regret is not an apology. Nonetheless, the "Bangladesh Government was swift to welcome the move" (BBC News 2002) probably because they did not expect even an expression of regret from the president of Pakistan. Continuing demands for an apology from Pakistan remain unsuccessful.[9]

An ecocritical reading of *Noor* emphasizes the landscape of Bengal through which the novel makes a substantial statement regarding Pakistan's debts to Bangladesh. Eventually, the reader must contemplate and question Pakistan's lack of a trial for the perpetrators of violence and its subsequent refusal to apologize. The novel centers on Ali, a Pakistani soldier who tries to atone for his past violence. After returning home from the war, Ali engages in multiple acts designed to punish himself, often physically. For example, on the night of his return, he shaves his head (54) and sits in a scalding hot bath (53), stops praying (129), gives up eating both meat (25, 142) and sweets (58), and never marries (36, 129).[10] But the only act that the novel refers to as an act of atonement is Ali's adoption of a five- or six-year-old Bengali girl named Sajida who lost her parents in the Bhola cyclone of November 1970 and lived through the subsequent war. Ali later realizes that he adopted her, a victim of both the cyclone and the war, more for his own sake than for hers. Khan writes, "In the shape of the child crouched over a curb in downtown Dhaka, Ali imagined making amends, atoning. Taking the child home, making her his daughter, Ali worried that in pretending to save her, he remained what he wanted, so badly, no longer to be" (172). While Ali gives Sajida a home where she lives happily with his mother, Nanijaan, and later with her husband, Hussein, and their three children, he still worries that he remains the same man he was during the war—"an officer in the Pakistani Army" (49).

The men who fought in 1971 have an especially fraught relationship to the violence since they are mostly its perpetrators. After interviewing in 2004–5 "123 Pakistani military personnel who represented different ranks" (186) at the time of the 1971 war, Yasmin Saikia (2010) concludes that the "armed violence in 1971 . . . became a site for personal transformation for some soldiers who had experienced the war first-hand. An ethics of humanity emerged, motivating them to question the call for 'duty,' i.e., commit violence. In short, one can say that the perpetrators were humanised in the war" (179). The personal transformation that some of the perpetrators experienced involved understanding their own mortality as they killed others. Saikia writes, "In their victims' death, perpetrators saw their own emotional and psychological fragility and vulnerability" (198). Ali can be read as the representation of a perpetrator who has been transformed by the war and becomes more aware of his own vulnerability. Khan describes "fancying his head a wall-sized cabinet of drawers that could be nailed closed. . . . He sat on the edge of the bathtub, slowly forcing his body into the water. . . . He submerged his feet, and just like that, he relegated the screams to one drawer, the pit of dead bodies and their scattered twitching into another" (53). Ali deliberately takes this bath to relegate the horrors of the war to various "compartments" that he believes will remain closed forever, thus enabling his rebirth.

However, other changes in Ali after the war seem less deliberate and more in keeping with Saikia's idea of soldiers becoming more human because of the war. As his mother recalls, "He'd learned to love" (130). His love for Sajida is so great that he cries publicly when she dislocates her shoulder. Nanijaan narrates, "The doctors said they'd never seen a father cry over a daughter's injury before and let him stay in the room" (130). But he did not only love Sajida; also, according to his mother, "he was an ocean of patience . . . he'd wait until eleven for dinner guests who should have been here at eight-thirty and then meet them in the driveway without a grumble" (130). The scalding hot bath and his love for Sajida and all humanity show that Ali is a new man and not the guilty officer he once was even though he accepts responsibility for what he did, punishes himself, and awaits further punishment.

Spatial Dreams, Spatial Drawings

Pakistan's actions against its own citizenry, as well as the actions of characters in this novel, are all social relations, which cannot be conceived of without the spatial relations. Massey (1994, 2) writes that we should be "thinking of space, not as some absolute independent dimension, but as constructed out of social relations: that what is at issue is not social phenomena in space but both social phenomena and space as constituted out of social relations, that the spatial is social relations 'stretched out.'" *Noor* is especially suited to this type of spatial analysis because it depicts vivid images of the East Pakistani vernacular landscape not only in the memories and dreams of various characters but also in the drawings of the eponymous character. Noor's drawings show the spatial context of social relations by what the drawings depict and by the memories they trigger in Sajida and Ali, the two characters who were in East Pakistan in 1971.

Even before Noor is born and begins drawing and painting the landscapes of East Pakistan, Noor influences Sajida from the womb. From the moment Noor is conceived, "Sajida had known immediately that her daughter would be different. But the recognition that her daughter was a thread to another world came to Sajida slowly, during the long nights of her pregnancy when she was frequently awakened by an aching bladder" (5). This other world is East Pakistan in 1971. During her pregnancy, Sajida begins to see and dream of color in more vivid detail, especially the colors of the landscape of East Pakistan. "Surrendering to deep sleep, Sajida's dreams grew more vivid than they had ever been. She pictured the landscape of East Pakistan—Bangladesh now—and her long-ago childhood in greens, each different from the last: rice paddies, banana leaves, palm trees, limes, sails of fishing boats" (6). Noor connects Sajida to the landscape of East Pakistan through dreams with vivid images that she never had before this pregnancy.

Kabir (2009) argues that fiction and narrative are part of the problem in representing partitions (1947 and 1971). This point is in keeping with Memon's (1983) assertion that most of the fiction regarding 1971 is "quite poor" (124). One of the problems with a narrative is that it usually follows a cause-and-effect structure that produces more condemnation than reconciliation. Memon criticizes most of the fiction he analyzes because it typically denounces Bengalis and Indians for the war and secession. He claims that short fiction writer Parvin Sarvar fails artistically because of her "haste to blame the Indians and East Pakistani Hindus for sowing the seeds of dissension and secession" (Memon 1983, 124). Kabir (2009), however, states that visual art and lyric poetry, such as Faiz's, lacks this problem because they do not follow the linear logic of cause and effect.

Ali's memories of East Pakistan are interspersed throughout *Noor* in italics. These snippets, while from Ali's perspective, do not provide a satisfying glimpse of that time and place. "Ali accepted that these conversations, if that is what such snippets were, were one-sided. Of course, Ali thought, he was speaking to himself. . . . When whiffs of stories rose like a stench from the file cabinets inside his head, he discovered that the only way to . . . return the details to where they had come from, was to put them into words—to himself . . . But the words were always wrong, lacking. They were never quite the memories, the sounds and smells, sharp and crystal clear" (182). Ali's one-sided conversation with himself fails because of its narrative form. The novel's embedded nonnarrative moments of ekphrasis rectify this problem by emphasizing reconciliation instead of blame.

Sorayya Khan's descriptions of drawings and paintings are especially important because, as Kabir (2009, 489) argues, such "embedded nonnarrative moments" can serve to counteract the "narrativization of Partition [which] mires reconciliation and understanding between collective identities." Kabir further notes that "South Asian authors have equally used ekphrasis to comment on the impossibility of narrativizing the post-Partition traumatized self: thus Sorayya Khan's *Noor* locates the traumatic impact of the 1971 war on Pakistanis within the eponymous [child character Noor], who . . . compulsively draws scenes of . . . life in the former East Pakistan" (491). While these embedded nonnarrative moments help us understand the legacy of 1971, Noor's production of visual landscape art, rather than lyric poetry or portraits, further conveys the complexity of that space. The landscape art that depicts space as social relations, location, and time is complex and cannot be simplified into a narrative of blame.

If we consider Massey's space-time and Kabir's critique of narratives of partition, then we can read the novel's many moments of ekphrasis as significant for reconciliation between a Bengali character and a West Pakistani soldier. Noor's devotion "to the vastness and complexities of colors" (27) in the context of landscape provides a representation that is more capable of healing than narrative alone. The multiple moments of ekphrasis, those descriptions of Noor's many drawings and paintings of the landscape of East Pakistan and its social relations in 1971, are not simple and linear. These nonnarrative, landscape-based moments provide the possibility of a politics that examines the political trajectory of the current divided Pakistan.

As noted, Pakistan has held no war crimes trial or issued any apology to Bangladesh. In fact, an official landscape, complete with extraction-oriented policies, has now been imposed on the province of Balochistan. As journalist Mahvish Ahmad (2014, 160–61) has pointed out, "Based on the lucrative Tethyan Belt that stretches into Waziristan and Afghanistan, Balochistan has extensive tapped and untapped resources (copper, gold, oil, gas, lead, and zinc)." This "resource curse," as Rob Nixon (2011) calls it, leads to a reduction in human development for peoples in the global south. Nixon writes, "In resource-cursed societies, a mineral strike, though less immediately spectacular than a missile strike, is often more devastating in the long term, bringing in its wake environmental wreckage, territorial dispossession, political repression, and massacres by state forces doing double duty as security forces for unanswerable petroleum transnationals or mineral cartels. In such societies, a highly concentrated revenue stream is readily diverted away from social and infrastructural investment and into offshore bank accounts" (70). While Nixon is discussing oil-rich Saudi Arabia, the same could be said of Balochistan, which is Pakistan's poorest province; its resources support the rest of Pakistan, just as East Pakistan's resources supported the rest of Pakistan before 1971. If we read the novel *Noor* ecocritically with attention to landscape, these parallels between then and now become more apparent.

Noor, whose name means divine light, has an undisclosed developmental disorder and a divine gift to be able to draw not only her parents' memories but Ali's as well. Noor mostly draws the landscape of East Pakistan when both Sajida and Ali were there, although her early drawings are interpreted differently by different characters, and later she produces a drawing of a shoe. Nonetheless, for the most part, her drawings open the closed compartments of Ali's mind. "His past had arrived. Soon it would be its own gallery, for all to see. However faint, there was a measure of relief in that. Looking at the walls of his house, considering how neatly Noor's drawings were ordered and hung, he knew he'd been wrong in the scalding bath on his homecoming to think he could pack it all away" (128). Even though Ali tries to leave behind the man he was and works hard to repress painful memories, he feels a faint measure of relief when Noor brings back his past in her drawings of the landscape of East Pakistan. More important, he realizes that he was wrong to try to leave his experience in that landscape behind. The novel proposes that what is owed to the people of Bangladesh is exactly this: examining the past, seeing its space, and remembering its relations in order to interrogate Pakistani authorities today.

Noor's drawings also enable Sajida to remember, contemplate, and question the narrative that Ali has told Sajida about how she came to live with him. Kabir (2009, 489) argues that a narrative is limited for two main reasons: "Post-Enlightenment modes of narrative typically rely on the concept of a singular perspective from which material is organized in order to produce the linear logic of cause and effect. Secondly, narrative in general privileges closure." Before Noor was born and started to draw, Ali had closed off the possibility of more discussion on the topic of his adoption of Sajida. The narrative that Sajida had repeated to Ali since she was a child was *You saw me. You found me. You took me*" (176, italics in original). This narrative has a singular perspective, Ali's, and implies that Ali took her because he saw her, realized he was looking for her, found her, and then adopted her. But Noor's drawings neither follow this linear logic nor provide closure. Instead, they lead to more questions, as the landscapes she draws are simply snapshots without cause or effect. The ekphrases in the novel are merely descriptions of the pictures, or moments in space-time. Without the beginning, middle, and end provided by narrative, descriptions of drawings cannot provide closure.

Because Sajida was only fix or six years old when Ali brought her home with him, she is not sure of her memories of East Pakistan. But Noor's drawings take her back to the space and helps her fill in the gaps. One day Noor draws the dented barrels on the road where Ali found Sajida and draws the landscape of the space. The narrator describes the drawing: "A pyramid of tin barrels. Thirty-six of them lying on their sides. . . . The barrels were knocked out of shape, dented and scraped as if they'd been lifted and dropped dozens of times. The sidewalk underneath crumbled, the curb shed rock. Bricks were missing from the whitewashed wall against which the pyramid of barrels was built. Electric wires and tree branches hovered behind. The sky was heavy with the city's dust" (103). While the narrator's description of the drawing emphasizes the sky, the tree, and the sidewalk, when Sajida looks at the drawing, she is taken aback when she remembers the barrels and what is written on them. "It took Sajida only a minute to see beyond the brushstrokes. She knew what had been there. *Joi Bangla*, Hail Bangladesh" (106). Sajida remembers this as she stares at the drawing and is instantly transported. "Sajida wiped her eyes with her fists, as if she were . . . in Dhaka, a city far, far beyond, rubbing away the exhaust from trucks and buses on a street with a crumbling sidewalk" (106). Once she imagines herself back on that sidewalk, Sajida remembers that she had "wandered from the house," a place where relief workers had given her clothes, when Ali took her (107). The bungalow was "lined with flowerpots," and the relief workers had spoken to her in a different language, but she and the reader realize that she was not homeless when Ali took her (107). In fact, Noor's drawing stirs Sajida's memories, which make her "adoption" seem more akin to an abduction. The drawing of the landscape of Dhaka, the place where Ali "found" Sajida, does not produce a story of cause and effect—just space and time and more questions. Why did Sajida wander away from the bungalow? Why did Ali take her? These questions are partially answered by the narrative, which states that Ali "adopted" Sajida to "make amends" (172) for his own actions, but the nonnarrative moment does not provide closure or answers.

Noor's drawings bring back the past and simultaneously the geography of East Pakistan by reminding Sajida of her family's connection to the Bay of Bengal. Living in Islamabad, Sajida is far from the ocean, but when Noor covers pages with the color blue, even though Nanijaan sees the sky, Sajida sees water. In fact, Khan reveals that Sajida can see more than water in Noor's drawings:

> One day, laying out Noor's drawings side by side until they were a carpet in the center of the living room, Sajida saw that Noor's blue was movement. Impatiently, she waited for Noor's drawings, examining and discovering a different pulse in each. Sajida could almost see ripples of water running away from the edge of a beach. She could feel the sweltering days and hear the grind of her father's fishing boat against the sand banks in the Bay of Bengal as it was pushed on land. More than anything else, she could make out fishing nets swimming and bending below the blue of Noor's crayons. (28)

Clearly Noor has drawn waves of blue in such a way that Sajida can imagine the movement, the ripples of water in the ocean, and her father's boat.

Noor's landscapes are vernacular in that they have little to do with West Pakistan's official landscapes, which are associated with a larger world of politics. John Brinckerhoff Jackson (1984, 150) writes that "underneath those symbols of permanent political power there lay a vernacular landscape—or rather thousands of small and impoverished vernacular landscapes, organizing and using spaces in their traditional way and living in communities governed by custom, held together by personal relationships." Jackson differentiates between landscapes that are imposed from above, which are more political, and landscapes that cannot be understood without some understanding of the communities that live on them and in relation to them. The novel's postcolonial ecofeminism shows that in her first drawings, Noor draws with a blue crayon, but her mother, Sajida, sees the water of the Bay of Bengal and fishing nets, and remembers the life of her fishing community in that vernacular landscape.

In a later orange-colored drawing, Ali sees sunsets. Khan writes, "When Nanijaan presented Noor with her first box of crayons . . . , Ali chose an orange one [drawing] (flat and long like sunsets he'd once seen) to hang on his door" (46). The novel hints that Ali is seeing the sunsets of East Pakistan. Later Noor's landscapes of East Pakistan include the devastation of the cyclone (chapter 5); the road where Ali picked up Sajida (chapter 7); the river, which is pink because of the bodies within it (chapter 9); and, most important, the mud pit, or mass grave, where Ali and Sajida see each other for the first time (chapter 12). As the drawings become more complex, the narrator states, "Noor's drawings were no longer simple words to be alphabetized on a wall. They were windows into another world, far away and distant, which might have ceased to exist without Noor" (106). Again it is significant that Noor's name means divine light because she is literally shedding light as she opens "windows" to reveal the vernacular landscape of East Pakistan in 1971, returning not only Sajida and Ali but also the modern Pakistani reader to that place and time, and forcing everyone to remember the devastation that resulted from the imposition of official landscapes.

This imposition began with West Pakistan's slow reaction to the Bhola cyclone of 1970 and continued when West Pakistan decided to terrorize the Bengalis in March 1971. The president of Pakistan at the time of the Bhola cyclone was Gen. Yahya Khan. According to Raghavan (2013),

On the night of 12 November, a cyclone hit the coastal areas of Bengal, with winds billowing forward at 150 miles an hour. . . . Hundreds of thousands perished in the worst natural disaster confronted by the province in the twentieth century. International assistance poured in, but the response from West Pakistan was languid and lackadaisical. Not a single political leader of any standing visited the eastern wing. Yahya had been on a trip to China and stopped in Dhaka on his way back. The president had been celebrating his freshly won commitment from Beijing for increased military assistance by a bout of drinking. He flew over the affected areas in an aircraft, downing several cans of beer to cope with a hangover and casting an alcoholic eye on the barely visible destruction beneath. Yahya concluded that the extent of the calamity had been blown out of all proportion. (32–33)

Raghavan does not provide any reason why no other political leader from West Pakistan visits the area. Surely international aid pouring in for widespread suffering otherwise would have led to visits from multiple West Pakistani leaders. This passage illustrates the criminal negligence of not only the president but all of West Pakistan.

Noor's drawings of the vernacular landscape of East Pakistan counter what Yahya Khan did or did not see by portraying what was left after the cyclone had moved through the area, killing Sajida's parents and five siblings. Noor draws a fisherman's boat over and over again, and Sajida sees her father's boat (74). Noor then dreams of the cyclone and draws the boat in a tree (75), but she does not draw Sajida scared in the tree (76), where she was found. Even though Noor behaves as if she is simply drawing and not seeing the meaning of her sketches, she later confides to her mother that she had seen Sajida in the tree but could not draw her there because as a child she needed to believe that her mother cannot be afraid. Noor's drawings remind Sajida of the events around the cyclone, of how her mother had told her to hold her baby brother, and of how she had eventually clung to a dead, bloated buffalo to stay alive. Noor's drawing accurately portrays Sajida's situation: "In Noor's drawing, Sajida saw a young girl, clothes ripped from her, clumps of hair plastered to her forehead and her neck. Her small hand disappeared into the buffalo's monstrous body. In the corner of the drawing, there was an outline of a baby" (80). The loss of her family, especially of her baby brother, is brought back to Sajida through Noor's drawings. It is only because of Noor that she remembers her baby brother's name; forgetting it had haunted Sajida for years.

The image of the dead, bloated buffalo that Sajida clung to returns at the end of the novel when Ali prostrates himself in front of Sajida and Noor and moans loudly. "The moan, deep and immense, rose gradually. It began in Ali's belly. It rode through his strained vocal chords and gaping throat. It hurled out of his mouth stretched wide like the dead buffalo's" (204). Ali's mouth is described as stretched as that of the dead buffalo's. His mouth magnifies the image of death that he, Sajida, and so many others in East Pakistan in 1971 have seen. Again, there is no linear logic of cause and effect. Death simply is. The novel's postcolonial ecofeminist outlook shows that Noor's landscape art also lacks the logic of cause and effect, and thus it elicits these moments of understanding.

When Ali sees the drawing, he immediately recognizes the landscape of East Pakistan even though he arrived after the cyclone. Ali notices that "the brown-black of the background, the images of torn, upside-down trees and shattered boats, were drawn from an odd perspective, as if from above rather than *inside* the scene. Yet there was a special mist of gray that ran across the picture—so certainly, Ali knew at first glance, that of East Pakistan's monsoons" (83–84, italics in original). The odd perspective is a reference to Noor's name. In this drawing, she sheds divine light and draws from above rather than from within. While Sajida is reminded of what she endured in the cyclone, Ali remembers the landscape and eventually the bloated bodies. By the time we hear Sajida's harrowing tale of survival, Yahya Khan's official landscape has been replaced by Noor's vision, with all the divine authority it implies.

Feminist Literary Fictions

Given that some 200,000 women were raped in East Pakistan in 1971 (Beachler 2007, 467), clearly women were again doubly victimized, as they had been in 1947. And while mass rape has been used as a weapon of war in "Cambodia, Haiti, Peru, Somalia, Uganda, Bosnia, Rwanda, Sierra Leone, Congo and Sudan" (D'Costa 2011, 5), it has not been used in places such as Palestine/Israel or El Salvador (8), thus demonstrating that sexual violence against women is not inevitable during war. D'Costa (2011, 8) argues that "the communal, ethnic and caste divisions of [South Asian] societies reflect the hyper-masculine and militarized structures and ideologies that form the basis of the region's nation-building projects." We can only assume that to a great extent neither El Salvador nor Palestine/Israel rely on ethnic divisions, masculinity, and militarized ideologies to explain the lack of gendercide in their conflicts. Further, the oppression of women continues in South Asia, as evidenced by the gender ratio. Even though women compose 51 percent of the population in most of the world, "the ratio of women to men in the population is dismally low in all three countries [India, Pakistan, and Bangladesh]—some 93 women to 100 men—evidence of acute discrimination along lines of gender" (Jalal and Bose 2011, 204).

This gender discrimination occurs regardless of a family's wealth. As Kumkum Sangari (2015, 3) writes, "The developmental narrative can barely account for why both rich and poor want to avoid daughters." This widespread sexism, however, clearly motivated the violence against and mass rapes of women in 1971.

Noor illustrates this gendered violence through its depiction of both the wartime atrocities of 1971 and Nanijaan's beatings at the hand of her husband, Ali's father. The novel also depicts Sajida and Noor as strong and empowered Bengali women who achieve their strength partly through their connection with the land of East Pakistan. The instances of violence against women in the novel create a strong indictment of West Pakistani patriarchy, while the characters of Sajida and Noor balance the depictions of Bengali women's suffering.

After Noor's drawing of the cyclone, italicized paragraphs start to appear at various points of the novel. These short narratives represent Ali's memories of East Pakistan in his own words. They are startling not only for their racism and sexism but also because they seem to be addressing someone. While Ali's memories contain multiple stories of the victimization of Bengali women, the novel also portrays the empowerment of Sajida and Noor, who are both Bengali in terms of ethnicity. Sajida's empowerment is made possible through Noor's drawings of the East Pakistan landscape in 1971, connecting Sajida to her identity. These landscapes also bring back Ali's memories of the war's sexually abused and tortured Bengali women. While none of the West Pakistani perpetrators of violence in East Pakistan are punished or disciplined in the narrative (or in life), the novel depicts Ali's punishing of himself, as well as the death of Ali's father, Nanijaan's abusive husband. This representation is important given the abject victimization of so many women: "Ali's father fell to the floor one day in the middle of a rage, and died" (64). Even though the novel contains Ali's narratives of brutalized Bengali women in East Pakistan in 1971 and Nanijaan's abuse at the hands of her husband in West Pakistan, Sajida and Noor's empowerment—along with Ali's self-punishment and the death of Nanijaan's husband—ultimately renders the novel as feminist.

Moreover, feminist social relations in space are evoked by Noor's drawing of the Sitalakhya River. "The river was wide, the banks, black and rich, were wider yet, the land flat. . . . The river was divided into two parallel streams. Half the river was pink, the other half gray. The pink was watercolor, the rest crayon. The textured banks of the river were oil paints squeezed roughly from a tube and gently patted down" (126). While Noor does not actually have dead bodies in her painting, Ali recalls that the river is pink from the dead bodies of men.

This river, which he refers to as "his river" (115), is also where Ali buried "the no-breasted woman" (127). Ali had met her at a train station, where she was *parading up and down the platform . . . and there were two huge pink infections oozing pus, yellow, where her breasts should have been. Chopped off, they were* (115–16, italics in original). The novel's ecofeminism links the river with the atrocities against women so we see more clearly that such violence is also linked to violence against the environment. From Ali's italicized memories, we learn that an officer insisted that the men care for the mutilated woman at headquarters. And they did. She told them stories of the terrors of the Bengali people: *The stories were packed with detail, down to the smell of a man's breath: acrid like rot. A story of a family that was slaughtered in broad daylight with a scythe. Another about a baby thrown into the air, caught by a bayonet . . . Men forced to eat their cut-off penises* (116). In describing the twenty-four-year-old no-breasted woman whose words and stories won over the West Pakistani military men around her and who dies despite their care, Khan illustrates the victimization of Bengali women in 1971. That the woman won the soldiers over is evident in that Ali and the others dig her grave twice to keep out the dogs and crows. *The first time a dog dug at the grave and stood still while we threw stones at it. Then we dug the grave again and covered it with rocks. The dogs, crows, didn't bother the grave after that* (117). Because of the novel's ecofeminist stance, her story is linked with Noor's drawing of the river near where she was buried. The drawing, which uses watercolor, crayon, and oil paints, creates a nonnarrative moment in the text that forces Ali to remember the river and the woman. There is no cause and effect, and there is no closure. After looking at the painting, Ali knows the woman is dead, but she lives in his memories. The cause of her death is torture, and the effect of her death is also torture.

Ali's memories of what he saw and what he did in that landscape include the story of a Bengali woman who is silent despite the atrocities that she endures. Unlike the no-breasted woman, she tells no stories and does not make a sound even while suffering excruciating pain. Ali reveals that it was his *"job on night duty to collect the girls and bring them to the officers"* (138). On one night Ali takes the silent woman, a young mother, to his superior officer to be raped and ripped open with *"scissors, pens, a metal ruler"* (141). She submits to all this without uttering a sound. Not only does Ali do nothing to stop the atrocities, but when he is left alone with her, he straddles her *"and thankfully, I couldn't enter her"* (141). It is not clear why he tries to do this when ultimately he is thankful that he could not. Perhaps he feels the need to prove something to himself after his superior officer questions his manhood for not raping her in his presence.[11] But clearly Ali feels guilty because he says, *"I knew what I'd done. I could never change that"* (141).

Rape was common in the 1971 war, and even though the text does not explicitly state it, we can assume that the breastless woman was also raped. Nayanika Mookherjee (2015) writes that although in Bangladesh these women are referred to as "war heroines," or *birangonas*, their experiences are still homogenized. She argues "that identifying raped women only through their suffering not only creates a homogenous understanding of gendered victimhood but also suggests that wartime rape is experienced in the same way by all victims" (6). In *Noor* we are shown two raped women: one who talks and another who is silent. Both talking and silence can be read as resistance. We are also shown two officers in the Pakistan Army: one who is caring and another who is savage. In depicting these varied representations of victims and perpetrators, Sorayya Khan goes out of her way to use a postcolonial ecofeminist stance to muddy the nationalist discourses of both Pakistan and Bangladesh. Noor's drawing of the poisoned river prompts the memories of oppression, showing that environmental justice is inseparable from social justice.

Ali's italicized narrative appears in the same chapter, which begins with Noor's drawing of the river, but it occurs after his mother asks him, "You killed someone?" (133). She too is silent about trauma and unable to ask him what else he did, while he thinks to himself that killing was not the worst of it. Khan's depictions of victimized Bengali women, both the breastless woman and the silent woman, are quite graphic; however, they serve the important functions of bringing such atrocities against women to light and breaking the silence, especially for a Pakistani readership. As Urvashi Butalia (2000, 20) has noted regarding the violence against women in 1947, "unless . . . we are able to talk about Partition, I fear we may not be able to put it behind us." The same holds true for the Bengali women in 1971. Moreover, they did not suffer from violence and rape only during the war; after the war, their own government forced them to have abortions, violating their bodies yet again. Saikia (2011, 52) writes, "After the war the Bangladeshi government mandated an abortion program to get rid of the 'bastard Pakistanis.' . . . The violence of rape was responded to with more violence by the Bangladeshi state. . . . Ideals of purity and impurity, belonging and exclusion, were worked out and physically enacted on the body of women."

In addition to the Bengali women of Ali's memories, the reader also learns his mother's story of domestic violence. Ali's father regularly beat Nanijaan for the entirety of their marriage. In one incident,

> her husband had grabbed her from the back, twisting her shoulders around, until her face was level with his. He wrapped his hands around her neck . . . shouting out of his narrowed mouth. . . . His grip became tighter and tighter until Nanijaan expected something in her neck to crack before he let go. . . . And then he punched her, slamming her face against the wardrobe. . . . Nanijaan pulled herself from the floor and waited until he had finished. He said some more things which . . . were nasty like his blows. (63–64)

The countless incidents of domestic violence that Nanijaan suffers at the hands of a West Pakistani male is reminiscent of the depictions of West Pakistani male violence against Bengali women, not because of its intensity or sexual nature, but rather because the perpetrator in each case feels the need to verbally abuse the women as well. In East Pakistan, "the commander pushed her [another Bengali woman] to the floor. . . . He laughed, called her a whore and much worse. . . . Then he forced his rifle into her mouth, tore her sari, and sat on top of her. When he was done, he stuffed his belt between her legs letting the oversized buckle catch and tear, laughing at how cleverly he had leashed her" (54). Nanijaan's husband also thought he was skillful, using "his gentlest voice to ask for help for his bleeding wife who, he said, had run into the cupboard, *squarely, imagine that!*" (64, italics in original). In both cases, West Pakistani men are depicted as violating women to whatever extent that they can. Apparently the only reason the violence was more horrific during the war is because the authority of the military made it more permissible.

While Nanijaan must wait for her husband to die, the raped woman is completely silent, and the breastless woman dies, Sajida is empowered, living happily in conjugal bliss with Hussein and her three children. The novel opens with the moment that Sajida conceives Noor, her third child, and Sajida's sexuality is not repressed or abused in any way. Moreover, the narrator tells us that when she tries to recall the moment of conception in her mind, it is similar to a memory "like the brief feel of a distant place she might have visited when she was a child" (1). On the novel's first page, we are shown how Noor's conception is related to East Pakistan, a distant place that Sajida can barely remember. The hint of that distant place is evoked by the scent in the air, which is "almost sweet by the faint smells of lovemaking" (1). Cilano (2011, 60) writes, "By including the detail that the room smelled faintly of sex, alongside Sajida's realization that she's just conceived her third child, the novel solidly and directly grounds the event in the materiality of Sajida's body." The novel grounds the event in the materiality of Sajida's body and the materiality of that "distant place" as well. Moreover, Khan is clearly juxtaposing the victimized Bengali women with the empowerment of Sajida as she learns and remembers more about East Pakistan and the truth of her own adoption.

Noor is also empowered by the end of the novel and, in the final scene, appears exactly as she did to Sajida in a vision when she was conceived. Instead of painting on paper, Noor decides to paint herself. Then she dances: "Gradually, in slow waves, her body began to move, from her shoulders to her arms, her chin to her neck, the heel of her foot to the toe, her good leg to her other one, and then, finally, into her hips, until she stood, in utter submission to her own private dance" (202). Thirteen-year-old Noor paints and dances as she pleases in front of a mirror for herself and no one else. When her mother arrives, the two of them laugh together. "Clutching each other, first by their hands and then their shoulders and arms, they shrieked with laughter, gasping for air, until they ached so much they collapsed on the floor and fell on top of each other" (203–4). This embrace is an evocative image of acceptance, love, and empowerment for Bengali women in the aftermath of the devastation of 1971 depicted in Noor's landscape art.

Forgiveness and the Future

Jacques Derrida (2001, 51) has argued that "pure forgiveness" is quite different from the actions that nation-states usually undergo following crimes against humanity. He too would find Musharraf's statement of regret to differ from pleas for forgiveness. Derrida writes, "Forgiveness is often confounded, sometimes in a calculated fashion, with related themes: excuse, regret, amnesty . . . forgiveness must in principle remain heterogeneous and irreducible" (27). Musharraf's statement was calculated to confound. It had nothing to do with forgiveness; it was merely a step toward reconciliation between two states. Derrida understands that nation-states do need a pragmatic way to move forward, but he does not consider it forgiveness. He writes, "Even where it could be justified, this 'ecological' imperative of social and political health has nothing to do with 'forgiveness', which when spoken of in these terms is taken far too lightly" (41). Pure forgiveness, according to Derrida, is to forgive the unforgivable and to do so unconditionally (32). His words are powerful because he makes us believe it is possible. *Noor*, however, deals with forgiveness so subtly that it is not completely clear if the unforgivable is actually forgiven.

Since the novel is written from a Bengali perspective (Cilano 2006, 223), we as readers spend a lot of time inside Sajida's head as she remembers and wonders about her past and her adoptive father. This personal history and engagement with the space of East Pakistan are inextricably bound up with the Pakistani state's political history. The novel builds toward a climax at which Sajida realizes, because of Noor's drawing, that she saw Ali at a mass grave before he adopted her. "Her drawing, almost a photograph, was in pencil on heavy paper. A cluster of troops stood in messy rows. . . . One officer was drawn in more detail than the others . . . Ali wore knee-high boots. Along with the others, he stood in ankle-deep mud, a shifting plane of mire dried to a thick slush" (179, 181). The drawing of the troops, including Ali, standing in mud does not include the blood because it is in pencil. As Ali tells Sajida, the troops were there to dig a mass grave in the April monsoon rain when Bengalis from a nearby camp appeared, with Sajida among them. This climax is especially painful for Sajida because Ali and the other troops fired into the crowd of Bengalis, killing everyone but her. The novel's ecofeminist stance shows that the West Pakistani military violated the land with the blood of its people just as the men violated the people, especially the women. At the end of the novel, Sajida must come to terms with this fact: "Ali, her father, might once have lifted his rifle and blindly aimed in a torrent of rain and rising waves of heated fog—and shot her dead" (200). While clearly Ali's actions, as well as those of the Pakistan Army, are unforgivable, the novel raises the question of whether Sajida could forgive Ali.

Sajida is prepared to deal with Ali's betrayal because before she even learns of her father's betrayal, her own husband, Hussein, betrays her, and she has to contend with Hussein's return. She ultimately takes Hussein back, but the narrator does not state that she forgave him. Khan writes, "Instead, she accepted him for what he had become, for the remorse he had shown that one single night" (99). In the same way that she accepts Hussein without forgiving him, we are told that she might accept Ali without forgiving him as well. Khan writes,

> Some years later, when Ali—her father—started speaking to her, really speaking to her, when his story rolled from his tongue, she recalled that night with Hussein and knew that in some vague and insufficient way, she'd been preparing for what was to come. As her father spoke, she appreciated the tenor of what forgiveness might mean and that life's pain, just like its love, was infinite and uncomprehending. That holes and emptiness were only one manifestation of sadness, and not even a great one at that. And, finally, that love, in its eternity and sincerity, its God-awful trueness, could be more exacting than anything she'd believed. Or dreamed. (99)

Even though Derrida imagines a forgiveness of the unforgivable, the novel does not necessarily represent the forgiveness that Sajida can bestow. It implies that one cannot forgive genocide because to appreciate "the tenor of what forgiveness might mean" is not necessarily to forgive. Instead, the novel depicts an attempt by Bengalis to face, accept, and possibly move on from the violence they have endured.

For Pakistanis now living in what used to be West Pakistan, trials of the perpetrators, reparations, and apologies are all in order. Sorayya Khan's novel begins a process of facing the past in time as well as in space to better understand important feminist social relations — particularly between peoples of different genders, ethnicities, cultures, and languages. The novel draws attention to the space of what is now Bangladesh not only in terms of "holes and emptiness" for Pakistanis but also in more concrete terms, such as where bloody rivers exist alongside mud pits that are actually mass graves. Noor's paintings and drawings are supplemented with Ali's memories, which include multiple raped and tortured Bengali women. The novel forces us to take the first step to simply remember that time and that space, to remember that situation of genocide, rape, and resource extraction.

To delve into that space and time is also to investigate current-day policies toward Balochistan, where the Pakistani state does not just extract Balochistan's natural resources but also dumps its toxic waste. "From Sui to Saindak, gas and gold leave the province. At the end of the past century, the Pakistani state is seen as having replaced these precious commodities with trash. At Chagai, in 1998, the state deposited atomic material into the province, devastating the health of nomads and cattle living in the region" (M. Ahmad 2014, 163). Remembering the time and space of East Pakistan in 1971 helps us examine the political trajectory of the post-Bangladesh Pakistani state's policies in the space of Balochistan in the present.

Balochistan is a province of Pakistan with an active separatist agenda based on ethnic nationalism. According to journalist Asad Hashim (2014, para. 29), it "has seen three localised uprisings against the state — in 1948, 1958 and 1963 — with broader armed movements taking place from 1973–77 and from 2005." While there may not be mass rapes of the Balochi people, the "disappearances" are increasing, as are the number of tortured bodies found. The mainstream press in Pakistan only started reporting on the plight of the Balochis since the summer of 2011, and, again, the official numbers are contested. *Dawn*, one of Pakistan's English-language daily newspapers, reported in 2013 that "592 mutilated dead bodies have been found in the last three years" from Balochistan (Shah 2013). But what about those who are not found? While the 2013 report claimed "132 cases of missing persons" (para. 5), the "Voice for Baloch Missing Persons (VBMP)—a non-profit rights group—claimed that thousands of Baloch missing persons were picked up from different parts of the province" (para. 8). In 2014 the families of these missing persons marched for more than a hundred days to meet with the UN Human Rights Council in Islamabad because the state of Pakistan does nothing about the thousands of missing persons. Regardless, according to Mahvish Ahmad (2014, 164), "Whether there is talk of a few hundred, or many thousands, there is little doubt that the security agencies are carrying out crimes against what the Pakistani state claims are its own people." This news reminds us of the Pakistani state's similar crimes against its own Bengali people in 1971, ones that led to war and the new state of Bangladesh.

Just as remembering the violence of 1947 in Punjab through a feminist eco-cosmopolitan lens helps us understand continuing violence against women and the land, as well as global capital's influence on food prices, revisiting the violence of 1971 against Bengalis through a more spatial postcolonial ecofeminist lens helps us understand both the violence of partition and the continuing oppression of resource-rich Balochis at the hands of the Pakistani state. In both cases, an attachment to the land and an understanding of space guide us to a more justice-oriented outlook toward place in the region of South Asia. To understand Pakistan's past in this way is to plan for a future that is more open to the rights of all others, nonhuman as well as human, living within the boundaries of Pakistan or even living in other states in the region such as India and Bangladesh.

Chapter 4 focuses on Pakistan's largest city and port, Karachi, by analyzing a novel that perceives the environment through the eyes of human others and nonhumans alike. It delves into the Sindhi nationalist movement, following indigenous Sindhi human and nonhuman characters, as well as those who have migrated to Karachi and displaced them.[12] The Arabian Sea, its animals, and its seashells, along with Karachi's history of migrations and displacements, ground my theorization of a specifically Pakistani eco-cosmopolitanism.

4

Karachi

Pakistani Eco-cosmopolitanism

A fiction writer's impulse is that of a child: to explore the world, to move beyond doors that are closed, regardless of who closes them. Her goal is to arrive at an artistic form that is true, for her. To do this in a country where to walk her own streets is a trespass is no small feat.
UZMA ASLAM KHAN

The three previous chapters focused on women's ideas of belonging to the regions of Punjab, Thar, and Bengal, respectively. In each case, I showed how their place-based identities confronted Pakistani religious nationalism by foregrounding the more-than-human land and water while simultaneously critiquing patriarchy and ethnic and religious discrimination. This chapter shows not only the inseparability of the land of Karachi, Pakistan's largest city and port, from the Arabian Sea and the inseparability of humans from other nonhuman animals but also the ways in which land and sea are one with humans and nonhumans alike. Uzma Aslam Khan's novel *Trespassing* (2003) is particularly appropriate for explaining these issues because of its human and non-human characters. As Khan states in this chapter's epigraph, the female human characters must live differently than the males do just as the nonhuman female turtle who opens her novel must also make sacrifices. In discussing this novel, Ananya Jahanara Kabir (2011) argues that Uzma Aslam Khan's focus on nature results in a cosmopolitan vision for the whole country by working

creatively through tropes of re-rooting . . . [which] circle around the possibilities offered by "nature" rather than "culture," including history, language and religion; they also tease out the limitations of a strict nature/culture binary, advancing instead new archives for the post-Partition nation that project a different affective circuit between subjectivity, space and the ability to belong. The evolution of Aslam Khan's writing suggests more than a presentist reaction to contemporary stereotypes of Pakistan as a near-failed, inward-oriented, Islamic state; rather, it provides a complete mode of imagining an inherent cosmopolitanism for this nation. (174)

Kabir focuses on nature in the novel to make an argument about the cosmopolitanism of the nation. Building on Kabir's important insights, I use ecocritical theoretical frameworks to consider the nonhuman animal characters in the novel.[1] In addition, I include the relationships between human and nonhuman animals in the novel to extend Ursula Heise's (2008) eco-cosmopolitanism to a more specific Pakistani eco-cosmopolitanism.[2]

Located on the Arabian Sea, Karachi has seen many humans and nonhumans come and go, as they migrate and are displaced. Easily Pakistan's most cosmopolitan city, Karachi's people are far more diverse in terms of religion, language, and ethnicity than in any other region of the country. Regarding the population of Karachi, feminist activist Anis Haroon (2001, 178) writes that it is a "multiplicity of ethnicities, religions, sects and political groupings"; therefore, "Karachi is in effect a mini Pakistan." Thus, unlike the other chapters, this one theorizes about both a local and a national identity. While the first chapter presents an eco-cosmopolitan feminism, this chapter advances a *Pakistani* eco-cosmopolitanism. Khan's novel is different from the other fictions discussed in this book; even though the novel is mostly set in Karachi, it makes connections across the country of Pakistan, creating a specifically Pakistani eco-cosmopolitanism that does not pertain to India or Bangladesh. Thus, this chapter moves the local-global nexus that I have been discussing to a more national theorization of a Pakistani eco-cosmopolitanism. This approach opposes, to some extent, the politics of some South Asian studies scholars who emphasize the similarities between Bangladesh, India, and Pakistan. Differences do exist between the nation-states of South Asia, and a focus on the particularities of Pakistan opens new types of discussions.

Khan's novel follows a romance between Daanish and Dia, two characters who are both drawn to nonhuman animals in Karachi. As the reader learns more about each of their families, it becomes clear that another character named Salaamat, the son of the family that works for Dia's parents, shares Daanish's love of the sea and likes turtles. In fact, the novel begins with the memories of a female turtle, taking us into her consciousness, so that a nonhuman animal also becomes a character in the novel; we see Karachi and the sea through her eyes. This decision by the author grounds the novel not only in the place of Karachi but also in its nonhuman animals.

The novel allows readers to share the experiences of human others and nonhumans such as turtles, and its Pakistani eco-cosmopolitanism ends up critiquing American, Pakistani, and Sindhi nationalism by showing the ways in which place-based belonging does not easily fit within these simplistic and dangerous frameworks. As literary critic Aroosa Kanwal (2015) points out, while the character of Salaamat "discards his Sindhi nationalist identity" (82), the character of Daanish "provides a critique of the reductive aspects of both American and Pakistani nationalisms" (83). These critiques of nationalism are inextricably linked to ideas of belonging in relation to nonhuman others. In delineating such a Pakistani eco-cosmopolitan viewpoint, I draw on both ecocriticism and postcolonial criticism, fields of study that have only recently been considered in tandem.[3]

While both Kabir and Kanwal draw heavily on postcolonial criticism to analyze *Trespassing*, neither uses ecocriticism even though the larger themes of the novel are linked to the environment, specifically to nonhuman animals. While Kabir's writing is from 2011 and Kanwal's is from 2015, Rob Nixon sensed a divide between postcolonial criticism and ecocriticism as early as 2005, noting that "the isolation of postcolonial literary studies from environmental concerns has limited the field's intellectual reach" (247). The previous year postcolonial eco-critic Graham Huggan (2004, 703) wrote, "Ecocriticism, at present, is a predominantly white movement, arguably lacking the institutional support-base to engage fully with multicultural and cross-cultural concerns." This was the case even though three years earlier Joni Adamson's *American Indian Literature, Environmental Justice, and Ecocriticism* (2001) "helped propel ecocriticism's twenty-first century turn—its expansion from a purview of EuroAmerican texts of nonfiction nature-writing—to the inclusion of the voices and struggles of marginalized minorities" (Adamson and Monani 2017, 5). Both Nixon and Huggan enriched and expanded Adamson's work in their articles theorizing about a postcolonial ecocriticism that was not predominantly white. In 2008 it seemed that Ursula Heise's book would be in line with Adamson's, Nixon's, and Huggan's premises because it "emphasizes the urgency of developing an ideal of 'eco-cosmopolitanism,' or environmental world citizenship, building on recuperations of the cosmopolitan project in other areas of cultural theory" (10). Given that theories of cosmopolitanism have been plagued with critiques that focus on the term's links to U.S. imperialism, Heise's eco-cosmopolitanism promised not only to consider environmental concerns within postcolonial studies but also to recuperate cosmopolitanism from allegations of a U.S.-centric nationalist focus.[4] Unfortunately, the vast majority of her primary texts are U.S.-based science fiction novels, although she insists that she did not initially "envision it as a particularly Americanist project" (Heise 2008, 8). This chapter builds on Heise's eco-cosmopolitanism and moves it in the direction that Adamson alludes to when she writes that "constructs such as race, class, and gender cannot be separated from concepts of 'nature'" (in Adamson and Monani 2017, 5). Here, I analyze a postcolonial Pakistani novel that emphasizes relationships between humans and the nonhuman in the context of multiple nationalisms, patriarchy, and the global economy.[5]

Shifting Ecocriticism and Postcolonial Studies

Postcolonial scholars often focus on migration and displacement, while scholars of ecocriticism have traditionally concentrated on nation and place (Nixon 2005, 235). This would seem to put them at odds; a concern with place appears to be the opposite of a concern with displacement. However, according to Cara Cilano and Elizabeth DeLoughrey (2007, 73), while "there are tensions between postcolonial and ecocritical approaches, they also share a commitment to social and environmental justice." This commitment to justice, though, is complicated when we consider the power of patriarchal nationalism, which has been used positively as well as negatively. Relying on nationalism to define cosmopolitanism may be seen as problematic by postcolonial critics, many of whom are deeply suspicious of nationalism (Gilroy 2004). Despite the potential effectiveness of nationalism in anticolonial struggles, nationalism continues to be contested in the field of postcolonial studies because of the rise of reactionary ethnic, religious, and, of course, patriarchal nationalisms in countries such as Pakistan.

Heise's eco-cosmopolitanism is overly close to nationalism. Heise (2008) defines the ideal of eco-cosmopolitanism as "an attempt to envision individuals and groups as part of planetary 'imagined communities' of both human and nonhuman kinds" (61). While the idea of a human-nonhuman community does resonate with the characters of Khan's novel, her use of political scientist Benedict Anderson's (1998) term for nations as "imagined communities" implies that, for her, eco-cosmopolitanism is a way of extending nationalism to include the planet and nonhumans. Heise suggests that eco-cosmopolitanism, as with Kwame Anthony Appiah's cosmopolitanism, comes out of and is not necessarily at odds with nationalism. In "Cosmopolitan Patriots," Appiah (1998, 106) states, "I have been arguing, in essence, that you can be cosmopolitan—celebrating the variety of human cultures; rooted—loyal to one local society (or a few) that you count as home; liberal—convinced of the value of the individual; and patriotic—celebrating the institutions of the state (or states) within which you live." I completely disagree. If the word means everything to everyone, then it has no meaning. Thus, eco-cosmopolitanism should not be regarded as similar to nationalism or patriotism as Heise (2008) implies.

Simplistically theorizing that eco-cosmopolitanism either is an extension of nationalism or is definitively anti-nationalist does not capture the complexity of our world and our relationship to it. Khan's novel is intriguing because it does not fall into this either-or trap. In fact, the distinct elements of her novel shift the significance of ecocriticism and postcolonial studies simultaneously. In my reading of the novel, *Trespassing* illustrates a Pakistani eco-cosmopolitanism that is much more nuanced than the one that is theorized by Heise. In the novel, eco-cosmopolitanism is neither an extension nor a rejection of nationalism because the ways in which humans and nonhumans navigate their homeplaces on our planet and the ways in which nation-states navigate within the forces of globalization are necessarily very complicated.

Some historical context is necessary. As discussed in chapter 1, Gen. Muhammad Zia-ul-Haq's regime began in 1977 and lasted eleven years. During this time, Zia tried to unite all Pakistanis under the banner of Islam and intensified a particularly religious form of nationalism. While this effort led to discrimination against Sikhs (chapter 1) and Hindus (chapter 2), it should not have led to ethnic conflicts among Muslims (this chapter) or even between Shia and Sunni Muslims. However, as Kanwal points out, the Iran-Iraq War (1980–88), as well as other conflicts in the region, was fought between Shia Iran and Sunni Iraq. When Zia imposed Islamization policies on Pakistan, he simultaneously aligned Pakistan with Sunni Saudi Arabia. As Kanwal (2015, 88) writes, "Zia, on the one hand, tried to create a unitary national (Pakistani) identity using Islam as the unifying factor and, on the other, negated the multi-ethnic and plural reality of the society by promoting discrimination between Shias and Sunnis, religious and secular-minded people, and other minorities such as Ahmadis." The Islam that Zia propagated was not only disastrous for non-Muslims but also for Shia Muslims. As Kanwal also points out, "It is important to note that these Shia-Sunni conflicts have been exacerbated by US interference in Muslim states" (93).[6] Pakistani nationalism is patriarchal and religious, and U.S. imperialism has resulted in short-sighted military strategies that regularly kill the most vulnerable civilians, women, children, and nonhuman animals. Neither nationalism nor imperialism is viable for Pakistanis. Set in Karachi of the 1980s and '90s, Khan's novel critiques the United States, Pakistan, and Sindhis by narrating a Pakistani eco-cosmopolitanism that is neither an extension of nationalism nor definitively anti-nationalist.

Trespassing also covers the violent ethnic conflict between Pashtuns and Muhajirs during the 1980s in Karachi as part of Pakistan's longer history. As the narrator states, "The bus-body-making business was one of the worst hit by the riots that began last year when a Muhajir student was run over by a Pathan bus driver. Members of her community insisted it was deliberate, and yet another way they were being exploited. They torched buses, smashed workshops, killed workers, learned to maneuver Soviet and American weapons" (233). This passage clearly references the history of the Cold War in Afghanistan, which brought many Soviet and American weapons to the streets of Karachi and led to increasing and extreme anti-Americanism in Pakistan. The Muhajirs resented the Pashtuns, and the Sindhis resented the Muhajirs. The violence continued, with weapons available for all. As Uzma Aslam Khan (2009b, para. 5) herself has stated, during the 1980s, Karachi was the site of "an ethnic war between the indigenous people of Sindh, where Karachi is located, and the Urdu-speaking migrants who'd settled in Karachi after Partition. Civil war, fueled and armed by the war between Empires, because by some accident of geography, the theater of their rivalry was Afghanistan, of which Pakistan had become an extension." The Cold War in Afghanistan brought civil war to Karachi and U.S. support for the brutal dictator General Zia. Anti-imperialism has historically been linked with religious nationalism in the region, creating pressure in the popular culture to choose one or the other. As a result, secular Pakistani intellectuals have had to reject both the religious nationalism of Zia and the imperialism of the United States.

Even though many theories of cosmopolitanism, including Heise's eco-cosmopolitanism, are oriented toward the reduction of the local in favor of expanding the global, the local and the global are by no means mutually exclusive. In Khan's novel, eco-cosmopolitanism becomes a way to think beyond the nation by rooting oneself in our planet, its geography, and its animals, all of which are both local and global. Khan posits an eco-cosmopolitanism that is rooted in the local in a way that implicates the planet globally. The local rootedness is not nationalism—this book refers to it as Pakistani eco-cosmopolitanism primarily for geographical purposes—but a materiality of place, and the global thinking is not necessarily imperialist cosmopolitanism but rather a kind of planetarity. This Pakistani eco-cosmopolitanism is an answer to the dilemma of Pakistani intellectuals who reject both nationalism and the more abstract theories of cosmopolitanism that focus on the global more than the local.[7] Thus, the novel illustrates a Pakistani eco-cosmopolitanism that is neither an extension of nationalism nor in opposition to a nationalism that can be co-opted by U.S. imperialism.

Trespassing, as noted, is set in Karachi in the 1980s and early 1990s and centers on three main human characters—Salaamat, Daanish, and Dia—of different genders, classes, and ethnicities and their connections to the nonhuman. These connections allow them each to trespass against the man-made boundary between humans and nonhumans, as well as the boundaries between humans of different ethnic origins in Karachi. The city is very diverse, but this diversity does not translate into tolerance. As Kanwal (2015, 77) writes, "Karachi has been convulsed by ethnic conflicts since the early years of independence."[8] However, this novel emphasizes trespassing against all kinds of boundaries between humans of different ethnicities such as Dia and Daanish, who are Sindhi and Muhajir, respectively. The novel also promotes trespassing against boundaries between humans and nonhumans, as Dia longs to become a silkworm, Daanish wants to be a nautilus, and Salaamat is saved by a turtle. In focusing on the deep relations between the human and nonhuman, the novel demonstrates the importance of peaceful relations between all beings.[9]

It is not surprising that *Trespassing* is so descriptive of the physical nonhuman world of Karachi and that it is situated in a very local materiality of place within a larger, global context. These descriptions of the physical world trespass against man-made ideologies of ethnic and religious nationalism and imperialism. Khan illustrates this more complex eco-cosmopolitanism by stating that she is most at home in the natural world. "I'm someone who's happiest in the natural world, not the world of drawing rooms, which I've always been skilled at avoiding. It's the physical earth—the flowers and the smells, the rain and the light—that moves and grounds me the most" (*Dawn* 2013, para. 6). Khan has lived in Pakistan, the United States, the United Kingdom, Morocco, the Philippines, and Japan. Being both rooted in the natural world and incredibly well traveled, she is therefore able to write in a way that speaks to the complexities on the ground without losing sight of the global. For example, *Trespassing* fills a silence about Pakistanis' attachment to the land, the sea, and the animals by showing Salaamat's being both healed by the sea and the land and saved by a turtle, just as he too tries to protect a turtle's eggs. Dia and Daanish also are entranced by the tiny creatures of the world. While Dia finds the divine in silkworms, Daanish feels as though his world has opened up when he includes nonhuman others and tries to understand them. These attachments are a kind of rejection of religious nationalism because they illustrate an environmental belonging that is deeper and greater than patriotism.[10] This environmental belonging is also a critique of U.S. imperialism because the novel describes not only racism in the United States but also the environmental damage the U.S. military caused in bombing Iraq. Last, the novel's emphasis on environmental belonging through attachments to nonhuman animals shows that postcolonial studies must move in the direction of ecocriticism to illustrate that the local and the global are not mutually exclusive.

Each of the three main characters is clearly connected with local animals and geographies in a global context. First, the Sindhi fisherman Salaamat becomes dispossessed and dislocated because foreign trawlers, mostly Korean, overfish the seas with the support of the Pakistani government. While global forces deprive him of his livelihood, Salaamat defends turtles and, at the lowest point in his life, appears to come alive in the presence of the beauty of the land and the sea. Even though he is pulled into a Sindhi separatist movement because of his dislocation from the sea, he eventually leaves the movement because he wishes to belong to the land without owning it. In doing so, he displays his attachment to the region's land, sea, and turtles and rejects nationalist political ideology. Salaamat's eco-cosmopolitanism becomes planetary rather than political. Next, Daanish, a Muhajir-Afghan middle-class boy in Pakistan who loves the sea and goes to the United States to study journalism, has a collection of seashells from around the world that sustains him in his travels. He found some of the seashells on the beaches of Karachi; his father brought back others after conference trips abroad. Daanish's connection to the local sea of his youth in Karachi helps him think globally about pollution in the context of the First Gulf War. His attachment to the sea and seashells, which are planetary and global, is also based on the geography of Karachi. Finally, Dia, a wealthy Sindhi, discovers the divine in observing the details of the lives of silkworms on her mother's silk farm. While connected to the local silkworms, she ponders the global history of silk. Moreover, her spirituality provides an eco-cosmopolitanism that does not fit with Pakistan's religious nationalism. Each of these characters displays the ideals of Heise's eco-cosmopolitanism by their connections to nonhuman aspects of the planet. Yet these characters also represent a more complex Pakistani eco-cosmopolitanism that is neither a simplistic extension of nationalism nor definitively anti-nationalist. Rather, it is based in the materiality of a local place within a global context.

In *Trespassing* eco-cosmopolitanism fosters an ability to think beyond the nation by developing an awareness of the environment in terms of its animals and geography—land, sea, cities, and villages—and rooting oneself in our planet. While Pakistan was conceived as "a Muslim nation which might transcend ethnic differences" (Jaffrelot 2004, 9), ethnic minorities such as Bengalis, Balochis, Sindhis, and Pashtuns, as well as those claiming the linguistic identity of Siraiki, have each had nationalist movements for self-determination and separatism in what is now Pakistan.[11] Khan draws our attention to these ethnic tensions when one of her characters states rather pessimistically, "We will always be divided. We'll always be Punjabi, Pathan, Pukhtun, Muhajir, Sindi, or what-have-you. But we will never be united. The Quaid's dream is slipping from our fingers. Our children won't even know he had a dream. They won't know why we're here. They will be rootless" (68–69). *Quaid* or *Quaid-e-Azam*, meaning "great leader," is often used in Pakistan to refer to Mohammad Ali Jinnah, the lawyer and politician who founded Pakistan as a homeland for the Muslims of South Asia after he and others concluded that independent India would lack equal opportunities for its Muslim minority after the British left in 1947. "The Quaid's dream" is posited as a dream of rootedness, but in Khan's novel, Pakistanis are portrayed as cosmopolitan and rootless because of the two partitions that displaced many from their homeplaces in India and Bangladesh. This portrayal is in tension with the three main characters, who are clearly connected with and rooted in the local animals and geographies. Ananya Jahanara Kabir (2011) calls it "re-rooting" as she also includes people such as the author, Uzma Aslam Khan, who are *mohajirs* or immigrants from what is now India (174). Thus, the novel shows that a divided country that lacks the expected nationalism can still be rooted in its environment. Despite the ethnic violence in Karachi in the 1980s, we are shown depictions of characters with deep attachments to the animals, the land, and the sea of that geographical region who are not necessarily attached to the nation of Pakistan.

These human characters' attachments to animals allow the reader to equate the human and nonhuman condition. According to postcolonial ecocritic Susie O'Brien (2001), one major difference between postcolonial criticism and ecocriticism is that the former is interested in resistance while the latter is interested in accommodation to survive. While Salaamat eventually rejects Pakistani and Sindhi nationalism in the postcolonial sense, his struggle for survival leads him to be less resistant and more accommodating in other ways. O'Brien writes that in ecocriticism, "survival . . . depends on an accommodation not just of human difference, but of the otherness of the physical environment" (148). Khan's novel begins and ends with both the marine turtles (known to nest on the Hawkes Bay and Sandspit beaches of Karachi) and Salaamat; both the endangered turtles and fisherfolk such as Salamaat are struggling to survive. The plight of the fishing community is similar to the plight of the endangered marine turtles.

According to Kabir (2011, 178), "*Trespassing* . . . opens with an account of turtles . . . [and] the fisherman's boy from whose perspective we see the scene." However, as Khan's novel begins, we see the scene from the perspective of a nesting female turtle. She recalls "how much safer it had been when the coastline belonged to the fishermen" (1). Her perspective lends a sense of history, and it is she that describes the violence that follows. She is the endangered and indigenous Sindhi we meet before we meet Salaamat, another indigenous Sindhi who is also endangered by the violence that begins the book. Khan sets up a binary where the Sindhi fisherfolk, who are natives of that area, and the turtle are on the same side while opposed by the visitors from the city.

As the nesting turtle lays her eggs on the beach, she watches Salaamat. Khan writes, "The turtle watches him watch her when most defenseless. But she knows him; all the turtles do" (1). That the turtles know Salaamat shows the depth of their relation to him. He does not want to interfere with the turtle's birthing process and eventually tries to protect her eggs from the city men. Both Salaamat and the turtle are presented as afraid of the city visitors, the men in the huts. Salaamat's attempt to protect the turtle's eggs leads the city men to beat him, pelt him with her eggs, and finally drag him out to sea. Khan writes, "And just when it seems the sea will swallow him, he touches a giant marbled shell. It carries him over watery hills till his path is smooth. He presses his cheeks into the turtle's hump of a home, going where she goes" (120). In struggling to survive, Salaamat accommodates the place and the nonhuman without accepting Pakistani or even Sindhi nationalism.

Salaamat illustrates a way of looking at the land that is strikingly reminiscent of environmentalist Aldo Leopold's famous land ethic. Salaamat would not have read Leopold, but resonances exist between them. Leopold (1987, 203) believed that a "land ethic" should move beyond "strictly economic" terms. When Salaamat joins a Sindhi separatist movement, Khan's novel illustrates that a land ethic in a global context needs to move beyond merely political terms as well. If our relationship to the land was based on something more than personal financial benefit, then we would not consider it only in terms of its economic and political potential. *Trespassing* depicts and condemns the violent nationalism of the Sindhis by showing Salaamat's engagement with and then rejection of the movement. While separatist movements are often focused on gaining land for their independent use, Salaamat has a different reaction. After his dislocation from the fishing village where he was born and raised, and after his disillusionment in the city of Karachi where he is an outsider even though his people were its "original inhabitants" (129), Salaamat joins a group of violent Sindhi separatist freedom fighters. His motives for joining the group are different from those of the other young men he meets there; while the others want to gain land to own and rule for themselves, Salaamat simply wants to die.

> He'd joined the camp thinking it would be his way at last to shrivel up and die, but if anything the opposite had happened. Salaamat was beginning to like his world again.
>
> The sand beneath his toes, the scent of the river, the way his hair blew out of the twine of grass binding it, the sky free of dust and haze, the feathery sisky leaves — all refreshed him. . . . Instead of distancing

himself from the land, he was entering it. And he grew unconvinced that the answer to all his troubles was a separate state. If anything, this land the others wanted to split was showing him how to glue back his splintered pieces. (344)

Salaamat's awareness that Sindhi separatism is not the answer leads him to resist both Sindhi nationalism and Pakistani nationalism because he has "entered" the land and has been healed. Khan's description of Salaamat's healing recalls Leopold's contention that "to the laborer in repose . . . [wilderness] is something to be loved and cherished, because it gives definition and meaning to his life" (1987, 188). Salaamat regains the definition and meaning he lost while living and working in the city. In Salaamat, Khan combines the ecological with theories of cosmopolitanism that move beyond nationalism and produces an ideal of eco-cosmopolitanism. Because this ideal is connected to local geography, it cannot be considered as simply anti-nationalist; nationalism is always based in local geography. Salaamat's Sindhi nationalist friend Fatah displays this kind of Sindhi nationalism when he draws the map of Sindh for Salaamat (344). Thus, an emphasis on land is not necessarily a complete rejection of nationalism, nor is it simply an extension of nationalism because Salaamat rejects the separate Sindhi state that they are fighting for.

In a way, Khan's novel complements Leopold's notion of place because they are both ambiguous about globalization. As Leopold (1987, 188) writes, "For the first time in the history of the human species, two changes are now impending. One is the exhaustion of wilderness in the more habitable portions of the globe. The other is the world-wide hybridization of cultures through modern transport and industrialization. Neither can be prevented, and perhaps should not be, but the question arises whether, by some slight amelioration of the impending changes, certain values can be preserved that would otherwise be lost." Leopold's phrase "perhaps should not be" shows that he is unclear about where he stands on globalization. Should globalization be allowed to continue unfettered? Should it be prevented? Philosopher Patrick K. Dooley (2003) argues that Leopold is also ambiguous about whether land exists for our use or whether it has its own intrinsic value. He calls this debate "a clash of homocentric versus biocentric world-views" (65). Geographer David Harvey (2004), however, has argued that if the biocentric worldview claims that "everything relates to everything else," then a biocentric or ecocentric vision should include both humans and cities. Harvey writes, "It also means that flows of money and of commodities and the transformative actions of human beings . . . have to be understood as fundamentally ecological processes" (330–31). He goes on to applaud the environmental justice movement for putting the "survival of people in general, and of the poor and marginalized in particular, at the center of its concerns" (345). In Khan's novel, the forces of globalization, economic as well as cultural, are treated ambiguously; while global networks provide weapons to Salaamat's extremist group, his transporting the weapons eventually provides Salaamat with a stable income. Together, economic globalization, Salaamat's struggle to survive, and his relations with the nonhuman complicate any answers to economic and environmental concerns. Here Khan shows that the local and the global are not mutually exclusive.

Khan both complements and contrasts with Leopold's notion of place because Salaamat is displaced both economically and politically. Heise (2008) critiques Leopold's and others' notions of place through the lens of globalization. "While cosmopolitanism has generally been understood as an alternative to nationally based forms of identity, it confronts more local attachments in the case of environmentalism in the United States, which have been articulated by means of such concepts as 'dwelling,' 'reinhabitation,' 'bioregionalism,' an 'erotics of place,' or a 'land ethic'" (10). Heise applauds the fact "that the increasing connectedness of societies around the globe entails the emergence of new forms of culture that are no longer anchored in place" (10) and that they are "superseded by the infinite possibilities of zooming into and out of local, regional, and global views enabled by, for example, the online tool Google Earth" (11). Khan's vision in the novel, however, is less abstract. Khan's eco-cosmopolitanism is grounded in the materiality of a particular place, its regional geography, its animals, and its plants while simultaneously engaging with the global environment and the global economy.[12] Google Earth does not allow us to see the realities on the ground as well as this novel does. The novel updates Leopold's land ethic within a more global context and, with its attention to one local place, calls for a more concrete and complicated theorizing of eco-cosmopolitanism.

This local place, Karachi, is on the sea. As Kabir (2011, 179) has noted, "*Trespassing* begins and ends with the sea." At the end of the novel, Salaamat is last seen by his nephew, who is "watching the older man saunter to the water's edge, take off his kameez, and slink into a swell" (426). The novel also begins and ends with turtles. The nephew who watches Salaamat also observes tiny baby turtles join Salaamat in the sea. We never learn whether Salaamat returns or drowns and joins the ecosystem of the sea. His resistance is not forceful because he does not join a campaign to save the turtles or end the violence of the freedom fighters. He escapes the violence simply by working for one of their weapons suppliers as a driver. He must accommodate forces beyond his control.

Similarly, one of the baby turtles heading to the sea is interrupted by Salaamat's nephew, who picks it up to look at it. After he puts it down, he notices that it is moving toward the huts. Salaamat's nephew picks it up and turns it around, and the novel ends with the sentence "Touching ground, the turtle immediately bursts forward, this time toward the sea, as though its course had never changed" (428). The ecosystem rights itself as the turtle goes to a place where it can survive.

Salaamat's stance is both rooted in his environment and displaced from it because of poverty and politics; unable to return to work in his village, he finds it "strangely soothing" when he sits in an unfinished house in the city because he feels as though he is "a little closer to being in a cottage by the sea" (386). Salaamat has an ecological desire to preserve the turtles and a cosmopolitan disregard for nationalism. Moreover, his struggle to survive does not lead to any grand gestures of resistance after he is beaten for trying to save the turtle's eggs. He accommodates the nationalist and global capitalist forces that marginalize him and the turtles by remaining in the city, where he can make enough money to survive. Eco-cosmopolitanism in this novel again is neither an extension of nationalism nor a complete rejection of it. Salaamat survives in a very material way that is associated with a particular place in a global context.

Another decidedly eco-cosmopolitan character in this novel is Daanish, the physician's son and collector of seashells who goes to the United States to study journalism and follow in his grandfather's footsteps. The children of physicians in Pakistan are not wealthy, and after he arrives in the United States, Daanish becomes a dishwasher. During his stay, he is confronted with U.S. nationalism during the First Gulf War, and as he observes U.S. dominance and capitalism, he becomes increasingly critical of the country's culture of imperialism. At the same time, Daanish discovers incredible natural beauty that he cannot help but admire on his college campus. As he ponders this beauty, his eco-cosmopolitanism can also be heard: "Such beauty in a country that consumed 30 percent of the world's energy, emitted a quarter of its carbon dioxide, had the highest military expenditure in the world, and committed fifty years of nuclear accidents, due to which the oceans teemed with plutonium, uranium, and God alone knew what other poisons. It had even toyed with conducting nuclear tests on the moon" (48). Daanish rejects the U.S. nationalism that has driven this consumption and military expenditure even before he returns to Pakistan and learns about the results of the First Gulf War. Dia tells him, "Last summer, a black rain fell. People said it was because of the bombed oilfields in Iraq. For months, soot covered the world and fell like ink. Ama said the rain destroyed our mulberry trees, but she'd had no way of confirming that. We ran short of food for the silkworms" (330). That the soot covers the world demonstrates that the war's effects extend far beyond the local.

The war affects people and environment alike. As a student of journalism, Daanish watches news coverage of the First Gulf War with great interest. Khan writes,

When the war began, television showed planes dropping missiles with absolute precision. At the same time, the print media disclosed that the Pentagon had rules for war coverage. In his journal, Daanish insisted that these rules amounted to deleting the war entirely. Absolutely no gore was shown. There were no wounded soldiers on either side, no schools in flames, no detonated sewage systems, no Iraqi civilians—the American public would not see even one, dead, dying, or alive. There were no war hospitals, no interviews with patients receiving any medication, no broken oil pipelines, no blown-up dams inundating thousands of square miles. None of that happened. The war was surgical and pure. There was no suffering. (157)

No suffering of humans or the land is allowed on American television, but we, as readers, are made aware of damage from the broken oil pipelines and flooding due to blown-up dams. Daanish's critique of the war and its media coverage thus also applies to U.S. nationalism and imperialism.

Another aspect of Daanish's eco-cosmopolitan ideal can be seen in his attachment to his seashells from around the world; he even wears the smaller ones around his neck wherever he goes. According to Kabir (2011, 179), "Seashells trigger moments of contemplation" (179) for Daanish; however, contemplation alone does not capture the extent of his attachment. As he flies to Pakistan to attend his father's funeral and see his mother, Anu, Khan writes, Daanish thinks about "the larger shells he'd left in Karachi. In about ten more hours, he would see them again. This filled him with more joy than the prospect of uniting with anything else at home, even Anu" (23). Thus, his shells, which symbolize his connection to the world's oceans, its global environment, are more important to him than his mother. He ponders what the lives of the creatures living in the shells must be like. When his father brought him a chambered nautilus from East Asia, "Daanish wanted to hold it in his palm, gaze at the iridescent whorl, picture the animal that had once lived inside the many rooms of mother-of-pearl. He wanted to follow it through each chamber with a feathery gill of light and watch how each was sealed off as the creature grew into the next one" (169). Daanish did not only want to follow and watch the animals but also "to be with the nautilus. No, to *be* the nautilus. With ninety arms to swim away and twenty cabins to roam" (171, italics in original). This connection between Daanish and his seashells is similar to Salaamat's connection with the turtles, although unlike the turtles in this novel, we never see the world through the nautilus's eyes.

As with Salaamat, Daanish needs to go to the beach to center himself. In fact, the first time Daanish and Khurram go to the cove with Salaamat, Khurram's driver, Daanish and Salaamat are both at ease while Khurram complains. Daanish's "footsteps were light as he clambered swiftly over the needlelike rocks on the western shoulder of the inlet, too elated to notice any cuts. Salaamat too crossed the mound with graceful ease; Khurram alone complained" (165). Even though Salaamat and Daanish come from different social classes, both men belong to Karachi's beaches in ways that make their visits a kind of homecoming. Daanish's concern for the poisoning of the oceans and his love for its seashells illustrate an eco-cosmopolitanism that is global because so much of the earth is covered in ocean. But his critique of the United States comes from a local Pakistani perspective because he grew up going to Karachi's beaches. Again, the local and global are not mutually exclusive. Khan's novel provides an eco-cosmopolitan stance that examines the reductive aspects of both Pakistani, American, and Sindhi nationalism and global capitalism to construct a richer, more nuanced, and less exclusive form of cosmopolitanism that considers our connection to our environment in multiply complex, material ways. I call these diverse eco-cosmopolitanisms Pakistani because they speak to the particular dilemmas of Pakistanis.

These very particular dilemmas result from the fact that Pakistani nationalism and cosmopolitanism are deeply rooted in religion. To be a Pakistani nationalist is to believe in a nation founded on Islam. But this sentiment can and has led to many different kinds of apologists for the Taliban. According to physicist Pervez Hoodbhoy (2009, para. 8), despite the violence of the Taliban, "few Pakistanis saw the Taliban as the enemy. Apologists for the Taliban abounded, particularly among opinion-forming local TV anchors that whitewashed their atrocities, and insisted that they shouldn't be resisted by force. Others supported them as fighters against U.S. imperial might. The government's massive propaganda apparatus lay rusting. Beset by ideological confusion, it [the government of Pakistan] had no cogent response to the claim that Pakistan was made for Islam and that the Taliban were Islamic fighters."

Pakistani intellectuals must reject religious nationalism for a number of reasons. Religion does not supersede language and ethnicity, as evidenced by Bangladesh's 1971 secession, and a nation-state based on religion does not work to provide legal citizenship to non-Muslim citizens, as evidenced by Pakistan's treatment of religious and ethnic

minorities. However, in rejecting Pakistani nationalism, Pakistani intellectuals inadvertently find themselves in a position that supports U.S.
imperialism, which is also equally untenable.[13] According to journalist
Ahmed Rashid (2009, xl), "Ninety percent of the $10 billion in aid that
the United States has provided Pakistan with since 9/11 has gone to the
military rather than to development." To support the cosmopolitanism
that is represented by the United States then is to support a kind of
imperialism in which U.S. national interests are more important than
those of both the human and the nonhuman. While Salaamat and
Daanish show the problems with Pakistani, Sindhi, and U.S. nationalism through their attachment to their environment, the character
of Dia expresses a spirituality that deals with religion more directly.

Muslim Ecofeminists

Dia, the third major character in the novel, is the only one who brings
religion and spirituality into her eco-cosmopolitanism. She shows that
any theory of eco-cosmopolitanism must have an understanding of the
particular histories of particular places. According to political scientist
Partha Chatterjee (1993), anticolonial Indian nationalism was spiritual
long before it was political. Though he examines Indian nationalism,
the same could be said of Pakistan because British India included the
geographical region of Pakistan. As Indians fought for independence
from the British, spirituality allowed Indian nationalism to express itself
as being different from colonial power. The same applies to Pakistan,
but here spirituality and the divine are defined as Muslim; thus, Islamic
nationalism continues to spread despite the calls for secularism. As
nationalists often associate this spiritual national identity with women,
it seems appropriate that Dia is the character who is most concerned
with the divine. According to Chatterjee (1993, 9), "It was undoubtedly
a new patriarchy that was brought into existence, different from the
'traditional' order but also explicitly claiming to be different from the
'Western' family. The 'new woman' was to be modern, but she would
also have to display the signs of national tradition and therefore would
be essentially different from the 'Western' woman."

Dia is modern, coming and going as she pleases; yet she displays the
signs of national tradition in her understanding of the *maghrib* (the

sunset call to prayer). Khan writes, "The muezzin had a thin plaintive voice, and when he sang Dia felt the day close around her. It was as if the call asked what the day had brought. The same errors? Yes, exactly the same. Even so, God hadn't lost hope entirely. There would be tomorrow, though one day tomorrow would run out. He would not keep spinning forever" (195). Here Dia clearly identifies with Islam, but she also thinks of God as a silkworm that is spinning. For Dia the divine is linked to the tiny details of life. While it would be tempting here to make links between Dia's Muslim spirituality, her connection with her environment, and the much older tradition of Islamic mysticism, or Sufism, Dia's spirituality is clearly not in the tradition of Sufism because her practice lacks the rituals and duties that are associated with a mystic. Instead, it is another example of a new, emerging eco-cosmopolitanism with a spiritual twist. Dia is conceiving of the divine differently than do both the Sufis and the fundamentalists, whose beliefs are often discussed as two versions of Islam (one syncretic and one orthodox).[14]

The press often focuses on the notion of Sufism's ability to resist the radicalism of fundamentalists such as the Taliban of Pakistan, but this ignores the fact that Muslims do not fit neatly into these two categories. Dia's spirituality likewise does not follow the prescribed modes of Islam and religious nationalism. She loves to watch silkworms as they spin their cocoons on her mother's silk farm, leading her to find the divine in their movements.

That it happened here, in her mother's farm, in the middle of the scorched Indus plain, amid the chaos of Sind, made all her ethical quandaries regarding the breeding of another life-form to suit human interests vanish. Standing in a room with eight thousand tiny creatures, witnessing them perform a dance that few humans even knew occurred; this was life. . . . They worked ceaselessly for three days and nights, with material entirely of their own, and with nothing to orchestrate them besides their own internal clocks. Each, a perfectly self-contained unit of life. When Dia watched one spin, she came closer to understanding the will of God than at any other time. (105–6)

For Dia the dance is so magical that it represents not only the divine but also life itself. When she goes to the farm, she compares herself to the silkworms, asking the cook, Inam Gul, to tell others that she is in her "cocoon and won't come out for weeks" (94). As with Salaamat and even Daanish, Dia seems to want to join the nonhuman.

Moreover, Dia's musings on the global history of silk lead to cosmopolitan thinking in a character who never actually leaves Pakistan. When she reads that silk was discovered by a Chinese empress, she wonders if the empress would have done anything differently if she had known the effects of her discovery on Persian silkworm smugglers, Sicilian kidnappers of Greek weavers, or the British torture of Bengali and Benarsi weavers (10–12). Here cosmopolitanism is associated with international relations and trade, and the focus is on commodification, exploitation, and conflict. Kabir (2011, 179) notes, "Aslam Khan inserts a mythic memory of precolonial contacts between present-day Pakistan and China, which had used the mountain routes over the Karakoram Range." This relationship between Pakistan and China is also evident when Dia imagines her parents as the Chinese emperor and empress who discovered silk. In her fantasy, Dia imagines her mother saying, "This is where I want to plant the lost dyes of this soil. The colors are faster than synthetic ones and they smell good. Plus, it'll help me feel that I'm at one end of a cord that leads back thousands of years" (422). Dia's mother revives the indigenous and ancient Indus Valley tradition of using "natural dyes for the yarn" (Kabir 2011, 179).[15] In imagining that her mother is the Chinese empress, Dia links China and the Indus Valley civilization in present-day Pakistan. As Kabir writes, "The threads in *Trespassing* that link . . . the Arabian Sea with the Silk Route trace a geography that bypasses regions now in post-Partition India, and the border between India and Pakistan, uniting sea and land in an attempt to forge a mythic geography for Pakistan's 'origins'" (179). Even though the novel is mostly set in Karachi, it makes connections across the country and creates a specifically Pakistani eco-cosmopolitanism that, unlike the other works discussed in this book, does not include India, Bangladesh, or Afghanistan.

Dia, seeing the parched riverbed of the Indus, finally realizes that the only way to know the history of this region of Sindh is to hear it from old men or books, which tell of "princesses like Sassi, dwelling in the glorious *lakhy bagh* on the banks of the river, surrounded by music, fountains, and burnished horses" (95). Her fascination with local and global history and with the nonhuman such as the Indus River and silkworms, and her ability to connect all of them can also be considered eco-cosmopolitan. However, Dia's stance is significantly different from those of Salaamat and Daanish because her character is the only one who mentions the divine and spiritual in connection with the nonhuman. This spirituality makes Dia appear to be the most nationalist of the three characters because Pakistan was created as a homeland for the Muslims of South Asia. However, she is similar to Daanish and Salaamat in that her views do not fall neatly into the category of Pakistani religious nationalism.

For Dia the spinning of the silkworms is divine, as are all the details related to the changing of the seasons and to plant and animal life. Her attention to detail gives her more in common with Daanish and Salaamat than with more religious characters such as Daanish's mother, Anu.

> Normally, the monsoons were Dia's favorite time of year. . . . Best was when the rainfall softened to a cool drizzle, driving the tiny furtive creatures she loved out into the open. . . . She'd step cautiously along her brilliant green lawn, absorbing it all: a residual raindrop on a single leaf, causing it to shudder like a hiccup; hoverflies swilling mist; bulbuls diving for dancing gnats. She'd feel things so poignantly it was as if the flaccid sky had sunk into her bones, teaching her to see life up close, closer than anyone else. When a thin flaxen light cut through the clouds—the clouds that were *in* her—she could hear earthworms die and aphids sweat honeydew. . . . At nightfall, she'd slip between deliciously chilled damp sheets that smelled of rain and think, as she so often did at the farm: God is here; God is detail. (289–90, italics in original)

Dia's attention to the tiny details of her environment, from creatures to raindrops to plant life, leads her to become one with her environment; the sky sinks "into her bones" and the clouds are "in her." Even though she relates the divine to her relation with her environment—an approach that makes her appear to be a Pakistani religious nationalist who turns to Islam to express her love of local geography—this too is a brand of eco-cosmopolitanism because she is describing the materiality of her place in relation to other tiny creatures that share the planet with her. In fact, when she first meets Daanish, she is entranced that he too is connected to the tiny beasts of the world. His response to her silkworms enchants her: "He was delighted, as if he'd gained simply by noticing. As if by sharing a fleeting moment with two tiny unsung beasts, his world had opened" (217). This opening of the world, however, cannot be read as religious nationalism. Amartya Sen (2006) has argued that we must stop overemphasizing the Islamic identity of Muslims. "There has been, in particular, a major loss of understanding in the failure to distinguish between (1) the various affiliations and loyalties a person who happens to be a Muslim has, and (2) his or her Islamic identity in particular. The Islamic identity can be one of the identities the person regards as important (perhaps even crucial), but without thereby denying that there are other identities that may also be significant" (61). Even though Dia's Muslim identity is crucial, her eco-cosmopolitanism is neither simply an extension of religious nationalism nor a simplistic anti-nationalism. She never gives up her Muslim identity.

Dia is a Muslim Pakistani eco-cosmopolitan, and she and her mother, Riffat, represent feminists in a largely patriarchal society. Dia speaks out against arranged marriages when her friend Nini agrees to one. Regarding men and women, Khan writes, "Dia was certain [that] . . . the most obvious yet neglected reason for their disparate positions in society [was] time. Women spent it on men; men spent it on men" (92). Riffat—"the plucky woman who revolutionized the production of silk in the country" (197)—also opposes arranged marriages and tells her daughter never to marry out of obligation (13). According to Kabir (2011), "Aslam Khan's depiction of Riffat and Dia as misfits within their social milieu aligns them to society's margins rather than its mainstream. Aslam Khan's favoured women are awkward, creatively intelligent and intelligently creative, insistent on feeling *and* thinking their way through the debris of Pakistan's past, and elated at the sudden recognition of the wonders inherent in the small picture" (182, italics in original). While for Kabir the small picture is related to marginalized narratives of indigeneity, it is also tied to nature, both silkworms and the plants needed for dying cloth. Riffat "discovered most colors could be obtained from plants easily grown here. She also learned which part of each plant needed to be harvested, how long this took, and what color it would give. Turmeric and myrobalan produced yellow; henna, madder, and pomegranate, red; indigo, blue; tamarind and onion, black; *chikoo*, brown" (98, italics in original). Riffat connects herself to an ancient three-thousand-year-old tradition of present-day Sindh while running a successful business. Thus, she is an indigenous feminist.

Khan is not only interested in critiquing patriarchy in Pakistan through strong female characters. She also critiques the ways in which "saving brown women from brown men" can become a rallying cry for Islamophobia in the United States (Spivak 1999, 285). As Kanwal (2015) writes,

> Khan's gendered focus aims at critiquing gender inequality within Pakistan's patriarchal society. But at the same time she delineates Pakistan as a land of opportunities for all those women of all classes who are willing to stand up for their rights. It also deconstructs the reductive tropes of *burqa*-clad Muslim women that have been used by the US to sanction its own illegal entry into Afghanistan, Pakistan and other Muslim countries. In doing so, Khan adds new dimensions to her writings by linking local gender discrimination to cross-cultural gender stereotyping in the West, in the service of "war on terror" rhetoric. This makes her work distinctive among second-generation writers of Pakistani origin. (75)

Kanwal foregrounds the many levels at which Khan is operating. On the one hand, her Pakistani eco-cosmopolitanism is functioning on a local, national, and global level, with reference to relations between human and nonhuman animals, the land, and the sea. On the other hand, her feminist stance critiques local patriarchy and U.S. imperialism. Kanwal finds that Khan tackles these far-reaching gender issues in unique ways.

Khan is also distinctive in her focus on sexuality. While none of the other writers and directors discussed in this book touch on the ways in which sexuality and gender exist on a continuum, Salaamat demonstrates them in his sexual longing for Dia and his sexual relations with Fatah (348). Salaamat trespasses against heteronormativity, and his gender identity is fluid; as a gender bender he crosses all kinds of man-made boundaries. Even though his grandmother's tearoom is "a place exclusively for women" (119), "the ease with which he did women's work—scouring pots, refiring hookahs, weaving fish baskets—endeared him to them. Some even enjoyed flirting with a youth who was neither man nor boy" (120). Khan's ecofeminist concerns can be seen through Salaamat, Dia, and Riffat, each of whom draws our attention to environmental, queer, and feminist issues, and illustrate the importance of intersectionality.

Khan's complicated eco-cosmopolitanism can be seen in her main characters' different gender, class, and ethnic backgrounds. Salaamat is a working-class Sindhi, Daanish is a middle-class Muhajir (even though his mother insists she is descended from Afghan royalty), and Dia is a wealthy Sindhi. Despite their differences, each of these characters is drawn to animals, to the land, and to the sea, the materiality of their place on the planet. Khan has touched on the issues of displacement, poverty, feminism, and spirituality all within an environmental, regional, and global context. In Khan's novel, eco-cosmopolitanism is grounded in a materiality of place that includes regional geographical features, animals, and plants while contemplating man-made borders of the nation-state and patriarchy. The novel's title alludes to the characters' trespassing against man-made boundaries. For these characters, the geographical materiality of place is far more important than the violent, divisive politics of Karachi, Sindh, Pakistan, in the 1980s.

Finally, through the character of Salaamat, Khan reminds us of the uneven development created by the forces of global capitalist imperialism. As noted previously, Salaamat is forced to leave his village because foreign trawlers have overfished the waters. Khan writes, "They say the foreign trawlers have stolen their sea. They trespass. Fish once abundant close to shore are now disappearing even in the deep. And the fishermen's boats cannot go out as far, even for the fish still left to catch" (2). Salaamat's lover, Fatah, who is also a Sindhi separatist, is aware of this injustice and knows that the Pakistani government does not stop the overfishing. When Salaamat says, "You can belong to the land, instead of forcing it to belong to you" (359), he is trying to convince Fatah that a relationship with one's environment does not have to involve violent nationalism. But Fatah's anger is focused on the state of Pakistan. "The Koreans took your sea, but you learned nothing. The Punjabis took your sweat; still you learned nothing. . . . It's not just land and sea they all want. They want the air we breathe. And what does this country do? It begs them to take it" (359). Fatah's frustration is understandable, given that the IMF and World Bank expect poorer nations with huge debt to earn as much foreign exchange as possible, and the "fishing industry makes a major contribution to the economy of Pakistan as a foreign exchange earner" (UK Department for International Development 2008). Salaamat may reject nationalism, but he is still not free from the tyranny of the nation-state.

Salaamat's eco-cosmopolitanism comes not from his support of the capitalist system but rather from his attachment to the turtles in Karachi. According to literary critic Fawzia Afzal-Khan (2001, 68), the economic situation in Pakistan continues to worsen. "Since the 1980s, developing and debtor countries, mostly situated in the Southern Hemisphere, have been undergoing a significant economic change initiated at the whims of developed and creditor nations of the North (hence the North/South divide has replaced the East/West colonial paradigm)" (68). These economic changes include structural adjustment programs that international lending agencies "devised in response to the debt crisis of the 1980s" (69), and they involve cutting "subsidies . . . on such products and essential services as water, public transport and electricity" (69). Khan documents Dia and Daanish's life in Karachi without electricity and water to show the effects of economic globalization on them and Salaamat, and she draws our attention to other national issues as well.

As Harvey (2004, 351) has pointed out, "Capitalism has intensely shaped [our contemporary world] to its own purposes over the past two hundred years." When thinking about environmental and social justice, we cannot ignore the imprint of the global economy on the ecosystem that we all share. Through the displacement of Salaamat from his fishing village, through Dia's family's attempts to adjust to power outages, and through Daanish's attempts to buy water when it stops flowing in their taps, Khan shows the effects of large global institutions such as the IMF on ordinary people in Karachi. People all across the postcolonial nation-state of Pakistan suffer from the scarcity of electricity and water.

The timely release of *Trespassing* helps scholars to explore different types of attachments to place between the human and the nonhuman in a global context. Writers such as Uzma Aslam Khan voice concerns for the planet that are neither an extension of nationalism nor a rejection of it. In this novel, Pakistani eco-cosmopolitanism is local in light of the global economy and the global environment. Chapters 1–3 focused on specific regions of Pakistan, and this chapter uses the region of Karachi to discuss the whole country of Pakistan. Chapter 5 examines displacement from multiple places and multiple countries to shift from the local to the national to the global. It analyzes the use of nonhuman animals and proposes ways to live with both the human and the nonhuman.

5

Displacement

Animalization

> Nomadism is the most attenuated concept in relation to location.
> Yet even theories of nomadic rhizomes include "nodes"—those sites
> of intersecting movements or "lines of flight." Thus most notions of
> displacement contain an oppositional notion of placement and vice versa.
> CAREN KAPLAN

After exploring four places in chapters 1–4, in this chapter I explore displacement because, as Caren Kaplan explains, notions of place contain oppositional notions of displacement, which is experienced by humans as well as nonhumans. War and nationalism, for example, have devastated both the land and families through violence and forced migrations. And our complete disregard for nonhuman animals is similar to the way in which we other some of our fellow humans. Nationalism and humanism oppress human and nonhuman others when we fight wars without regard for the land and all who live there.[1] Kamila Shamsie's novel *Burnt Shadows* (2009) engages with these issues by describing the nuclear bombing of Nagasaki, the violence of partition in Delhi, the war in Afghanistan in the 1980s, and the attacks in the United States on September 11, 2001. In addition to exploring these places and the effects of war and violence, the novel also describes three human characters who are displaced from Nagasaki, Delhi, and Kandahar. Their displacement is a theme that sheds light on the horrors of animalization and on the love of place. In this chapter, I argue that the novel's critique of nationalism among humans is embedded in and inseparable from its resistance to humanism.

Feminist geographer Doreen Massey's (2005) concept of space-time sheds light on this novel. She argues that because we cannot grow without others, we have to conceptualize space as open, multiple, and relational. History can then be open rather than predetermined. "Conceptualising space as open, multiple and relational, unfinished and always becoming, is a prerequisite for history to be open and thus a prerequisite, too, for the possibility of politics" (Massey 2005, 59). Like Massey, I hope for change, particularly when it comes to social and environmental justice. I am indebted to her idea of "throwntogetherness," which forces us to consider the ways in which we must negotiate with the space that we occupy. "Place, in other words does—as many argue—change us, not through some visceral belonging (some barely changing rootedness, as so many would have it) but through the *practicing* of place, the negotiation of intersecting trajectories; place as an arena where negotiation is forced upon us" (Massey 2005, 154). According to Massey, we must negotiate with everyone and everything—namely, human others, as well as nonhuman rocks and trees and animals. Massey's critical framework leads us to ask, how does place affect the characters in the fictions we read? How is the negotiation of intersecting trajectories forced upon these characters, women and men, human and nonhuman? How does it shape them?

In her book *For Space* (2005, 140), Massey's position regarding space is not "hostile to place or working only for its dissolution into a wider space." Instead, she insists, "what is special about place is precisely that throwntogetherness, the unavoidable challenge of negotiating a here-and-now (itself drawing on a history and a geography of thens and theres); and a negotiation which must take place within and between both human and nonhuman" (140). This understanding of place is much more useful than "some romance of a pre-given collective identity or of the eternity of the hills" (140) because Massey provides a framework for imagining time-space as ever changing. She believes that we must negotiate a here and now in the context of a there and then, keeping in mind that places change over time. Massey writes, "Reconceptualising place in this way puts on the agenda a different set of political questions. . . . [P]laces . . . implicate us, perforce, in the lives of human others, and in our relations with nonhumans they ask how we shall respond to our temporary meeting-up with these particular rocks and stones and trees. They require that, in one way or another, we confront the challenge of the negotiation of multiplicity" (141). Places ask what we shall do on this planet in the context of others. According to Massey, our politics must imagine and take into consideration the human, the nonhuman, and the here and now in all of its ever-changing multiplicity. Massey's goal is always politics. What would we do differently if we understood and accounted for all of this? What would we do if our understanding and accounting were the result of reading fiction?

As a geographer who is interested in cultural theory, Massey cites Jacques Derrida but critiques him by insisting that the world is not like a text; rather, a text is like the world. Derrida's angle as a philosopher is different from hers. Massey (2005, 54) writes, "Coming at it from [my] angle hints at what it might mean to argue *not* that the world (space-time) is like a text but that a text (even in the broadest sense of that term) is just like the rest of the world" (italics in original). I believe that a text can shape our imagination of the world, and, by extension, a text can shape our politics.

Massey's imagination of the world, of space-time, is useful for understanding texts—specifically, Kamila Shamsie's novel *Burnt Shadows*, which begins in 1945 and ends post-9/11. The novel spans multiple continents, covers multiple wars that affect the human and nonhuman in a space-time of throwntogetherness, and demands that we reconsider our future politics. *Burnt Shadows* focuses on displacement as a result of nationalist violence and comments on the violent displacement from homeplaces, especially from attachments to the nonhuman. Embedded within its critique of nationalist violence is a critique of humanism through a trope of animalization, which Shamsie uses to powerful effect. Even though the novel's characters are forced to migrate as if they are nomads, they each have nodes, or locations where they intersect, per feminist theorist Caren Kaplan's (1996) observation in this chapter's epigraph.

Burnt Shadows follows Hiroko Tanaka from the bombing of Nagasaki, when her fiancé dies, to Delhi, where she meets and falls in love with Sajjad Ashraf during partition. As Hiroko has been displaced from Nagasaki, Sajjad is displaced from Delhi when together they are forced to migrate to Karachi, Pakistan.[2] Later, their son, Raza, befriends Abdullah Durrani, an Afghan refugee who was displaced during the

Cold War from Kandahar, first to Karachi and eventually to New York, where Abdullah and Hiroko live post-9/11. Shamsie focuses on a type of resilience despite loss through the characters of Hiroko Tanaka, Sajjad Ashraf, and Abdullah Durrani, all of whom were immigrants in Pakistan. While the other novelists and filmmakers discussed in this book focus on a local sense of place in Pakistan within a global sense of the planet, Shamsie's novel also emphasizes local places outside Pakistan: Nagasaki, Delhi, Kandahar, and New York. Despite each of her characters' displacement, they reaffirm commitments to place in ways that subvert nationalism through the nonhuman and through a global vision. Their narratives of belonging look past the insular to the global without losing the sense of a materiality of place, which I have discussed throughout this book. For Abdullah this sense of place is manifested in his love of Kandahar's pomegranate orchards and New York's cab drivers, while for Hiroko and Sajjad this global yet nonhuman vision is manifested in a powerful image of birds. In this way, Shamsie's novel is a catalyst for social and environmental action within and beyond Pakistan.

Nationalist Violence and Place-Based Nonviolence

While Kamila Shamsie's novel *Burnt Shadows* does not actually focus on birds, its animalization of both violent and nonviolent human characters as birds suggests that Shamsie's critique of human nationalist violence and displacement is routed through an equal critique of what ecocritic Raymond Malewitz (2014, 544) describes as "absolute divisions between human subjects and nonhuman objects." In my discussion of the character of Hiroko, I use the term "animalization" in the same way as literary critic Sundhya Walther (2014, 595), who uses it to "refer to the process by which a being, human or nonhuman, is classified as being 'animal,' especially in opposition to the category of the 'human.'" She goes on to say that she is "engaging with the cultural constructs of human and animal, rather than the actual characteristics of real nonhuman animals" (595). According to postcolonial ecocritics Graham Huggan and Helen Tiffin (2015, vii), "The so-called *animal turn* . . . has inevitably informed recent developments in postcolonial ecocriticism, one of whose tasks is to ask what makes us human in the first place—

what elevates us above other animals." In the novel, human characters are associated with birds in a way that does not elevate humans; as violent humans animalize others, real birds lead the character of Sajjad to ponder nonviolence. As religious studies scholar Aaron Gross (2012, 5) points out, "Across time and across cultures humans imagine themselves through animal others," and Sajjad does so exactly by imagining himself through pigeons and sunbirds. Birds in this novel, similar to the images that the protagonist Hiroko has burned onto her back in 1945, represent both the perpetrators of nationalist violence and those who resist it through animalization, which challenges both nationalist violence and the dominant discourse of humanism.

References to birds are repeated throughout the novel, often as metaphors of not only U.S. violence but Japanese and Afghan violence as well. Hiroko is a Japanese survivor of the bombing of Nagasaki whose perceptions of nuclear risk, especially in South Asia, are very high. Hiroko's sense of the planet is the result of the deterritorialization she experiences throughout her life.[3] Hiroko is educated and middle class, but Abdullah is not. Thus, when Hiroko and Raza meet Abdullah, a survivor of the war in Afghanistan, his experiences inspire deep sympathy in both. Postcolonial critic Victor Li (2009, 275) argues that when both Arundhati Roy in *The God of Small Things* (2008) and Amitav Ghosh in *The Hungry Tide* (2006) create subaltern male characters who die at the end of their novels, "the immortalization of the subaltern involves a troubling logic of sacrifice and necroidealization that replaces the messiness and ambiguity of struggle with the reassurance of an aestheticized political ideal." Li (2009, 291) is right to ask, "What is the cost of this sacrifice? Why should death be the price of idealization? Is there a danger that the subaltern's death is made to serve purposes other than the subaltern's own?" As an ecocritic, I would add that these deaths serve the purpose of teaching readers environmental lessons. Shamsie's novel moves away from such necroidealization because she does not end her novel with the sacrificial death of Abdullah. He does not die so that we can learn environmental lessons about deterritorialization.

In *Burnt Shadows* Shamsie's descriptions of the bombing of Nagasaki are terrifying; she explicitly details its effects on both the people and the planet. Soon after the bombing, Hiroko notices that her kimono has fused with the skin on her back. As she looks out the window, she realizes that the damage to her valley reflects the damage to herself. "Fire and smoke and, through the smoke, nothing. Through the smoke, land that looks the way her back feels where it has no feeling. . . . Her fingers can feel her back but her back cannot feel her fingers. . . . Urakami Valley has become her flesh. Her flesh has become Urakami Valley" (28). Hiroko cannot separate the violence against the people from the violence against the land because the land has become her flesh, as have the birds of the land.

According to Malewitz (2014, 544), "One central challenge of post-humanism . . . revolves around a difficult question: given our status as human beings embedded within a deep tradition of humanism, how can we collect and share information about nonhuman agents from their points of view? Since animals lack an easily identifiable interiority . . . how can we . . . think through animals?" For instance, why are birds so prominent in Shamsie's novel? Is it because they fly? Migrate? Move from place to place as do many of the main characters? Possibly, but there is more to it. As literary critic Sarah Dowling (2013, 735) writes, "If some tame creatures fade into the background, other animals are more insistent, more disruptive, harder to ignore." When Hiroko is wearing the kimono, the narrator describes her this way: "Her body from neck down a silk column, white with three black cranes swooping across her back" (23). This image of migratory birds in motion is burned onto her during the bombing: "There could be no mistaking the three charcoal-coloured bird-shaped burns on her back" (92). In the case of Hiroko, the cranes eventually come to suggest her forced migrations from Nagasaki to Tokyo, then to Delhi, Karachi, and finally New York.

Avian migrations also imply the fluid interconnectedness of ecosystems, but in each of her migrations, Hiroko is forced to leave because of war, violence, or the threat of violence. The cranes on her back serve as a continuous reminder of the nuclear bomb and its violence. "Some days she could feel the dead on her back, pressing down beneath her shoulder blades with demands she could make no sense of but knew she was failing to meet" (50). The cranes come to represent the dead of Nagasaki and their silent demands for justice; Hiroko carries them with her wherever she goes. In Karachi, where she spends most of her life, Hiroko becomes a fierce opponent of Pakistan's nuclear program.

While cranes represent Euro-American violence against the Japanese, Hiroko soon learns about the nationalism that is linked to the violence. After the bombing, she goes to Tokyo and works for Americans there, including a man with a gentle face whom she comes to respect. Hiroko states, "And then one day—near the end of '46—the American with the gentle face said the bomb was a terrible thing, but it had to be done to save American lives" (63). American nationalism is shown as the reason for the bombing of Hiroko's homeplace, and the cranes burnt onto her back both represent that American nationalist violence and her flight from Nagasaki and later Tokyo.

Eventually Hiroko is able to connect the bombing of Nagasaki with U.S. post-9/11 policy, and, interestingly, Shamsie references birds again. When a well-meaning Euro-American named Kim Burton calls the police to report Abdullah as an illegal immigrant, Hiroko states, "In the big picture of the Second World War, what was seventy-five thousand more Japanese dead? Acceptable, that's what it was. In the big picture of threats to America, what is one Afghan? Expendable. Maybe he's guilty, maybe not. Why risk it? Kim, you are the kindest, most generous woman I know. But right now, because of you, I understand for the first time how nations can applaud when their governments drop a second nuclear bomb" (370). Hiroko's moment of understanding becomes a major connection for the reader. As literary critic Sachi Nakachi (2012, 138) writes about this passage, "Through Hiroko's voice, Shamsie asserts that American Islamophobia after 9/11 has the same root as the American attack on Nagasaki. Both come from American fear and prejudice against non-whites." The connection is also illustrated through the nonhuman—specifically birds—when the narrator states, "The silence that followed was the silence of intimates who find themselves strangers. The dark birds were between them, their burnt feathers everywhere" (370). These burned feathers emphasize that those same cranes burned on Hiroko's back in 1945 also show the distance created by U.S. nationalist fear again post-9/11. The cranes, the dark birds with burned feathers, disrupt our understanding of history by emphasizing the U.S. nationalism in the violence.

In the novel, birds do not represent only American violence; Hiroko also dreams of a violent bird that she associates with both Japanese and

Afghan suicide bombers. Hiroko has a dream in which a Japanese boy wishing to die for his nation in World War II becomes an Afghan boy wishing to die for his in the 1980s. "In her dream, Raza was speaking to an Afghan boy but the boy, although an Afghan boy, was also her ex-student, Joseph, the kamikaze pilot. 'Maybe I won't join the Air Force,' Joseph, who was also the Afghan boy, said. Raza sneered. 'Scared, little boy?' Joseph stood up taller, unfurling his black wings, and when he opened his mouth desiccated cherry blossom cascaded out, blanketing the dry soil of Afghanistan" (228). The Afghan boy becomes the kamikaze pilot Joseph, but when he is pushed and taunted, when his masculinity is questioned, he becomes animalized as a bird representing Japanese and Afghan nationalist violence.[4] And when he opens his mouth, he does not speak. He is silent because, according to postcolonial theorist Kalpana Rahita Seshadri (2012, 13), "the site of animalization or brutalization is primarily one where language as representation and legitimate speech becomes inaccessible." This bird with black wings can be read as the link between American, Japanese, and Afghan nationalist violence because, as with the cranes on Hiroko's back, the bird in her dream cannot speak.

Shamsie also depicts the earth as confused by humans who become more practical during wartime. Even though some might assume that functionality, especially during crisis, should be applauded, the earth is mystified. "Hiroko Tanaka . . . walked past the vegetable patches on the slopes a few days ago and saw the earth itself furrowing in mystification: why potatoes where once there were azaleas? What prompted this falling-off of love? How to explain to the earth that it was more functional as a vegetable patch than a flower garden, just as factories were more functional than schools and boys were more functional as weapons than as humans" (7).

Through the cranes on Hiroko's back and the dream where an Afghan/Japanese boy becomes a bird, Shamsie uses animalization to connect U.S., Japanese, and Afghan nationalist violence, all of which involves discrimination and racism. According to Seshadri (2012, ix), "If we understand modern discriminatory practice as a functioning of what Foucault terms biopower, we can immediately discern that what is termed 'racism' is synonymous with the practice of dehumanization, whereby the victim is disqualified from being a full member of the elite company of human beings." The earth is depicted as mystified because only a falloff of love can explain the use and value of boys as weapons. The comparison between birds and bomb-dropping fighter planes piloted by mere boys is implicit here. In Hiroko's dream, Joseph's animalization is shown to result from his lack of power; he is just a cog in the larger machinery of war. In writing about Bhanu Kapil's *Human-imal*, Dowling (2013, 751) states that she "maintains that the opening and closure of the gap between human and animal is an effect of power in which the animalized are shut out from language and society, but her work also reveals that in pursuing this gap, in tracing its openings and closures, the possibility of thinking and writing differently springs forward." Joseph is animalized and silenced, shut out from language.

Images of birds abound in this novel. Not only are they associated with Hiroko, her life experiences, and her dreams but also with the two men she loves. As the novel opens, Hiroko is engaged to a German named Konrad Weiss living in Nagasaki. Konrad writes about and researches a time when European and Japanese architecture mixed as easily as the people did; however, as the war continues, he must hide his notebooks. "Ever since Germany's surrender shifted his status in Nagasaki from that of ally into some more ambiguous state which requires the military police to watch him closely[,] the lifeless words have become potent enough to send him to prison" (9). While Konrad thinks of his words as lifeless and Hiroko picks the notebooks up and flies them around as if they are birds, their friend Yoshi Watanabe reminds him that writing "*about a Nagasaki filled with foreigners . . . longingly* [is] *one step away from cheering on an American occupation*" (9, italics in original). As a result of Hiroko's playfulness and Yoshi's warnings, "the night Germany surrendered, Konrad constructed a mobile of strong wire[,] hung each of his eight purple-leather notebooks from it . . . and attached the mobile to a tree. The wind twirled the purple-winged birds in the moonlight" (9). These "birds" represent Konrad's longing for a time before war when he and Hiroko could have been together "uncomplicatedly" (6).

The novel lends substantial power to birds that are man-made: Konrad's purple-winged birds protect him from violence while the cranes burned onto Hiroko's back are the result of violence. The threat of violence compels Konrad to fashion his birds, while the violence of the bomb makes Hiroko move across the world, reflecting her charcoal-colored burns of migratory birds. Unreal cranes and purple-winged birds are associated with nationalist violence and the bomb, but the real birds in the novel do not connote any type of human violence.

After Hiroko's fiancé, Konrad, dies when Nagasaki is bombed, Hiroko meets Sajjad in British India while visiting Konrad's sister and her husband, Elizabeth Burton (née Ilse Weiss) and James Burton. Even though Sajjad will eventually be forced to migrate and experience the pain of deterritorialization, when we first meet him, he behaves as if he is a nonmigratory bird and thinks of himself as a homing pigeon that is able to return home. Thus, he too is animalized. Sajjad has a deep and abiding love for his *moholla*, or neighborhood, Dilli. Even as talk of partition becomes more and more heated, he insists that his attachment to his homeplace is greater than any kind of nationalism. Regarding the possible creation of Pakistan, he states, "Either way it won't matter to me. I will die in Dilli. Before that, I will live in Dilli. Whether it's in British India, Hindustan, Pakistan—that makes no difference to me" (40). This devotion will not be enough to help him reach his goal.

Sajjad takes Hiroko to Istanbul in 1947 during the partition of British India to spare her the pain of yet another violent conflict, but he and Hiroko are unable to go back to India. Upon returning from the Indian Embassy in Istanbul, he says, "They said I'm one of the Muslims who chose to leave India. It can't be unchosen. They said, Hiroko, they said I can't go back to Dilli. I can't go back home" (127). Sajjad must learn to live in the newly created state of Pakistan due to forces he cannot control: the forces of Muslim nationalism in British India, the forces of British colonial power, and the forces of Indian Hindu nationalism. The map of India and Pakistan that these other forces created means nothing to him. Sajjad's sense of place is related to the history and culture of "Dilli: his city . . . the place to which his ancestors had come from Turkey over seven centuries earlier" (33).

Sajjad's animalization is not a representation of violence but of nonviolence and a better way for humans to live. When pondering the boundary between Dilli and Delhi, Sajjad compares himself to pigeons, which are known for their ability to return home. "I am like those occasional pigeons, Sajjad thought. At home in Dilli but breaking free of the rest of my flock to investigate the air of Delhi" (34). In India rock pigeons are usually referred to simply as pigeons, and even though they do not migrate, they can fly very long distances and return home. Sajjad's thinking here shows pigeons voluntarily exploring the world around them before heading home. The image is instructive for its focus on voluntary exploration and investigation. Thus, the pigeon, unlike the crane, does not represent violence and oppression; instead, it represents both a resistance to forced migrations by emphasizing flights by choice and the importance of a sense of a homeplace for one's return.

Animalization actually works differently in Sajjad, who provides a possibility of thinking in another way. Instead of representing violence, Sajjad is animalized as a bird to represent resistance not only to the displacement caused by partition-related violence but also to colonialism. Thus, the metaphor of the bird as representing resistance becomes even stronger when Sajjad behaves as if he is one. After observing a sunbird in his British employer's hollyhocks, he tries to sample the nectar, just as the birds do. "Angling his back so that James Burton couldn't see what he was doing, Sajjad leaned forward and flicked his tongue into the hollyhock, trying to sample its nectar, but without any success" (38). Sajjad loves birds and hopes someday to attract them to his home with a garden. That he imitates the sunbird shows his connection to this nonmigratory animal. Sajjad does not want James to see this mimicry, as James represents the British colonizers in India while Sajjad is the colonized. Sajjad knows that if James were to see him, James would interpret his behavior as animal-like and "uncivilized." As anticolonial philosopher Frantz Fanon (2004, 7) points out, "The colonized subject . . . is reduced to the state of an animal. And consequently, when the colonist speaks of the colonized he uses zoological terms." James, as the colonizer, would only be able to read Sajjad's actions through those colonial stereotypes.

However, both moments with the pigeons and the sunbirds show an interspecies identification on Sajjad's part that resists forced migration, nationalist violence, and colonial stereotypes. Jacques Derrida (2008, 3) refers to this as "'the crossing of borders' between man and animal." He goes on to write, "Passing across borders or the ends of man I come or surrender to the animal in me and the animal at unease with itself" (3). Feminist theorist Donna Haraway (2008) suggests that we cross these borders when thinking through animals. She states, "The discursive tie between the colonized, the enslaved, the noncitizen, and the animal—all reduced to type, all Others to rational man, and all essential to his bright constitution—is at the heart of racism and flourishes, lethally, in the entrails of humanism. . . . Companion species must instead learn to live intersectionally" (18). The two moments that Sajjad has with birds are attempts to live intersectionally, but he is limited by the racism and humanism of British colonialism.

For Hiroko, the trope of animalization is akin to the brutalization of racism. As Seshadri (2012, 17) writes, "I approach modern racism as dehumanization or 'animalization.'" The type of animalization she discusses helps her to "discover the continuity in terms of structural violence among institutions that have vastly differing histories and economies, such as Southern slavery, the Nazi concentration camp, the Middle East crisis, and the contemporary war on terror" (68). Seshadri's theorization of animalization as brutal and racist captures Hiroko's experience in Nagasaki, the birds burned onto her back, and her dreams of the dark birds. Historian Ronald Takaki (1995) also writes that race played a role in the use of the atomic bomb in Japan. "For the United States during the years between Japan's attack on Pearl Harbor and America's atomic bombing of Hiroshima, there were two wars—the European war and the Pacific war. In Europe, the enemy was identified as Hitler and the Nazis, not the German people. In the Pacific, on the other hand, American anger was generally aimed at an entire people—the 'Japs.' During the war, the Japanese were condemned as demons, a monkey race, savages, and beasts" (8). Many Americans are of German ancestry, and, as a result, it was easier to demonize the Japanese than it was the Germans. Takaki shows that Euro-American racism against the Japanese involved animalizing them at times as beasts or monkeys. Recognizing Hiroko's process of animalization as a result of racism fits with Takaki's argument because she was animalized when the bird design on her kimono was burned onto her back during the bombing. The animalization associated with Hiroko is thus violently racist and nationalist.

Through Sajjad, the novel presents another kind of animalization. His displacement is in stark contrast to his animalization as a bird in both his behavior and his thinking. In Sajjad's case, he is not animalized by violence and trauma but by his encounters with birds. Philosopher Matthew Calarco (2008, 3) argues that *"the human-animal distinction can no longer and ought no longer to be maintained"* (italics in original). Sajjad does not maintain this distinction; therefore, his animalization is much closer to that in Haraway's work on companion species. She (2008, 19) writes, "Species interdependence is the name of the worlding game on earth, and that game must be one of response and respect. . . . I am who I become with companion species." Sajjad's animalization is expressed through his awareness of other species of birds. His response to them and respect for them provide him with a nonviolent philosophy that emphasizes a voluntary exploration of land followed by a return home instead of a forcible displacement of humans from their homeplace due to violent nationalism. While Hiroko's unreal and man-made birds torment and make demands on her, Sajjad's birds show him a way to live that resists British colonialism and the nationalisms that lead to displacement. Sajjad's animalization is place-based nonviolence, while Hiroko is, herself, animalized by violent humans and dreams of the animalization of others because of nationalism.

Theorizing about animalization and migration together helps fill the gap between postcolonial theory and ecocriticism in the way that the editors of *Global Ecologies and the Environmental Humanities* (DeLoughrey, Didur, and Carrigan 2015) suggest. They write that they are "committed to accounting for the more-than-human and multispecies world, while at the same time identifying the hierarchical processes that led certain humans to be reduced to 'nature' (or other species) and examining the significance of this for present-day experiences of environmental racism" (11). Through Hiroko and Sajjad, we thus see our connection to the multispecies world as well as the hierarchy of racist animalization between humans.

Deterritorialization, the Nonhuman, and a Global Sense of Place

What are the losses and possible gains of deterritorialization, which is a type of homelessness? As Mitchell Thomashow (1999, 123) has stated,

"We must consider the potential of widespread, global migrations of peoples and species as the shadow of globalization . . . a grim reminder of the transience engendered by forced uprootedness. Homelessness takes many shapes and forms." Humans and nonhumans are forcefully uprooted all over the world for economic reasons, war, nationalism, and climate change. A global sense of place must include an understanding of all these complicated dynamics. Shamsie's characters heighten our awareness of the complexities of migration even though they display a global sense of place. We must include in our understanding of these complicated dynamics the novel's critique of nationalism among humans, and we must read the novel ecocritically to grasp the ways in which this critique is embedded in and inseparable from its resistance to humanism.

Shamsie considers the trauma of wars and violence through the issue of forced displacement. The nonhuman element of birds, trees, spiders, reptiles, and land adds poignancy to her descriptions of forced migrancy because of human animalization and attachments to the nonhuman. According to Thomashow (1999, 122), "When habitats are transformed by commercial, industrial and agricultural developments, natural resource extraction, tourism and war, a chain of ecological and cultural disruptions is initiated. Indigenous societies must either adapt to the changing circumstances, migrate to a new habitat, or face extinction." Human and nonhuman migration is not chosen freely when habitats are transformed by war, and the ecological and the cultural are equally affected by violence. While one could argue that Shamsie's primary concern is not with environmental issues per se, her depiction of the aftereffects of the nuclear bombing in Nagasaki, the war in Afghanistan, and the violence in Karachi should be read through both an ecocritical and a postcolonial lens. Shamsie draws attention to the ecological consequences of violence, particularly nuclear violence, while simultaneously countering the multiple nationalisms of Pakistan, Japan, Afghanistan, and the United States.

An ecocritical approach can be far more illuminating within a postcolonial framework because postcolonial critics can avoid some of the pitfalls of much U.S. ecocriticism. According to postcolonial ecocritics Elizabeth DeLoughrey and George B. Handley (2011, 16–17), "Postcolonial ecology's concerns are differently inflected than mainstream American environmentalism and tend to emphasize access to arable land and potable water, public health, the threats of militarism and national debt. . . . Postcolonial . . . nations . . . firmly place the human in nature, a significant difference from dominant Anglo-American environmental trajectories. Moreover, postcolonial ecology has presented some of the most important critiques of American empire."

Through fiction, these critiques of empire are often situated locally in postcolonial spaces that are described at length and in resistance to the more global forces of capitalism and cultural imperialism. For instance, postcolonial ecocritic Byron Caminero-Santangelo (2011, 294) argues that a South African novel "affords an ideal opportunity to explore . . . 'a transnational ethics of place.'" He states that even though he is considering the global, "the category of place is still privileged" in his analysis (307). While I am sympathetic toward Caminero-Santangelo's position of privileging place even when exploring the transnational, and I have certainly tried to do it in earlier chapters, I find that in *Burnt Shadows*, Shamsie's emphasis shifts to a global position both to depict the forced displacement of war for humans and nonhumans alike and to resist nationalisms of all kinds, including U.S. militarism. This seems counterintuitive because a global sense of planet can be very abstract, and most change in or direct exploration of issues usually happens locally. Nonetheless, *Burnt Shadows* helps us imagine a planetary sense of self through the displaced characters of Hiroko, Sajjad, and Abdullah. Each of these characters suffers the effects of forced migrations in different ways and shows how that image of the migrating bird can have both positive and negative layers of meaning. Hiroko's migration, as well as the movement and migration of other characters, makes the stance of the novel cosmopolitan in the way that Carol Breckenridge and the other editors of *Cosmopolitanism* (2002, 11) describe it: "ways of living at home abroad or abroad at home—ways of inhabiting multiple places at once, of being different beings simultaneously, of seeing the larger picture stereoscopically with the smaller." Both the larger and the smaller pictures are presented in this novel through the nonhuman. By emphasizing the nonhuman in my reading of this novel, I am furthering the work of DeLoughrey, Didur, and Carrigan in *Global Ecologies and* the *Environmental Humanities* (2015). They write that "a truly 'ecological' humanities needs to be relational and interconnected, deconstructing hierarchies between the arts and the sciences and encouraging modes of thinking that move across cultural as well as human and nonhuman boundaries" (9).

The movement across human and nonhuman boundaries is clearly presented in the bombing of Nagasaki; it is described as hellish partly because Hiroko cannot recognize her father's humanity. Just as with Hiroko, the bomb dehumanizes and animalizes him. Hiroko's deterritorialization is caused when neither the place nor her father is familiar to her because they are so irrevocably changed. "Hiroko looks down, sees a reptile crawling up the path towards her house. She understands now. The earth has already opened up, disgorged hell" (28). Hiroko does not recognize her father because he looks and crawls like a reptile. After he dies, Hiroko remains haunted by his animalization. When she gives birth to her son, Raza, she is unable to tell him that her many migrations from Tokyo to Bombay to Delhi were acts of desperation. "Why tell him of the momentum of a bomb blast that threw her into a world in which everything was unfamiliar, Nagasaki itself become more unknown than Delhi? Nothing in the world more unrecognisable than her father as he died" (227). Hiroko is displaced by the bomb even before she migrates because it animalizes her father and completely alters her homeplace.

Hiroko is displaced not once but twice because of nuclear weapons. The first is in 1945, and the second occurs in 1998 when India and Pakistan both conduct nuclear tests. Before the testing, her friend Yoshi arrives in Karachi "with a group of hibakusha [or people who are affected by the nuclear bomb] determined to say what he could to turn Pakistan away from the idea of nuclear tests. Hiroko had translated the words of the hibakusha into Urdu through the press conference, spent an afternoon filled with tears and laughter with Yoshi afterwards, and then boarded the plane to New York" (297). After thirty years of residency, Hiroko leaves Pakistan just before the tests because she knows what they can mean for Pakistan and the whole region. Hiroko's deterritorialization thus leads to her critique of both nationalism and nuclear weapons.

In 1945 Hiroko's sense of place is defamiliarized in a harmful way, but her sense of the planet becomes more constructive as she becomes a strong critic of nuclear weapons. For her, deterritorialization has both negative and positive effects. As Heise (2008, 10) has pointed out, "Undoubtedly, deterritorialization, especially when it is imposed from outside, is sometimes accompanied by experiences of loss, deprivation, or disenfranchisement that environmentalists have rightfully resisted and should continue to oppose. Yet deterritorialization also implies possibilities for new cultural encounters and a broadening of horizons that environmentalists as well as other politically progressive movements have welcomed, sometimes without fully acknowledging the entanglements of such cultural unfolding with globalization processes that they otherwise reject." I do not agree with Heise's valorizing of the global over the local. Hiroko does become more global in her thinking after she experiences the loss of Nagasaki and all that is familiar to her. When she meets Rehana in Pakistan, and Rehana says that she is "at home in the idea of foreignness," Hiroko knows immediately that she has found a friend (143). Hiroko's deterritorialization is what leads to her planetary consciousness, which includes her ability to embrace people such as Rehana who are not necessarily rooted in a sense of place that corresponds with the boundaries and borders of nation-states. This argues against an uncritical valorization of the global over the local because globalization is, first and foremost, economic; but Hiroko and Rehana's relationship is not based on economics.

When Hiroko goes with Elizabeth and James Burton to Mussoorie, one of India's hill stations, she realizes that the floral life of that region is the same as Nagasaki's. The bioregion is the same even though the borders of nation-states do not align with it.

Each day, sitting in this tree, eyes drifting over Mussoorie's trees and flowers, some as familiar as the texture of tatami beneath her feet, she strung together different memories of Nagasaki as though they were rosary beads: the faint sound of her father preparing paint on his ink stone, the deepening purple of a sky studded by clusters and constellations of light in an evening filled with the familiar tones of her neighbours' voices . . . the walks along the Oura with Konrad, dreaming of all that would be possible after the war. (97)

Mussoorie and Nagasaki merge in her mind, and Hiroko develops a positive global sense of place despite its having resulted from war. The novel, however, never denies Hiroko's accompanying sense of loss; after all, she has lost her homeplace, her father, and even her dreams of a postwar life with Konrad.

Also, regardless of her global sense of place, nationalist racism haunts her son in Pakistan. Hiroko and Sajjad's son, Raza, who is ethnically Japanese and South Asian, is born and raised in Karachi but looks as if he is from Afghanistan. As he comes of age in Karachi, he becomes friendly with Afghan refugees in the city who assume that he is one of them. *Burnt Shadows* offers another critique of nationalism as the narrator states about Hiroko: "It didn't bother her in the least to know she would always be a foreigner in Pakistan—she had no interest in belonging to anything as contradictorily insubstantial and damaging as a nation—but this didn't stop her from recognizing how Raza flinched every time a Pakistani asked him where he was from" (208).[5] This critique shows the damaging effects of othering and exclusion that nationalism demands. Hiroko's global sense of place cannot protect her son.

Nonetheless, the novel shows that Elizabeth and James Burton's American son, Harry Burton, can only think of all that Hiroko and Sajjad have overcome. Harry emphasizes the positive over the negative. But the novel implies, through Hiroko, that no one ever fully recovers from such things as war and displacement; in fact, the word "overcome" is insufficient.

"Partition and the bomb," Harry said, interrupting her. "The two of you are proof that humans can overcome everything."

Overcome. Such an American word. What really did it mean? But she knew he meant it generously, so it seemed discourteous to throw the word back in his face with stories of a "not right" foetus which her body had rejected, or the tears Sajjad wept after his first visit to his collapsed world in Delhi. (184)

Hiroko's global sense of place and all that is positive about it comes with a very high price, and while the American Harry thinks that the effects of the partition and the bomb can be overcome, the narrator tells us that Hiroko knows better. The divisions between people that led to the partition and the bomb are the boundaries that continue to grow and develop in impenetrable ways.

Long before the international border was established between Pakistan and India, a boundary separated Sajjad's neighborhood of Dilli and British Delhi. Sajjad sees this boundary as the point where trees in courtyards are replaced with flowerpots. "Delhi: city of the Raj, where every Englishman's bungalow had lush gardens, lined with red flowerpots. That was the end of Sajjad's ruminations on British India. Flowerpots: it summed it all up. No trees growing in courtyards for the English, no rooms clustered around those courtyards; instead, separations and demarcations" (33). These separations and demarcations show the differences between how his people live in Dilli and how the British live in Delhi, and lead to more superimposed mapping at partition. As Thomashow (1999, 129) points out, "The delineation of hard and fast boundaries is the cause of much human suffering, as clashing tribes or nation-states argue about who belongs where. Bioregionalism must avoid the shadow of extreme regional identification. Rather, strong communities allow for permeable boundaries, and recognize the connections between places as intrinsic to the well-being of any one place." As discussed in chapters 1 and 2, this particular boundary is *not* penetrable and has caused and continues to cause much suffering.

Sajjad's regional identification with Dilli and its Muslims shifts over time from an extreme regional identification to a recognition of connections through passable boundaries. For instance, as the partition riots rage through the city, Sajjad becomes closer to James Burton's Muslim bearer Lala Buksh. "In all the years he'd been coming here he and Lala Buksh had barely spoken to each other beyond Sajjad conveying some request of James's to his bearer or wishing him a perfunctory *Eid Mubarak*. But in the last few weeks, as riots continued and the creation of a new state seemed increasingly likely, the two men had started to drink a cup of tea together in the morning while discussing what news the previous day had brought with it of death and politics and freedom"

(88). Partly because the violence is based on religion, Sajjad draws closer to Lala Buksh, but even at this point in the novel, his moral compass continues to guide him. "In talking to Lala Buksh, Sajjad realised that atrocities committed on Muslims touched him far more deeply than atrocities committed by Muslims—he knew this to be as wrong as it was true" (89).[6] Meanwhile, Sajjad grows to love Hiroko and marries her even though she is not a Muslim. He also grows to love Karachi even though it is not Dilli. The novel shows that boundaries can be crossed and should be crossed but willingly, not forcibly.

Similar to Sajjad's experience, Abdullah is forced to leave Afghanistan after fighting the Soviets because "peace never happened" (319). As a refugee of war, he drove a truck in Pakistan for four years but could not earn enough money. He tells Hiroko, "My brothers said one of us had to go to America where you can earn a real living" (319). Hiroko finds him in a library in New York, looking at photographs of Afghanistan. He states, "'Kandahar. Before the wars.' He ran his palm across the photograph, as though he could feel the texture of the ripening pomegranates pushing up against his skin. 'First they cut down the trees. Then they put landmines everywhere. Now—' He bunched his fingers together and then sprang them apart. 'Cluster bombs'" (317). Abdullah's love for the fruit trees and fruit of Kandahar is also equated with his love for his son. Recalling the monthly conversations between Abdullah and his son, Abdullah's brother Ismail states, "When they speak on the phone once a month Abdullah says tell me when your hand is big enough to fit around the largest Baba Wali pomegranate" (325). Baba Wali is the Sufi saint whose tomb Abdullah's family visits on Fridays and where a grove of pomegranate trees grows. Even when he thinks of his growing child, whom he has never met, Abdullah wants to put him in the context of the nonhuman trees that he loves.

Abdullah's displacement from and continuing devotion to the fruit trees of Kandahar are significant details because the multiple wars have created a food crisis in Afghanistan. According to Susie O'Brien (2004, 160–61),

In looking even cursorily at the ecology of food in Afghanistan—a country in which eighty-five percent of the population is directly dependent on agriculture—it is almost impossible to ignore the way it has been shaped by war. . . . Since much of Afghanistan is dry, agriculture depends on a vast series of underground channels (*kanez*) for irrigation. Extremely vulnerable to silting and cave-ins, these channels became direct targets for bombing, starving the orchards of Kandahar of water. . . . In conjunction with the widespread deployment of landmines, these tactics contributed to a steady erosion of the agricultural economy, in addition to the killing and displacement of more than two million people.

Abdullah's displacement from his homeplace is connected to the wars' effects on the nonhuman landscape and agriculture. These wars are global in nature, beginning with the Cold War and continuing through the war on terror. Hiroko immediately recognizes Abdullah's displacement as being similar to Sajjad's because "he had looked at the photographs of Kandahar's orchards as Sajjad used to look at pictures of his old moholla in Dilli" (319). Both the neighborhood and the orchards represent the materiality of each of these places—Dilli before partition and Kandahar before the Cold War. Massey's insistence that a place is space-time is even more clearly illustrated by the places from which Abdullah, Sajjad, and Hiroko have been displaced.

When Sajjad and Hiroko's son, Raza, goes to Kandahar as an adult, he has a hard time reconciling the Kandahar that Abdullah described to him as a child and the city after 9/11. "Twenty years ago, in Sohrab Goth, in highway restaurants, in the cab of the truck decorated with the dead Soviet, Raza had listened to Abdullah rhapsodise about the beauties of his city—the emerald in the desert whose fruit trees bore poems, whose language was the sweetness of ripe figs. But Raza's brief glimpse of Kandahar had shown him only dust, fierceness and—a month after the Taliban's defeat—not a single unshrouded woman" (322). Abdullah's deep nostalgia for the "orchards, the fleet river and the mountains beyond" is juxtaposed with the aftermath of war and the Taliban (323). The novel's postcolonial ecofeminist stance shows that Raza's displacement, which leads to his time in Afghanistan running from the Central Intelligence Agency, makes him painfully aware of all the privileges he has lost, but not being able to *see* any women is among the most difficult. As a result, Raza sees the Taliban, as do most Westerners, as absolutely evil.

However, a conversation with Abdullah's brother Ismail sheds some light on how ordinary Afghan men were persuaded by the Taliban. The brother whom Abdullah idolizes tells Raza:

> I'm a farmer. I want to plant crops and harvest them. Do you understand? I need peace for this. I need security. In exchange for that, there's much that I'll give up. . . . This is what I fought for [against the Soviets]. The right to . . . farm. . . . To watch my sons measure handspan against a pomegranate, not a grenade. But the Taliban—they don't know Sufis or orchards. They grew up in refugee camps, with no memory of this land, no attachment to anything except the idea of fighting infidels and heretics. So when they came they brought laws different to the laws I grew up with. So what? (326)

Raza does not understand how Ismail and other Afghan men can give up the freedom of women for a Taliban-style peace that comes with laws that oppress women. But Ismail's speech has to be understood in the context of perpetual war. According to anthropologist Mahmood Mamdani (2004, 161), "The Taliban provided the [Afghan] population effective protection against the likes of Gulbuddin Hikmatyar, warlords turned drug lords. . . . The promise that made the Taliban popular and brought it to power was that it would establish law and order." This is exactly what Ismail tells Raza when he refers to the importance of peace. Raza, however, is right: The price of this kind of gendered peace is far too high. As Mamdani notes, "Once the Taliban began to run the state, its brutality took the form of a harshly patriarchal rule" (177).

In effect, this patriarchal rule displaced the women of Afghanistan from their place in their own society. Unfortunately, it was acceptable to many Afghans; to the Pakistan military, which feared Afghan nationalism; and to the United States, due to its interest in oil. Mamdani (2004, 160–61) writes, "After a State Department meeting with a visiting Taliban delegation on February 3, 1997, a senior U.S. diplomat explained his government's point of view: 'The Taliban will probably develop like Saudi Arabia. There will be Aramco, pipelines, an emir, no parliament and lots of Sharia law. We can live with that.'" Afghans are also victims of the resource curse that Rob Nixon (2011) describes and is discussed in chapter 3. According to feminist anthropologist Lila Abu-Lughod (2013), members of the Revolutionary Association of Women of Afghanistan (RAWA) "have courageously worked since 1977 for a democratic secular Afghanistan in which women's human rights are respected, against Soviet-backed regimes or U.S.-, Saudi-, and Pakistani-supported conservatives" (41). As Mamdani has, Abu-Lughod writes that RAWA members "consistently reminded audiences to take a close look at the ways policies were being organized around oil interests, the arms industry, and the international drug trade. . . . Unfortunately, only their messages about the excesses of the Taliban were heard, even though their criticisms of those in power in Afghanistan had included previous regimes" (50). Abu-Lughod makes this point to show that President George W. Bush used the women's suffering as another reason to bomb the Taliban even though they had suffered under many previous regimes as well.

Nonetheless, this passage shows that Ismail is attached to the land in a way that the Taliban, which consists of generations of young men born in refugee camps, are not. In emphasizing Abdullah's love for Kandahar's fruit trees, the novel lays bare the consequences of war on the landscape and natural resources and on the women who are easily sacrificed as the men try to farm peacefully under the Taliban and the warlords-turned-drug-lords. The final irony of Abdullah's deterritorialization from Kandahar is that when he is forced to leave New York (because he has been reported as an illegal immigrant and agents with the Federal Bureau of Investigation have come looking for him after 9/11), he tells Raza, "New York is my home. The taxi drivers are my family" (359). As with Hiroko, Abdullah is displaced more than once by forces outside his control: war, poverty, and xenophobia.

Abdullah's sense of place is beautifully captured by his love for the nonhuman: Kandahar's pomegranate orchards, rivers, and mountains. While the other novelists and filmmakers discussed in this book focus on a local sense of place in Pakistan within a global sense of the planet, Shamsie's novel also emphasizes local places outside Pakistan, such as Nagasaki, Delhi, Kandahar, and New York. For instance, Abdullah loves the fruit trees of Kandahar as much as he loves his community of cab drivers in New York. In teaching us about the effects of the war in Afghanistan on both the local trees and the local women, the novel critiques both nationalism and humanism; it shows the consequences of war on the humans and the nonhuman alike. But unlike narratives that decenter the nation and nationalism via the local, Shamsie's novel decenters the nation via a much more global vision. As literary critic Harleen Singh (2012, 34) writes, "By decentering the nation and privileging the global relationships of colonialism, culture, and history, Shamsie unsettles the seamless singularity with which temporal and religious binaries (modern/regressive, secular/fundamentalist, western/non-western) are enacted to justify the war on terror." In addition to unsettling these temporal and religious binaries, Shamsie also unsettles the binary human-nonhuman, resulting in a more expansive critique of war itself.

Burnt Shadows is strikingly different from Shamsie's prior works. While all four of her previous novels were mostly set in Karachi and had protagonists who were all born in Pakistan, *Burnt Shadows'* protagonist, Hiroko, is Japanese and is displaced from Nagasaki, Delhi, and Karachi at different times in her life. Abdullah, an Afghan, is displaced from Kandahar, Karachi, and New York, while Sajjad is born in British India and displaced from Dilli. These global forced displacements deconstruct notions of the self and the other. As Aroosa Kanwal (2015, 146) points out, "Sajjad's compatibility with Hiroko despite their affiliation to different religions and communities, Raza's friendship with Harry, Kim's friendship with Raza, and Ilse's affiliation with Hiroko reveal the contingency and heterogeneity of global societies in which the whole concept of otherness crumbles; it is not only South Asians who are shown to be displaced. Neat divisions of margin and centre are blurred in such a way that both are revealed as steeped in constructions of otherness." With Hiroko's migrating within Asia first and then to the United States and with Abdullah's being forced to leave the country after migrating there, Shamsie resists the typical narrative of an immigrant who comes to the United States to pursue happiness.

The novel also blurs neat divisions of the human and the nonhuman as it depicts all these multiple affiliations through the Muslim story of the spider that protected Prophet Mohammed. Initially, Sajjad tells this old legend to Konrad, who tells it to Hiroko, who then tells it to Ilse. Hiroko tells the story to Ilse in this way: "Have I told you about the spider? How it wove its web—quick as lightning—over the mouth of the cave where Mohammed and his friend were hiding when they fled from Mecca, and so convinced their pursuers that no one had entered the cave in a long time?" (110). Sajjad uses the story to convince Konrad that the spider is beloved by Muslims. It shows the values of loyalty and protection between humans and a nonhuman spider; however, the story eventually comes to represent the protection and allegiance that the two families feel toward each other. "There was the spider, and there was its shadow. Two families, two versions of the spider dance. The Ashraf-Tanakas, the Weiss-Burtons—their story together the story of a bomb, the story of a lost homeland" (362). The story of the spider is imagined through the stories of the families and vice versa, and the story of displacement as the result of violence in multiple places is imagined through the story of the nonhuman. But the nonhuman is also present through descriptions of Urakami Valley, the reptile, the birds, the pomegranate orchards, and many other references to the more-than-human in this novel.

Shamsie's novel opposes both nationalist violence and humanism. The birds that are burned onto Hiroko's back, animalizing her and her dreams, are the result of manmade nationalist violence that leads to her forced migration; thus, as noted, it makes sense that the dark birds or burns are migratory cranes. The novel, however, offers an important challenge to both forced migration and humanism because the sunbirds and pigeons show Sajjad a place-based and nonviolent way to live. They eat, explore, and return home—actions that are described as natural in the novel for humans and for birds. Thus, the boundaries between humans and birds are blurred, making it easier to see how humans and nonhumans are equally affected by wars, violence, displacement, and environmental degradation. The deterritorialization of Abdullah, Sajjad, and Hiroko is the result of nationalist violence, which *Burnt Shadows* depicts as the devastation during the partition of British India, as well as in the attacks on Nagasaki, New York, and Afghanistan. That Hiroko's sense of risk is imagined as birds on her back and in her dreams emphasizes the ways in which nuclear risk, as with migratory birds, are not limited within national borders.

Burnt Shadows ends up critiquing nationalist violence in all its manifestations—that is, against people and against the planet. Global and social inequalities intersect with the environment. As Huggan and Tiffin (2015, 12) elegantly state, "What the postcolonial/ecocritical alliance brings out, above all, is the need for a broadly materialist understanding of the changing relationship between people, animals and environment. . . . This suggests (1) the continuing centrality of the imagination and, more specifically, imaginative *literature* to the task of postcolonial ecocriticism and (2) the mediating function of social and environmental *advocacy*, which might turn imaginative literature into a catalyst for social action and exploratory literary analysis into a full-fledged form of engaged cultural critique." As with Massey, Huggan and Tiffin are concerned about advocacy and politics. They see literature as a catalyst for social action and literary criticism as a form of cultural critique. So we must ask, what can imaginative literature such as *Burnt Shadows* teach us if we pay close attention to the nonhuman, to animality, to place, and to displacement? This novel critiques both nationalism and humanism in a larger and longer historical and geographical context, forcing us to ponder what it means to be displaced and animalized on a much more vast, global scale. In doing so, the novel is a catalyst for social action within and beyond Pakistan.

Conclusion

Justice for All

Karl Marx . . . recognized capitalism's "irreparable rift" with "the natural laws of life itself," while feminist scholars have long recognized that patriarchy's dual war against women's bodies and against the body of the earth were connected to that essential, corrosive separation between mind and body—and between body and earth—from which both the Scientific Revolution and Industrial Revolution sprang.
NAOMI KLEIN

The ongoing effects of climate change make it vitally important to link environmental and social justice issues around gender in Pakistan. Reading Pakistani women's literary and cinematic fictions through a lens of postcolonial ecofeminism is one way to bring these issues together. Throughout this book, I have shown that to bridge issues of social justice with environmental justice, we must create an idea of belonging that is separate and different from national belonging. We must decenter the nation from notions of belonging to centralize the environment. Even though none of the writers and filmmakers I study depicts environmentalism directly in their works, it is critical to imagine what it means to belong in a sustainable and inclusive way. Sabiha Sumar, Mehreen Jabbar, Sorayya Khan, Uzma Aslam Khan, and Kamila Shamsie provide fictions set in Pakistan that I read as alternate visions of belonging to local environments that are affected by gendered global and state-sponsored agendas. The phrase "to belong" includes *both* social and environmental justice in terms of distribution of natural resources and political participation. Just as more scholars of South Asia need to include ecological justice in their analyses, environmentalists in the global north also need to consider global social inequality as well as the way in which Islamophobic and other racist discourses impact the human and the nonhuman alike around the world. To read in a postcolonial ecofeminist way opens up new possibilities for thinking about social and environmental justice together because the place-based discourses that emerge from such readings oppose patriarchal religious nationalism. What we find instead are attachments to the land, the sea, and the animals of the place that is Pakistan.

Even though this place-based sense of belonging is in line with that of deep ecologists such as Arne Naess (1993) who first articulated the idea that the land, the sea, and the animals have intrinsic worth and should be protected, especially from humans who seek only to benefit economically from them, it is crucial for us, when we think globally, to move away from deep ecology. Naess did not consider vast global differences in material wealth, consumption, and population as part of his vision of environmental justice; however, taking these differences into account acknowledges global social inequalities. As ecofeminist sociologist Erika Cudworth (2005, 23) writes, "Without an analysis of intra-human domination deep ecological politics, although radical in tactics, tends to fall into a conservationism that does not question the basis of consumer capitalism which it so despises." Without a critique of capitalism, it becomes hard to see the structures of global inequality.

Even if we understand that incredible poverty in the global north and incredible wealth in the global south exist, what is possible for a North American with means is not possible for a Pakistani who is poor, and deep ecologists have not considered many of these realities. Postcolonial ecocritic Upamanyu Pablo Mukherjee (2010, 26) points out some of the problems with deep ecology when he writes,

It is conservative both because it sees "nature" as something separate from and threatened by the human, the vestiges of which are to be conserved; and because its vision of solitary pioneer-poets or at best small communities of enlightened rural farmers offers versions of a bucolic utopia that are constantly subsumed by the actual force of historical capital. Further, this nature/culture dualism found at the core of deep ecology's conservationist thrust seems to dispute its own principle of relationality—if everything is indeed connected to everything else, to what extent is it possible to strain after a vision of nature emptied of humans?

Humans are animals, after all. We are not separate from the environment. And our shared environment includes the forces of global capitalism, which we cannot escape. Deep ecological thinking that separates humans and capital from an idealized conception about nature might only be possible, theoretically, in less densely populated parts of global north countries where it might be easier to imagine uninhabited space. But deep ecology as a framework is completely unsuited for and biased against the global south.

My postcolonial ecofeminist readings of Pakistani women's literary and cinematic fictions are in line with academics from the global south such as economists Ramachandra Guha and Joan Martinez-Alier (1997, 59), who insist "that wealth is a greater threat to the environment than poverty." They disprove many of the assumptions of deep ecologists, including the idea that the rich are more concerned about the environment than the poor are. As Elizabeth DeLoughrey and George Handley (2011) suggest, activists and scholars from the global south are critical of a wide range of issues because of their location. "In short, critiques of capitalism, technology, neoliberalism, modernization, biopiracy, and empire demonstrate that environmental concerns are not the exclusive prerogative of the privileged north" (16).[1] A wider vision of social and environmental justice is needed for us to solve our problems. The move from deep ecology to environmental justice has led to an infusion of postcolonial theory into ecological thinking; consequently, we can no longer think of social and environmental justice, humans and nonhumans, and the global north and global south separately.

Once we understand this linkage, it becomes clear that Pakistan's low human development index makes the effects of climate change, such as heat waves, droughts, and floods, much worse than they would otherwise be.[2] In Pakistan, these recurrent catastrophes include the 2010 floods, which were the worst in Pakistan's history.[3] According to a report by the Asian Development Bank and World Bank (2012, 18),

The 2010 floods were assessed to be the worst since 1929. The United Nations (UN) termed the disaster as greater than the 2004 tsunami, the 2005 Pakistan earthquake and the 2010 Haiti earthquake, combined. At the time, NDMA [National Disaster Management Authority] had estimated that the floods affected 78 districts and covered over 100,000 sq. km. The floods affected approximately 20 million people, (more than one-tenth of Pakistan's population) with over 1,980 reported deaths and nearly 2,946 injured. About 1.6 million homes were destroyed, and thousands of acres of crops and agricultural lands were damaged with major soil erosion happening in some areas.

While the causes of the flood are varied, they are mostly man-made and include "the cumulative effect of erratic weather forecast by climate change models, massive deforestation, and lax attention to infrastructure maintenance and engineering standards" (Gronewold 2010, para. 10). Decision-making people are responsible not just because the Industrial Revolution has led to climate change but also because even now there are policy-making people behind decisions that lead to deforestation and inattention to infrastructure maintenance.

The ordinary people of Pakistan are aware of their vulnerability and lack of readiness, even as many of them are unfamiliar with the term "climate change." Pakistanis interviewed by Climate Asia between March 2012 and January 2013 revealed how they feel:

> Life has got worse in the past five years.... This is in stark contrast to the citizens of five of the other six Climate Asia countries [where Asians were also interviewed] who believe that life has improved. Nearly half of people in Pakistan (44%) also feel that changes in climate and environment have an impact on their lives now—a higher percentage than in any other Climate Asia country. This includes the inter-related effects of increased temperatures, erratic rainfall, increased extreme weather events and increased pests and mosquitoes. (Zaheer and Colom 2013, 4)

While most of the people from other countries who were interviewed felt that life had improved, Pakistanis stated that life had become worse.

In terms of man-made environmental changes to our planet, Pakistanis cause less of that change but feel some of its worst consequences. Yet the dominant academic discourse about Pakistan tends to focus on security issues, and news reports often cover Taliban attacks and bombings. The Taliban shot Malala Yousafzai in 2012, although she survived; killed 150 other people, mostly children, at a school in Peshawar in 2014; attacked Christian minorities in a park in Lahore, killing 70 and injuring hundreds—mostly Muslims—in 2016; and bombed a shrine in Sehwan, killing 90 men, women, and children Sufi worshippers in 2017. As a result, media coverage has presented Pakistan as a dangerous place for women, children, and minorities. While Rob Nixon (2011) does not explicitly discuss Pakistan, his points about violence are salient to this context. He insists that crisis reportage of "fast violence" distracts from the "slow violence" of climate change and its effect on the most vulnerable: women, children, and minorities, as well as the nonhuman animals and the environment. He writes, "As the journalistic chestnut has it, 'if it bleeds, it leads.' And as a corollary, if it's bloodless, slow-motion violence, the story is more likely to be buried, particularly if it's relayed by people whose witnessing authority is culturally discounted" (16).

Donations were higher for the 2010 Haiti earthquake than for the 2010 Pakistan floods, even though the damage was greater in Pakistan. Pakistanis unquestionably received less aid than Haitians did because Pakistanis are mostly Muslims. According to postcolonial critics Peter Morey and Amina Yaqin (2011), "Images of Muslims that are repeatedly circulated in the cultures of Western countries . . . in the present time" consist mostly of "the distortion of particular features of Muslim life and custom, reducing the diversity of Muslims and their existence as individuals to a fixed object—a caricature in fact" (2, 3). Morey and Yaqin insist that these stereotypes of the "bearded Muslim fanatic, the oppressed, veiled woman, the duplicitous terrorist who lives among 'us' the better to bring about our destruction" (2) have reemerged after 9/11 with renewed force and affect the lived experience of actual Muslims. Regarding the lower donations from the global north for Pakistani flood victims than for Haiti's earthquake victims, journalist Brett Neely (2010, para. 20) writes, "The campaign to halt a planned Islamic cultural center in Lower Manhattan and anti-Muslim remarks by politicians may have made some Americans wary of giving money to Muslim Pakistan." Thus, the slow violence of floods in Pakistan, affecting people who are stereotyped and culturally discounted, led to a natural disaster that was much more lethal than the mainstream media in the global north reported.

Given the country's high rates of corruption and its relatively few democratic elections of officials, that ordinary Pakistanis do not rely on their government to help them during natural disasters is not surprising. According to Climate Asia's Pakistan report, "Pakistanis have the lowest level of confidence in government among Climate Asia countries (70%) and people see lack of water, food and disrupted energy supplies as a failure of government. However they are taking more action than people in many other Climate Asia countries to deal with the impacts they face. This includes supplementing income, using technology to improve soil fertility, recycling water and using renewable energy" (Zaheer and Colom 2013, 4). Because their government is unreliable, Pakistanis now are engaging with their environment, dealing with climate change, and preparing for natural disasters. They must find ways to deal with global climate change with minimal help from their government. But even today, when environmental degradation is a pressing global concern, the dominant paradigm in the global north when thinking about Pakistan continues to be security issues and Islamist political parties, with some attention being paid to women's issues.

Those of us who are ecocritics and environmental humanists more generally, who are interested in issues of inequality and justice, and who are concerned about Pakistan should understand that social justice and environmental justice cannot and should not be separated. This is sometimes an area of concern for international nongovernmental organizations when they consider poverty and the environment.[4] However, the World Wildlife Fund–Pakistan's (2015, 12–16) ongoing 2014–15 projects, which cover categories such as forests, freshwater, sustainable agriculture, species, and climate change, do not include any linkages with women's development. This is also the case with both international and Pakistani NGOs. Generally, women's NGOs and environmental NGOs in Pakistan do not overlap their concerns and their work.[5] However, part of linking social justice with environmental justice is to consider women's relationships with their environments.

In neighboring India, these concerns have been brought together, as activists such as writer Arundhati Roy (Comfort 2008) and environmental thinker Vandana Shiva regularly draw attention to both environmental and women's issues.[6] In academia in the global north, theorists have been thinking and writing about women and the environment since the 1970s. Pakistan also needs feminist academics and feminist activists to emphasize environmental justice. One example from India that could be helpful in Pakistan has to do with women's land rights. Bina Agarwal (2002) argues that both environmental and social justice can be served if more Indian women owned and controlled land. Unfortunately, the emphasis in development circles is on securing microcredit for women.[7] Agarwal suggests an alternative approach. She insists that we should "link land and micro-credit by providing rural women who depend on land-based livelihoods with credit for leasing in or purchasing land in groups. . . . Here micro-credit would complement rather than substitute for efforts to enhance women's land rights" (9). Agarwal's suggestions are equally valid for Pakistan. It is crucial that we start to see gender as central in social and environmental justice movements.

My goal in writing this book has been to encourage scholarship about and activism in Pakistan that connect conversations about women to conversations about the environment. In so doing, I aim to work toward a more sustainable future not only in the global south but also everywhere on our shared planet. I hope that my postcolonial ecofeminist readings of Pakistani women's literary and cinematic fictions are a catalyst for change, not only in the way those inside Pakistan think about the women's movement and all that is possible within it, but also in the way people outside Pakistan think about the global south, in general, and Pakistan, in particular. After all, fictions are what help us imagine and think in new ways. Outsiders who wonder about Pakistan should know that while oppression in Pakistan does exist, people are resisting. Pakistanis and others in the global south are not merely passive consumers. Those in Pakistan should know that more fruitful contestations of dominant paradigms will happen when the environmental movements and the feminist movements join hands.

Notes

Introduction

1. While creative and scholarly work on partition in Pakistan has focused on the division of the land and people, it has thus far eschewed a larger ecocritical stance that includes the sea, the animals, and the plants. In India, Vandana Shiva (2014) and Arundhati Roy (1999) have been thinking ecologically for quite a while.

2. According to ecocritic Greg Garrard (2016, 61), ecocriticism is, "like feminist and Marxist criticism, a politicized reading practice that challenges ecocidal attitudes." For more on how ecocritical approaches to literature developed, see his book *Ecocriticism* (2011).

3. According to ecocritics Joni Adamson and Kimberly Ruffin (2013, 12), "Questions of belonging have long been central to the interdisciplinarities among AS [American studies], ethnic studies, and ecocriticism." I would add that belonging is also central to postcolonial studies, especially for questions of national belonging, diaspora, and refugees. My own work on belonging builds on all of this analysis in a postcolonial Pakistani context.

4. Ecocritic Adamson (2016, 135) defines the environmental humanities as "history, philosophy, aesthetics, religious studies, literature, theater, film and media studies informed by the most recent research in the sciences of nature and sustainability." Even though work in the environmental humanities is informed by the sciences and social sciences, Adamson writes that environmental humanists do not abandon "the subject-matter strengths and specific tools that are the hallmark of their discipline, such as critical analysis" (139). Similarly, while my humanities-based research is informed by research in other disciplines, my work continues to be literary and film criticism.

5. For more on postcolonial ecofeminism, see literary critic Youngsuk Chae (2015, 520), who explains that "the development project in postcolonial societies and its impact on marginalized women and other subjugated people necessitates an examination of postcolonial environmental issues from an ecofeminist viewpoint." I agree with her completely.

6. In this formulation, I am indebted to historian Wendy Harcourt (2016, 164), who insists that "our attachments to place are about social, spiritual, and cultural meaning and identity as well as economic need."

7. While my postcolonial ecofeminist work is based on mostly English-language research, I am aware that this focus is limiting. I leave to others more proficient in other languages of Pakistan to explore the role of the nonhuman in other Pakistani literary and cultural productions.

8. Economists Pradeep Bhargava and Manju Balana (2007, 289) write that even though "both India and Pakistan have made great progress in food production and are almost self-sufficient as far as cereals are concerned . . . the incidence of food poverty is high."

9. According to development consultant Nira Ramachandran (2007, 230), "Research in several developing countries of Asia, Africa and Latin America has found that improvements in household food security and nutrition are associated with women's access to income and their role in household decisions on expenditure. This is because women tend to spend a significantly higher proportion of their income than men on food for the family." Nonetheless, the problem of child nutrition, especially in South Asia, continues. According to economists Jean Drèze and Amartya Sen (2013, 47), "More than 40 per cent of South Asian children . . . are underweight in terms of standard WHO [World Health Organization] norms, compared with 25 per cent in sub-Saharan Africa."

10. Pakistan is in the category of "low human development," and there has been no change in its ranking since 2009 (UNDP 2015, 214).

11. A cursory look at the list reveals that the poorest countries are the least prepared for floods, droughts, and hurricanes. Regarding Pakistan, it states, "Pakistan is the 50th most vulnerable country and the 41st least ready country" (ND-GAIN 2018).

12. As literary critic Munazza Yaqoob (2015, 258) has argued, "The narrative of *Trespassing* both acknowledges and privileges the presence of nature and non-human life in human settings. Nature does not merely serve as the background or as the provider of symbols and images to illustrate human affairs, but nature and non-human creatures form a consistent part of the text."

13. To give only a few examples, cinematographer Mushtaq Gazdar (1997) provides a review of fifty years of Pakistani films since partition. Film scholar Rahat Imran (2016) provides the only other single-author book on Pakistani activist documentary film. In addition, anthropologist Ali Khan and historian Ali Nobil Ahmad (2016) have edited a collection of

essays on Pakistani film and social change. Anthropologists Irna Qureshi (2011) and Gwendolyn S. Kirk (2014) both consider gender in Pakistani films. None, however, take an ecocritical approach to Pakistani film.

14. Urban and regional planning scholar Keith Pezzoli (2016, 26) writes that "a bioregion is a fruitful place-based organizing concept." I use this concept in chapter 2 on bioregionalism. See Pezzoli's work about the commitments, initiatives, and development of this field of study.

15. Exploring the role of the nonhuman in Pakistani men's fictions would also be a very fruitful line of inquiry, especially if the focus was on the land. In the Urdu-language partition fiction of Saadat Hasan Manto's (1997) story "Toba Tek Singh," the protagonist wishes to sit on a tree because a tree belongs to no one and dies in the no-man's-land between India and Pakistan. Here a Pakistani author is intervening in political notions of the state and its man-made boundaries to ponder attachments to the land outside of imposed nation-state borders.

16. Farzana Shaikh (2009) states that at the time of independence, when an "estimated 7–9 million Muslims" (50) migrated to Pakistan, the battle lines sharply divided the migrants, or *mohajirs*, from those "who saw themselves as the native sons of the soil" (48). But this has changed to such an extent that Shaikh now finds both the migrants and the locals are completely denationalized, with both looking outside the nation for a sense of identity.

17. My work is critical of both cosmopolitan global Islam and the patriarchal nationalism of the "sons of the soil" rhetoric used by indigenous ethnic groups in South Asia. See chapter 4, "Karachi: Pakistani Ecocosmopolitanism," for more on how this rhetoric inspires a violent Sindhi nationalist group in the novel *Trespassing*. For more on the conflicts that arise from this rhetoric, see political scientist Myron Weiner's classic *Sons of the Soil: Migration and Ethnic Conflict in India* (1978).

18. In grounding this theory in the environment of Pakistan, I also include nonhuman animals, especially in chapter 4, where my use of eco-cosmopolitanism illustrates many of the claims currently being advocated by the cosmopolitical movement around the world. This discussion of cosmopolitics in ecocriticism is based on the idea that "we are entering a moment in politics that takes as its goal . . . the recognition of the 'rights' to life for all humans and nonhumans" (Adamson and Monani 2017, 7). While I agree with this sentiment wholeheartedly, my work is more in keeping with that of postcolonialists who "position the nature/human binary as political, and do not necessarily see the dismantling of this divide as the foremost intellectual priority due to the

already historical imbrication of the human with nonhuman nature and place" (DeLoughrey, Didur, and Carrigan 2015, 11).

19. Toor (2011, 110) writes that these "intellectuals understood that only a nationalist project that drew on the cultures and histories of the various regions that were now part of the state, as opposed to the de-territorialized ideology of 'Muslim nationalism' which was the cornerstone of official nationalism, held out any hope for a just social and political order in Pakistan." In her excellent analysis of leftist discourses in Pakistan, Toor shows how the religious right, represented by the political party Jama'at-i Islami and its founder, Maulana Maududi, actively tried from the late 1960s onward to use their "vast propaganda machinery" to argue that "Islam and socialism were fundamentally incompatible, because socialism—like capitalism—was an essentially materialist philosophy which not only rejected spirituality and religion, but was antithetical to them" (101, 102). This anti-secular argument was conveniently in line with Pakistan's military and bureaucratic establishment, which chose to side with the Right against the Left, even though this establishment was mostly secular at the time. Pakistan's national culture came to be dominated by Islam, even though many leftist intellectuals such as poet Faiz Ahmed Faiz argued during the late 1960s that the national culture of Pakistan was an amalgamation of many parts. Faiz and others have tried to include minorities in a nationalist project that is unique to the nation-state of Pakistan, while the religious right has tried to show the importance of Islam to any sense of Pakistani identity.

20. According to Gaard (2010, 643), "In the two book-length introductions to ecocriticism to date, Lawrence Buell's *The Future of Environmental Criticism* (2005) and Greg Garrard's *Ecocriticism* (2004), the retelling of ecocritical roots and developments marginalizes both feminist and ecofeminist literary perspectives." While it is true that in Buell's telling, ecofeminism comes across as a separate development in ecocriticism, he does list many of the most important and canonical figures of the movement, including Donna Haraway, Annette Kolodny, and Val Plumwood (2005, 19). Moreover, Buell refers to ecofeminism as a "multiverse" where "inquiry starts from the premise of a correlation between the history of institutionalized patriarchy and human domination of the non-human" (19). Gaard's list of canonical works of feminist ecocriticism published between 1975 and 2000 is much longer than Buell's and is even longer than Garrard's (2011). She argues that these works do not receive enough attention in Garrard's book at all (Gaard 2010, 645).

21. For more on postcolonial ecocriticism, see Susie O'Brien's article "Articulating a World of Difference" (2001), Graham Huggan's article "'Greening' Postcolonialism" (2004), Rob Nixon's chapter "Environmentalism and Postcolonialism" (2005), and Cara Cilano and Elizabeth DeLoughrey's article "Against Authenticity" (2007). This work was followed by Upamanyu Pablo Mukherjee's monograph *Postcolonial Environments* (2010); Bonnie Roos and Alex Hunt's edited collection *Postcolonial Green* (2010); Laura Wright's monograph *Wilderness into Civilized Shapes* (2010); Elizabeth DeLoughrey and George Handley's edited collection *Postcolonial Ecologies* (2011); Rob Nixon's monograph *Slow Violence* (2011); Graham Huggan and Helen Tiffin's monograph *Postcolonial Ecocriticism* (2015); Elizabeth DeLoughrey, Jill Didur, and Anthony Carrigan's edited collection *Global Ecologies and the Environmental Humanities* (2015); and Erin James's monograph *The Storyworld Accord* (2015).

22. Cultural geographer John Brinkerhoff Jackson (1984) was the first to use the term "vernacular landscape" to discuss people's relationship to landscape. Joni Adamson introduced Jackson's work into ecocriticism in her groundbreaking book *American Indian Literature, Environmental Justice, and Ecocriticism* (2001), making her the first to tease out the importance of Jackson's ideas and use them as an ecocritic. I am indebted to and build upon Adamson's work by using her definitions of both vernacular landscape and official landscape and relating them to East Pakistan before 1971. In my work, I show how official landscape masks the vernacular when postcolonial borders are drawn without any regard for the people who live on the land.

23. It should be noted that Bengal was another province of British India that was partitioned in 1947. According to anthropologist Delwar Hussain (2013, 7), "While the particulars of Partition concerning Punjab and Bengal have been widely written about in novels and academia as well as filmed, much less is known of the severing of Sylhet [East Pakistan in 1947, Bangladesh since 1971] from Assam [independent India since 1947]." Hussain's *Boundaries Undermined* (2013) fills this gap and adds to all of our work on the borderlanders of South Asia.

24. Comparatively little ecocritical literary and film criticism covers partition's relation to people's attachment to the land. To give just one example, film critic Bhaskar Sarkar (2009) focuses on the different ways in which Indian partition films mourn the nation over a sixty-year period, finding that the films change over time. In discussing his approach to the films, he writes, "Chapters 1 through 3, which focus on the early years after

1947, adopt a sympathetic approach to mainstream commercial films. In contrast, the concluding chapter on the sharp rise in the incidence of Partition films in recent years takes a more critical stance, denouncing an overarching and banal historicist mode that paradoxically promotes forgetfulness, and whose continuing lack of self-consciousness now has disquieting political implications" (33). While the importance of Sarkar's work cannot be denied, he has focused less on the images of land in these films even though it was land that was partitioned. The deep connection between land and people, and the fact that land is home, suggests this important area requires further study through an ecocritical lens.

25. Even though most people of the world do not live in rural areas anymore, those who do, as with the characters in the film, are oppressed in multiple ways. "Agrarian reform," according to ethnobotanist Gary Paul Nabhan (2016, 7), "in Latin America, Europe, and Asia [is] a movement to keep peasant societies from becoming increasingly landless and in greater servitude to capitalistic institutions by enacting the redistribution of land and other wealth." See Nabhan's work for more on agrarian ecology and the elements that define new agrarianism.

26. I use the word "indigenous" in the way that philosopher Kyle Powys Whyte (2016, 146) defines it: "The concept of indigeneity, then, can refer to the aboriginality of many possible individuals or groupings, from particular species to governments or knowledges. It is important to recognize that indigeneity is seldom used to express 'coming before' in a basic sense; rather, it is more often used to express intergenerational systems of responsibilities that connect humans, nonhuman animals and plants, sacred entities, and systems." In keeping with Whyte, not only do I refer to human and nonhuman Sindhis as indigenous to Sindh (in chapters 2 and 4) but I also consider precolonial South Asian sacred religious practices to be indigenous (in chapters 1 and 2).

27. I agree with geographer Noel Castree (2016, 155) that "'nature' is, and should remain, a contested idea because it allows us to disagree about *both* the 'questions' and the 'remedies' we might otherwise assume to be obvious." As long as nature is a contested idea, it can be transformed.

28. The five books of literary criticism are Tariq Rahman's *A History of Pakistani Literature in English, 1947–1988* (2015), Cara Cilano's *Contemporary Pakistani Fiction in English: Idea, Nation, State* (2013), David Waterman's *Where Worlds Collide: Pakistani Fiction in the New Millennium* (2015), Aroosa Kanwal's *Rethinking Identities in Contemporary Pakistani Fiction: Beyond 9/11* (2015), and Muneeza Shamsie's *Hybrid Tapestries: The Devel-*

opment of Pakistani Literature in English (2017). The two books on Pakistani film are Mushtaq Gazdar's *Pakistan Cinema, 1947–1997* (1997) and Rahat Imran's *Activist Documentary Film in Pakistan: The Emergence of a Cinema of Accountability* (2016).

1. Punjab

1. In the province of Punjab, administrator Penderel Moon (1962, 293) estimated there were 200,000 casualties.
2. Sumar has made a number of feminist documentary films dealing with Islamization in Pakistan. For excellent analyses of many of them, see Rahat Imran (2008, 2016).
3. See Jill Didur's *Unsettling Partition* (2006), Ritu Menon's *Women Writers on Partition of Pakistan and India* (2006), and Ritu Menon and Kamla Bhasin's *Borders & Boundaries* (1998).
4. Ritu Menon and Kamla Bhasin (1998) and Urvashi Butalia (2000) have described the dilemmas of women who were abducted and raped by men from other religious communities and those who were forced to commit suicide by their own fathers and brothers during the partition of British India. As Indian historians, they have put partition violence against women in the context of Indian history, but as Butalia (2000, 17) notes, "I have had no access to information, interviews or anything else from Pakistan."
5. While the film focuses on Zia as the originator of Islamization in Pakistan, this is too easy and not completely accurate. Even though Zia did implement many Islamization policies, such as the Hudood Ordinances, the Islamization of Pakistan can be traced back to Maududi, who was against the creation of Pakistan in 1947 but then led the religious right in Pakistan to keep Islamist ideas in the public eye. See Saadia Toor (2011) for more on how his political party pressured different leaders in Pakistan before Zia's rise. For example, in 1974, before Zia came to power, the religious right coerced Zulfikar Ali Bhutto to declare Ahmadis were not Muslims.
6. Here I refer to nationalism as a popular sentiment that is more concerned with the well-being of one's fellow citizens than that of those perceived as others.
7. See Olivier Roy (2004) for more on "globalised Islam," which I read as being cosmopolitan.
8. For more on the ways in which South Asian Muslims are cosmopolitan, see art historian Iftikhar Dadi (2010, 30) who writes, "Due to minority sta-

tus in India and Muslim memory of belonging to the larger Muslim world during the early modern Persianate and Islamicate cosmopolitanism and since the later nineteenth century under pan-Islamic movements, South Asian Muslim experience differs from other experiences of nationalism."

9. See Shazia Rahman (2007) for both the pitfalls of the term "cosmopolitan feminist" and the ways in which it can be reinscribed.

10. An eco-cosmopolitan feminist reading of this film is particularly significant at this time, given the continued honor killings in Punjab. One of the most famous cases occurred in 2016 when Pakistani internet celebrity Qandeel Baloch was murdered by her brother for allegedly bringing dishonor to her family. She was born in Dera Ghazi Khan, Punjab. At the same time, also in 2016, the problem of honor killings got international attention when documentary filmmaker Sharmeen Obaid-Chinoy won an Academy Award for her film *A Girl in the River: The Price of Forgiveness* (2015), which follows the story of a teenage girl who survives an attempted honor killing by her father and uncle in Gujranwala, Punjab. Honor killings in Punjab continue today and must therefore be dealt with, critiqued, and resisted.

11. I agree with Jaikumar's reference to sympathy here. But in creating a distinction between empathy and sympathy, I think ecocritic Salma Monani (2014, 227) is right in arguing that empathy is even better than sympathy, because "sympathy, as primarily a concern *for*, is motivated . . . by a sense of charity [which] signals a sense of concern that is hierarchical, and inherently patronizing."

12. For example, women in the 1970s covered up less than they did in 2002. The shift can be seen in *Khamosh Pani*, particularly in comparing the way Ayesha's neighbor Zubeida dresses in the film's early scenes and in the later ones. While no law in Pakistan dictates what women should wear (such as in Saudi Arabia or Iran), unwritten laws do dictate the lives of ordinary women.

13. For more on the significance of food, see Parama Roy's *Alimentary Tracts* (2010) and Anita Mannur's *Culinary Fictions* (2009).

14. The land was divided in a remarkably counterintuitive manner. Historian Yasmin Khan (2007, 126) states, "The line zigzagged precariously across agricultural land, cut off communities from their sacred pilgrimage sites, paid no heed to railway lines or the integrity of forests, divorced industrial plants from the agricultural hinterlands where raw materials, such as jute, were grown." For literary criticism of partition fiction and film, see Kavita Daiya (2008), Jill Didur (2006), and Niaz Zaman (2001).

15. The music in the film sounds very obviously local even as it crosses the India-Pakistan border. Local instruments such as the tabla, sarangi, and dholak (drum) can be heard, and vocals are in regional languages such as Punjabi.

16. For more on the ways in which Pakistanis argue about sainthood, see anthropologist Katherine Pratt Ewing's *Arguing Sainthood: Modernity, Psychoanalysis, and Islam* (1997). With regard to the Zia era, she writes, "Many of the Islamicists who supported Zia, particularly the Jama'at-i Islami, were themselves hostile to Sufism, pirs, and shrines" (76). These different belief systems are illustrated in Sumar's *Khamosh Pani*.

17. According to the International Fund for Agricultural Development, "The government of Pakistan does not recognize indigenous peoples but refers to them as tribal" (IFAD 2012). While I discuss the tribal peoples of Sindh in chapter 2 as well as the fisherfolk of coastal areas in chapter 4 as being indigenous, here I use the term "indigenous" to mean a religious practice that is precolonial, sacred, and engaged in by people from multiple religious groups.

18. One recent example of this rejection of local religious practice was the suicide bombing of the tomb of the saint Lal Shahbaz Qalandar in Sehwan, Pakistan, in 2017. This attack is not an isolated case, however. According to journalists Asad Hashim and Alia Chughtai (2017, para. 16), at least ten attacks on shrines across Pakistan have occurred since 2005: "Armed groups such as the Pakistani Taliban and others have often targeted shrines for not conforming to their strict, literalist interpretation of Islam."

19. According to economist Amartya Sen (2006, 76), "The religious partitioning of the world produces a deeply misleading understanding of the people across the world and the diverse relations between them, and it also has the effect of magnifying one particular distinction between one person and another to the exclusion of all other important concerns."

20. My analyses of food are inspired by literary critic Anita Mannur (2009, 24), who writes, "It is important to examine how food is an equally important vector of critical analysis in negotiating the gendered, racialized, and classed bases of collective and individual identity."

21. I refer here to the anti-corporate globalization movement, which supports fair trade over free trade and human rights over the prerogatives of transnational capital. Arundhati Roy is one of the spokespersons for this movement.

22. Legal scholars Shaheen Sardar Ali and Javaid Rehman (2001, 3) write that, in Pakistan, "most ethnic groups constitute a majority in their area

of origin and are indigenous to it, but constitute a minority in comparison to the entire population of the country." In this sense, both Punjabi and Sindhi are indigenous languages in Pakistan.

2. *Thar*

1. As Wendy Harcourt (2016, 161) writes, "Our understanding of the environment is first and foremost informed by our experience of place." We often think of environment and place together just as we think of social justice and belonging together. However, as Joni Adamson and Kimberly N. Ruffin (2013, 16) state in their book on ecocriticism, it is important to put place and environmental justice together with belonging and social justice so that "academic and public discourse about citizenship and belonging in both local and global contexts might become more accessible and clear, and thus, more transformative."

2. Even though the government of Pakistan does not recognize indigenous peoples, Pakistan did ratify the International Labour Organization Convention 107, which protects indigenous populations from oppression and discrimination (ILO 1957). According to Shaheen Sardar Ali and Javaid Rehman (2001, 106), "Sindhis are the indigenous peoples of the province of Sindh with an ancient history going back at least 5,000 years." Moreover, "tribal peoples of Sindh" include "Haris," or Dalits who are landless farmers (IFAD 2012). Throughout this chapter, I refer to the Kohlis as Dalits because this term is associated with current progressive movements.

3. I use the term "homeplace" here as a broader term than "life place," which denotes only one bioregion. "Homeplace" helps me discuss a landscape that feels as if it is a home to its inhabitants.

4. While this film is set in 2002, recently the number of women farmers in Sindh has increased. In March 2011 journalist Rick Westhead (2011, A32) reported the "ruling Pakistan People's Party gave away . . . 37,231 hectares" of farmland, adding to the "38,445 hectares of farmland" that they gave to "5,729 peasants" over the previous two years. Also, "4,500 of those involved in the land grant program so far have been women, and the March allotment was reserved for women only" (A32).

5. According to social scientist Srinath Raghavan (2009, 242), "The crisis was precipitated by a terrorist attack on the Indian Parliament in December 2001 carried out by a Pakistan-based group. India responded by mobilizing its forces to the border, threatening to impose costs on Pakistan unless it cracked down on the terrorist groups operating from

its soil. The ensuing stand-off lasted for ten months until India pulled back its forces from the border in October 2002." The part of the border Raghavan is referring to here is not in the Thar Desert.

6. In 1987 Chicana feminist Gloria Anzaldúa wrote that a "borderland is a vague and undetermined place created by the emotional residue of an unnatural boundary" (25). She writes here of the borderlands between the United States and Mexico, considering them unnatural. As literary critics Debra Castillo and Kavita Panjabi (2011, 1) explain, the borderlands represent "the violent division of a nation: Mexico in 1845 with the annexation of Texas, and then the 1848 Treaty of Guadalupe Hidalgo that forced the young nation to cede over half of its remaining territory to the United States." Many countries, including Palestine/Israel, Ireland, and others, have been violently divided. In each case, a border becomes disputed and is viewed as unnatural politically, physically, and metaphorically.

7. This situation of extreme poverty is exacerbated by the feudalism of Pakistan. According to journalist Issam Ahmed (2010, para. 8), "While India managed to largely abolish feudalism, powerful landlords in the provinces of Punjab and Sindh who chose to side with the . . . party led by Pakistan's founding father, Muhammad Ali Jinnah, were rewarded by being allowed to keep their land and titles. The situation has remained mostly unchanged."

8. In contrast, Nabhan (2016, 8) writes that while the new agrarianism "draws heavily on past agrarian practices and thinking, it is not bound by them because [it] is focused on building the future." This future must include migrants, as Janet Fiskio (2012) explains.

9. Writing about Bolsena, Italy, Harcourt (2016, 162) insists that "place is not static but is shaped by the changing experiences of the people living in the place." Similarly, we must think of the place of Thar not as a static desert but in terms of the experiences of the people living there.

10. This friendship develops after resolving a number of conflicts, usually involving Shankar's concern for Ramchand and the possibility of Ramchand's being violated sexually or otherwise. The larger group bonds through their desire to protect the child.

3. Bengal

1. While the focus of this chapter is East Bengal, I have titled it "Bengal" because, as historian Joya Chatterji (2007, 5) notes, "over the centuries, accidents of human and environmental history produced a certain cohesiveness in the region. Long periods of being governed as

a separate province, whether by the Mughals or by the British, and interregnums during which Bengal asserted its autonomy had given its territories a measure of administrative integrity. Geography, too, in particular the dominance of the delta by two great river systems of the Ganges and the Brahmaputra, helped to shape its distinctive character."

2. For more on West Bengal and India, see the work of Joya Chatterji (2007, 9), who writes, "Curzon's actions provoked a furore in Bengal which in 1911 forced the viceroy of the day to rescind the partition of 1905."

3. In fact, anthropologist Annu Jalais (2010) finds this same separation between humans and nonhumans in the Sundarbans of Bengal. She writes, "The Sundarbans thus has two parallel but segregated histories, one relatively well-endowed relating to wildlife; the other, rather sparse, concerning the region's human inhabitants" (5).

4. Regarding film, see Bangladeshi director Chashi Nazrul Islam's Bangla-language film *Hangor Nodi Grenade* (The mother, 1997). For Bangladeshi films that deal with women's experiences of the 1971 war, see Nasirud-din Yousuff's Bangla-language film *Guerrilla* (2011) and Bangladeshi woman director Rubaiyat Hossain's film *Meherjaan* (2011). For literature, see Niaz Zaman and Asif Farrukhi's anthology *Fault Lines* (2008) for short stories about 1971 that were originally written in Bangla by writers from Bangladesh. Shaheen Akhtar's Bangla-language novel *Talaash* has been translated into English as *The Search* (2011). Akhtar's novel, as well as English-language novels by Bangladesh-born writer Tahmima Anam, grapple with 1971 from a woman's perspective. Finally, for an analysis of memorial sculptures in Bangladesh, see Nayanika Mookherjee (2007).

5. For an example of this kind of feminist film criticism, see Elora Halim Chowdhury's "When Love and Violence Meet" (2015, 761), which analyzes the film *Meherjaan* "in association with themes of trauma, . . . the . . . relationship of nation to gender and sexuality, and the notion of humanizing the Other."

6. According to political scientists Jalal Alamgir and Bina D'Costa (2011, 38), "For the last four decades, Bangladesh's attempt to interpret the brutalities of 1971 has been couched largely in narratives of nationalist glory. This provided the unity of discourse that a war-ravaged coun-try needed." They go on to question the simplicity of this Bangladeshi nationalist narrative and insist that Bangladesh, India, and Pakistan cooperate to bring war criminals to trial. While I agree completely, it should be noted that Bangladesh has many narratives while Pakistan has very few.

7. Urdu-language newspapers were quick to write about Bengali violence. According to Yasmin Saikia (2011, 50), "The story of violence committed by Bengalis is less well known and is poorly represented in the news media, except the Pakistani Urdu news press, which obviously toed the line of their leaders to vilify the Bengalis."

8. The International Crimes Tribunal was set up in 2009.

9. According to Bina D'Costa (2011, 81), "Although Bangladeshi human-rights groups, political activists and women's organizations occasionally raise rape charges, Pakistan has repeatedly denied such accusations. In 1996 and 2001 several Pakistani feminist organizations publicly apologized for the atrocities committed by the army and their collaborators against Bengali women in 1971, but no official apology from Pakistan has thus far been offered."

10. "God and meat, Ali thought. Both were off limits, in the same category, since coming home. God because nothing Ali had seen—or done—could have been divined by God. And meat because he'd smelled flesh in every possible manifestation. Freshly dead, not-so-freshly dead, rotted, singed, burned, baked and every variety in between, and he never wanted to set eyes on it, much less his tongue on it, again" (142).

11. In analyzing four memoirs by Pakistani military generals, Bina D'Costa (2014, 457) tries to determine "how Pakistani genocidal masculinity was constructed and manifested during the independence struggle of Bangladesh." Her analysis sheds some light on this issue.

12. The indigenous peoples I discuss in chapter 4 are the Sindhi coastal fisherfolk who are considered the "most vulnerable tribal group in Sindh province" in "terms of economic livelihood, legal rights and human rights" (IFAD 2012).

4. Karachi

1. In some ways, the Pakistani eco-cosmopolitanism that I theorize about is similar to the cosmopolitics that anthropologist Marisol de la Cadeña (2010, 361) calls "pluriversal politics," which "would accept what we call nature as multiplicity and allow for the conflicting views about that multiplicity into argumentative forums." Her focus on Andean indigeneity, however, is different from the context of South Asia, where indigenous, tribal, and ethnic identities are harder to define clearly.

2. According to literary ecocritic Laura Dassow Walls (2016, 47), "cosmos" is "humanity's oldest ecological vision of our planet" because the concept goes back to many ancient cultures. She writes that it "ties together

our future hopes with our deepest past" (50). In keeping the cosmos in Pakistani eco-cosmopolitanism, I too hope to tie the future with the past and the human with the nonhuman, because as philosopher Bruno Latour (2004, 454) writes, "If *cosmos* is to mean anything, it must embrace, literally, everything—including all the vast numbers of nonhuman entities making humans act."

3. When it comes to South Asia specifically, I know of only one monograph of postcolonial ecocriticism. See Upamanyu Pablo Mukherjee's *Postcolonial Environments: Nature, Culture and the Contemporary Indian Novel in English* (2010).

4. In his insightful essay "Cosmo-Theory," literary critic Timothy Brennan (2001, 682) states, "Cosmopolitanism is the way in which a kind of American patriotism is today being expressed."

5. After Heise's book, Rob Nixon published the monograph *Slow Violence and the Environmentalism of the Poor* (2011) and Graham Huggan and Helen Tiffin published the book *Postcolonial Ecocriticism: Literature, Animals, and Environments* (2015). These and other postcolonial works furthered Adamson's attempts to move beyond Euro-American texts.

6. Kanwal (2015, 93) goes on to explain, "For example, during the Afghan war, Saudi Arabia and other Arab Gulf states, with U.S. support, provided billions of dollars to Pakistan in order to train Afghan guerrillas for the Soviet-Afghan War, which was fought under the banner of Islamic ideology. However, the US changed its policy towards *mujahideen* after the Afghan War. *Madrassas* (Islamic seminaries) for the training of *mujahideen* in Pakistan during Zia's regime have produced targets for the U.S. Army since the Soviet-Afghan War, as some radicals trained in these morphed into al-Qaeda and other terrorist groups that are currently confronting the West."

7. I agree with Antonio Gramsci (2008, 9) that "all men are intellectuals" and that "one cannot speak of non-intellectuals, because non-intellectuals do not exist." When I write of Pakistani intellectuals, I mean all of us humans, of all gender identifications, who contribute "to sustain a conception of the world or modify it, that is, to bring into being new modes of thought" (Gramsci 2008, 9).

8. Kanwal (2015, 77) explains, "As a result of the massive influx of Urdu-speaking Muslim *muhajir* (immigrants) at the time of the 1947 Partition, the local Sindhi population was outnumbered. The 1960s marked a second wave of domestic migration when Pakistani Pashtun/Pathan people started migrating to Karachi for economic reasons. They were later

joined by Afghan immigrants in 1979. Karachi, consequently, became a battleground for various ethnic and sectarian groups. Unfortunately, no politicians or state representatives have ever made any efforts to engage with the social, ethnic, sectarian and religious problems or to combat the rise of intolerance within Pakistan."

9. This aspect of the novel is to some extent in keeping with cosmopolitics in the context of indigenous struggle, as Joni Adamson and Salma Monani highlight in their anthology *Ecocriticism and Indigenous Studies: Conversations from Earth to Cosmos* (2017). Their introduction argues that the essays they have gathered "serve as philosophical engagements to navigate the everyday ethics of living in wider worlds with humans and nonhumans alike" (8). My analysis, however, is not restricted to specifically indigenous characters. Of the three characters I discuss in this chapter, Salaamat and Dia are Sindhis and therefore indigenous to Sindh. Even though Daanish is not indigenous, however, I argue strongly for his equal attachment to Karachi's beaches and seashells.

10. Uzma Aslam Khan's novel *The Geometry of God* (2009a) also deals with religious fundamentalism in Pakistan by focusing on the physical world; one of the main characters is a paleontologist working during a time of heightened Islamization policies in the 1980s. On the back cover, a blurb by Pakistani novelist Nadeem Aslam reads, "No one writes like Khan about the body, about the senses, about the physical world."

11. For more on the ethnic and linguistic rights of Siraiki speakers, see literary critic Nukhbah Taj Langah (2012). She writes, "The speakers of Urdu and Punjabi together fulfil the role of challenging the political status of a . . . group, comprising the Sindhis, Balochis, Pashtoons and Siraikis. This second group brings together the three provinces which assert political rights through their respective mother tongues, as well as the aspirations of a new language-based political group, 'Siraiki'" (23). She insists that "Siraiki is the most widely spoken language in Pakistan" because it is spoken in three out of four of its provinces (23).

12. This Pakistani eco-cosmopolitanism is a step toward the cosmopolitics in Peru that de la Cadeña (2010) discusses. She describes the activist Mariano Turpo's world as one in which "political skills include the relations between human beings and other-than-human beings that together make place: mountains, rivers, . . . sheep, . . . rocks. . . . And as the new liberal state . . . dismisses this place . . . to make room for mining and the economic benefits it would potentially generate, people . . . concerned about the destruction of their place, bring their concern to

politics" (356). While none of the main characters in this novel become cosmopolitical activists, their concerns are marked in the novel's descriptions of their relations with place.

13. Here I am referring to a much more recent phenomenon. Historically, Pakistani intellectuals who rejected religious institutions were not necessarily considered aligned with the United States. For instance, in discussing Urdu-language poets, M. A. R. Habib (2003, xxv–xxvi) describes Faiz Ahmad Faiz and N. M. Rashed as being more humanist than religious. However, Saadia Toor (2011) has documented the ways in which Faiz's leftist humanism was systematically delegitimized by the religious right. Ongoing tensions with India have increased along with Pakistan's interference in Afghanistan. This, in part, has led to increased military expenditure, which has led to the erosion of public educational institutions and, of course, to much greater U.S. involvement in Pakistani affairs. Thus, the allegation of pro-U.S. imperialism rings far truer now than it did forty years ago.

14. Since 2005 the fundamentalists have increased their attacks on the Sufis. Regarding the 2017 suicide bombing of a Sufi saint's tomb at Sehwan in Pakistan, historian William Dalrymple (2017, para. 8) writes, "Hardline Wahhabi and Salafi fundamentalism has advanced so quickly in Pakistan partly because the Saudis have financed the building of so many madrasas that have filled the vacuum left by the collapse of state education."

15. Kabir (2011, 180) writes that Uzma Aslam Khan's fiction shows that "there exists an archive of Pakistaniness beyond Islam's advent."

5. Displacement

1. By "humanism" I mean a human-centrism that disregards the needs of nonhuman animals.

2. For more about the displacement's impact on the Muslims of Delhi and on the Hindus of Karachi, see Vazira Zamindar (2007). She writes, "Delhi and Karachi became the two capitals of the post-independence states, and although the two cities were dramatically different before independence, it is Partition itself that binds them together" (5).

3. Gilles Deleuze and Félix Guattari are most famous for their use of the term "deterritorialization," but I use it as Ursula Heise (2008, 51) does: "It refers to the detachment of social and cultural practices from their ties to place that have been described in detail in theories of modernization and postmodernization."

4. Ronald Takaki (1995, 72–73) writes that the Japanese were also racist against Americans and Europeans: "In their war against the United States, the Japanese people were told by their leaders that they had a glorious mission. . . . A uniquely 'pure' race, the Japanese had to fight against the 'brutes,' 'wild beasts,' monsters, devils, and demons of America and Europe. The Japanese dehumanized the enemy in what they considered a race war." Thus, racialized animalization was not only practiced by one nationality, and Shamsie connects them all through this description of Hiroko's dream.

5. Both Hiroko and Sajjad reject nationalism to such an extent that their son's eventual rebellion against them leads him to insist on patriotism. They "hadn't known whether to howl with laughter or with tears to think that their son's teenage rebellion was asserting itself through nationalism" (132).

6. This lies in stark contrast to Harry, who mourns for New York during 9/11 while staying in the Democratic Republic of Congo. Harry realizes that far more lives are being lost in the Congo every year but does not acknowledge this to be "wrong." Instead, the narrator states that Harry "couldn't find any way to connect those numbers to his emotions" (276); yet he wept for New York even though two thousand people had died every day for more than three years in the Congo. He even tells his daughter that all this death is "good for business, very definitely" (276) given his work for a security company.

Conclusion

1. As poorer countries travel down the path of industrial development, they deal with problems of industrialization including air pollution and smog, which lead to many diseases and death. According to journalist Damian Carrington (2017, para. 3), "There is no doubt that air pollution is a global crisis: it causes 6.5 million early deaths a year." Human children's developing lungs are the most affected, but undoubtedly nonhuman animals also suffer. "Exposure to smog for long hours . . . affects the immune system of animals to fight against harmful bacteria in the respiratory tract" (Abubakar and Raza 2016, para. 16).

2. When it comes to the Global Climate Risk Index 2017, "countries like the Philippines and Pakistan that are recurrently affected by catastrophes continuously rank among the most affected countries both in the long term index and in the index for the respective year for the last six years" (Kreft, Eckstein, and Melchior 2016, 4).

3. The waters from the 2010 floods were actually visible from space. According to journalist Nathaniel Gronewold (2012, para. 47), "At its height, the floodwaters could be seen from space, with the Indus spreading more than 20 miles wide at some parts."

4. The World Wildlife Fund (WWF)–Pakistan's 2015 annual report states, "Poverty and environmental degradation are strongly interlinked, particularly in developing countries like Pakistan and WWF-Pakistan works to improve management of the country's natural resources while ensuring better livelihoods for the rural poor" (50). In this way, WWF-Pakistan does consider social justice with environmental justice.

5. Of course, there are always exceptions. For instance, in 2003, a Swiss NGO Women's World Summit Foundation gave its prize for women's creativity in rural life to a Pakistani woman named Khalida Bibi Awan for creating a local seed bank. The group's website states that Khalida Bibi is "very active in biodiversity conservation and her great knowledge of indigenous seeds made her popular in the village. She can evaluate seed quality and water requirements by only holding them in her hands. Her household became a village seed bank with more than 70 kinds of seeds from different crops" (WWSF 2003).

6. See Vandana Shiva's books *Seed Sovereignty, Food Security: Women in the Vanguard of the Fight against GMOs and Corporate Agriculture* (2016a), *Staying Alive: Women, Ecology, Development* (2016b), and *Ecofeminism* (2014).

7. Agarwal (2002, 7) writes, "The present thrust of most national and international agencies is not on land rights but on micro-credit programs which are being promoted as a panacea, especially (but not only) for poor rural women."

References

Abubakar, Syed Muhammad, and Mohsin Raza. 2016. "Smog Gets in Your Eyes." *Dawn*, updated November 21. http://www.dawn.com/news/1297726/smog-gets-in-your-eyes.

Abu-Lughod, Lila. 2013. *Do Muslim Women Need Saving?* Cambridge MA: Harvard University Press.

Adamson, Joni. 2001. *American Indian Literature, Environmental Justice, and Ecocriticism: The Middle Place.* Tucson: University of Arizona Press.

———. 2016. "Humanities." In Adamson, Gleason, and Pellow, *Keywords for Environmental Studies*, 135–39.

Adamson, Joni, and Kimberly N. Ruffin. 2013. Introduction. In *American Studies, Ecocriticism, and Citizenship: Thinking and Acting in the Local and Global Commons*, edited by Joni Adamson and Kimberly N. Ruffin, 1–17. New York: Routledge.

Adamson, Joni, and Salma Monani. 2017. "Cosmovisions, Ecocriticism, and Indigenous Studies." In *Ecocriticism and Indigenous Studies: Conversations from Earth to Cosmos*, edited by Salma Monani and Joni Adamson, 1–19. New York: Routledge.

Adamson, Joni, William A. Gleason, and David N. Pellow, eds. 2016. *Keywords for Environmental Studies*. New York: New York University Press.

Afzal-Khan, Fawzia. 2001. "Exposed by Pakistani Street Theater: The Unholy Alliance of Postmodern Capitalism, Patriarchy, and Fundamentalism." *Social Text 69* 19 (4): 67–91.

Agarwal, Bina. 2002. "Are We Not Peasants Too? Land Rights and Women's Claims in India." SEEDS 21:2–30.

Ahmad, Iftikhar. 2004. "Islam, Democracy and Citizenship Education: An Examination of the Social Studies Curriculum in Pakistan." *Current Issues in Comparative Education* 7 (1): 39–49.

Ahmad, Mahvish. 2014. "Balochistan Betrayed." In *Dispatches from Pakistan*, edited by Madiha R. Tahir, Qalandar Bux Memon, and Vijay Prashad, 150–67. Minneapolis: University of Minnesota Press.

Ahmed, Issam. 2010. "Biggest Hurdle to Pakistan Flood Recovery: Wealthy Landowners." *Christian Science Monitor*, September 29. https://www

.csmonitor.com/World/Asia-South-Central/2010/0929/Biggest-hurdle
-to-Pakistan-flood-recovery-Wealthy-landowners.

Akhtar, Shaheen. 2011. *The Search*. Translated by Ella Dutta. Delhi: Zubaan Books.

Akmam, Wardatul. 2002. "Atrocities against Humanity during the Liberation War in Bangladesh: A Case of Genocide." *Journal of Genocide Research* 4 (4): 543–59.

Alaimo, Stacy. 2000. *Undomesticated Ground: Recasting Nature as Feminist Space*. Ithaca NY: Cornell University Press.

Alaimo, Stacy, and Susan Hekman. 2008. "Emerging Models of Materiality in Feminist Theory." In *Material Feminisms*, edited by Stacy Alaimo and Susan Hekman, 1–19. Bloomington: Indiana University Press.

Alamgir, Jalal, and Bina D'Costa. 2011. "The 1971 Genocide: War Crimes and Political Crimes." *Economic and Political Weekly* 46 (13) (March 26–April 1): 38–41.

Ali, Shaheen Sardar, and Javaid Rehman. 2001. *Indigenous Peoples and Ethnic Minorities of Pakistan: Constitutional and Legal Perspectives*. New York: Routledge Curzon Press.

Ali, Tariq. 1983. *Can Pakistan Survive? The Death of a State*. New York: Penguin.

Anam, Tahmima. 2007. *A Golden Age*. London: John Murray.

———. 2011. *The Good Muslim*. London: John Murray.

Anderson, Benedict. 1998. *Imagined Communities: Reflections on the Origin and Spread of Nationalism*. Brooklyn: Verso.

Anzaldúa, Gloria. 1987. *Borderlands/La Frontera: The New Mestiza*. San Francisco: Aunt Lute Books.

Appiah, Kwame Anthony. 1998. "Cosmopolitan Patriots." In *Cosmopolitics: Thinking and Feeling beyond the Nation*, edited by Pheng Cheah and Bruce Robbins, 91–114. Minneapolis: University of Minnesota Press.

———. 2006. *Cosmopolitanism: Ethics in a World of Strangers*. New York: Norton.

Asian Development Bank and World Bank. 2012. "2011 Pakistan Floods: Preliminary Damage and Needs Assessment." Washington DC: World Bank Group. https://openknowledge.worldbank.org/handle/10986/17565.

Athique, Adrian M. 2008. "A Line in the Sand: The India-Pakistan Border in the Films of J.P. Dutta." *South Asia: Journal of South Asian Studies* 31 (3): 472–99.

BBC News. 2002. "Musharraf Boosts Bangladesh Ties." July 30. http://news.bbc.co.uk/2/hi/south_asia/2157891.stm.

———. 2014. "India PM Narendra Modi Visits Siachen Glacier on Diwali." October 23. http://www.bbc.com/news/world-asia-india-29735292.

———. 2016. "Qandeel Baloch: Murdered Pakistan Celebrity's Parents Speak of Pain." July 21. http://www.bbc.com/news/world-asia-36858317.

Beachler, Donald. 2007. "The Politics of Genocide Scholarship: The Case of Bangladesh." *Patterns of Prejudice* 41 (5): 467–92.

Bhargava, Pradeep, and Manju Balana. 2007. "Realizing the Right to Food in South Asia." In *Food Insecurity, Vulnerability and Human Rights Failure*, edited by Basudeb Guha-Khasnobis, Shabd S. Acharya, and Benjamin Davis, 286–307. New York: Palgrave Macmillan, United Nations University.

Blair, David. 2002. "Musharraf Apology to Bangladesh." *Telegraph*, July 31. http://www.telegraph.co.uk/news/worldnews/asia/bangladesh/1403185/Musharraf-apology-to-Bangladesh.html.

Bose, Sarmila. 2011. "The Question of Genocide and the Quest for Justice in the 1971 War." *Journal of Genocide Research* 13 (4): 393–419.

Bourke-White, Margaret. 1949. *Halfway to Freedom: A Report on the New India in the Words and Photographs of Margaret Bourke-White*. New York: Simon & Schuster.

Breckenridge, Carol A., Sheldon Pollock, Homi K. Bhabha, and Dipesh Chakrabarty, eds. 2002. *Cosmopolitanism*. Durham NC: Duke University Press.

Brennan, Timothy. 1997. *At Home in the World: Cosmopolitanism Now*. Cambridge MA: Harvard University Press.

———. 2001. "Cosmo-Theory." *South Atlantic Quarterly* 100:659–91.

Buell, Lawrence. 2005. *The Future of Environmental Criticism: Environmental Crisis and Literary Imagination*. Oxford: Blackwell.

Butalia, Urvashi. 2000. *The Other Side of Silence: Voices from the Partition of India*. Durham NC: Duke University Press.

Calarco, Matthew. 2008. *Zoographies: The Question of the Animal from Heidegger to Derrida*. New York: Columbia University Press.

Caminero-Santangelo, Byron. 2011. "In Place: Tourism, Cosmopolitan Bioregionalism, and Zakes Mda's *The Heart of Redness*." In *Postcolonial Ecologies: Literatures of the Environment*, edited by Elizabeth DeLoughrey and George B. Handley, 291–307. Oxford: Oxford University Press.

Carrington, Damian. 2017. "The War against Air Pollution Has Begun — and It Will Be Fought in Cities." *Guardian*, February 13. https://www.theguardian.com/cities/2017/feb/13/war-air-pollution-fought-cities?utm_source=esp&utm_medium=Email&utm_campaign=GU+Today+USA+-+Collections+2017&utm_term=213077&subid=9497831&CMP=GT_US_collection.

Castillo, Debra A., and Kavita Panjabi. 2011. Introduction. In *Cartographies of Affect: Across Borders in South Asia and the Americas*, edited by Debra Castillo and Kavita Panjabi, 1–47. Kolkata: Worldview Publications.

Castree, Noel. 2016. "Nature." In Adamson, Gleason, and Pellow, *Keywords for Environmental Studies*, 151–56.

Chae, Youngsuk. 2015. "Postcolonial Ecofeminism in Arundhati Roy's *The God of Small Things*." *Journal of Postcolonial Writing* (51) 5: 519–30.

Chashi, Nazrul Islam, dir. 1997. *Hangor Nodi Grenade* (The mother). Bangladesh: Chashi Chalachchitra.

Chatterjee, Partha. 1993. *The Nation and Its Fragments: Colonial and Postcolonial Histories*. Princeton NJ: Princeton University Press.

Chatterji, Joya. 2007. *The Spoils of Partition: Bengal and India, 1947–1967*. Cambridge: Cambridge University Press.

Chaudhuri, Kalyan. 1972. *Genocide in Bangladesh*. New Delhi: Orient Longman.

Cheah, Pheng. 2006. *Inhuman Conditions: On Cosmopolitanism and Human Rights*. Cambridge MA: Harvard University Press.

———. 2008. "Universal Areas: Asian Studies in a World in Motion." In *The Postcolonial and the Global*, edited by Revathi Krishnaswamy and John Hawley, 54–68. Minneapolis: University of Minnesota Press.

Cheah, Pheng, and Bruce Robbins, eds. 1998. *Cosmopolitics: Thinking and Feeling beyond the Nation*. Minneapolis: University of Minnesota Press.

Cheney, Jim. 1989. "Postmodern Environmental Ethics: Ethics as Bioregional Narrative." *Environmental Ethics* 11:117–34.

Chester, Lucy P. 2009. *Borders and Conflict in South Asia: The Radcliffe Boundary Commission and the Partition of Punjab*. Manchester: Manchester University Press.

Chowdhury, Elora Halim. 2015. "When Love and Violence Meet: Women's Agency and Transformative Politics in Rubaiyat Hossain's *Meherjaan*." *Hypatia* 30 (4): 760–77.

Cilano, Cara. 2006. "An Interview with the Author." In *Noor*, by Sorayya Khan, 211–25. Wilmington NC: Publishing Laboratory.

———. 2011. *National Identities in Pakistan: The 1971 War in Contemporary Pakistani Fiction*. New York: Routledge.

———. 2013. *Contemporary Pakistani Fiction in English: Idea, Nation, State*. New York: Routledge.

Cilano, Cara, and Elizabeth DeLoughrey. 2007. "Against Authenticity: Global Knowledges and Postcolonial Ecocriticism." *ISLE: Interdisciplinary Studies in Literature and Environment* 14 (1): 71–87.

Cohen, Stephen P. 2006. *The Idea of Pakistan*. Washington DC: Brookings Institution Press.

Comfort, Susan. 2008. "The Hidden Life of Things: Commodification, Imperialism, and Environmental Feminism in Arundhati Roy's *The God of Small Things*." *Postcolonial Text* 4 (4): 1–27.

Crawford, Chiyo. 2013. "Streams of Violence: Colonialism, Modernization, and Gender in Maria Cristina Mena's 'John of God, the Water-Carrier.'" In *International Perspectives in Feminist Ecocriticism*, edited by Greta

Gaard, Simon C. Estok, and Serpil Oppermann, 87–100. New York: Routledge.

Cudworth, Erika. 2005. *Developing Ecofeminist Theory: The Complexity of Difference*. New York: Palgrave Macmillan.

Dadi, Iftikhar. 2010. *Modernism and the Art of Muslim South Asia*. Chapel Hill: University of North Carolina Press.

Daiya, Kavita. 2008. *Violent Belongings: Partition, Gender, and Postcolonial Nationalism in India*. Philadelphia PA: Temple University Press.

Dalrymple, William. 2017. "In Pakistan, Tolerant Islamic Voices Are Being Silenced." *Guardian*, February 20. https://www.theguardian.com/commentisfree/2017/feb/20/islamic-state-foothold-pakistan-government-sehwan-bombing-saudi-fundamentalism.

Das, Veena. 2000. "The Act of Witnessing: Violence, Poisonous Knowledge, and Subjectivity." In *Violence and Subjectivity*, edited by Veena Das, Arthur Kleinman, Mamphela Ramphele, and Pamela Reynolds, 205–25. Oakland: University of California Press.

Dawn. 2013. "Interview: Uzma Aslam Khan." January 27. http://www.dawn.com/news/781645/interview-uzma-aslam-khan.

D'Costa, Bina. 2011. *Nationbuilding, Gender and War Crimes in South Asia*. New York: Routledge.

————. 2014. "*Once Were Warriors*: The Militarized State in Narrating the Past." *South Asian History and Culture* 5 (4): 457–74.

de la Cadeña, Marisol. 2010. "Indigenous Cosmopolitics in the Andes: Conceptual Reflections beyond 'Politics.'" *Cultural Anthropology* 25 (2): 334–70.

DeLoughrey, Elizabeth, and George B. Handley. 2011. "Toward an Aesthetics of the Earth." In *Postcolonial Ecologies: Literatures of the Environment*, edited by Elizabeth DeLoughrey and George B. Handley, 3–39. Oxford: Oxford University Press.

DeLoughrey, Elizabeth, Jill Didur, and Anthony Carrigan. 2015. "Introduction: A Postcolonial Environmental Humanities." In *Global Ecologies and the Environmental Humanities: Postcolonial Approaches*, edited by Elizabeth DeLoughrey, Jill Didur, and Anthony Carrigan, 1–32. New York: Routledge.

Derrida, Jacques. 2001. *On Cosmopolitanism and Forgiveness*. New York: Routledge.

————. 2008. *The Animal That Therefore I Am*. Edited by Marie-Louise Mallet. Translated by David Wills. Bronx NY: Fordham University Press.

Devji, Faisal. 2013. *Muslim Zion: Pakistan as a Political Idea*. Cambridge MA: Harvard University Press.

Dharejo, Salam. 2014. "Thar Crisis: Living a Nightmare." *Newsline*, April 19. http://newslinemagazine.com/magazine/thar-crisis-living-a-nightmare/.

Didur, Jill. 2006. *Unsettling Partition: Literature, Gender, Memory*. Toronto: University of Toronto Press.

Dooley, Patrick K. 2003. "Biocentric, Homocentric, and Theocentric Environmentalism in *O Pioneers!*, *My Antonia*, and *Death Comes for the Archbishop*." *Cather Studies* 5:64–76.

Dowling, Sarah. 2013. "They Were Girls: Animality and Poetic Voice in Bhanu Kapil's *Humanimal*." *American Quarterly* 65 (3) (September): 735–55.

Drèze, Jean, and Amartya Sen. 2013. *An Uncertain Glory: India and Its Contradictions*. Princeton NJ: Princeton University Press.

Dwyer, Rachel. 2006. *Filming the Gods: Religion and Indian Cinema*. New York: Routledge.

Ebrahim, Zofeen T. 2015. "Expensive Water Plants Won't Quench Thirst in Pakistan's Thar Desert." *TheThirdPole.net: Understanding Asia's Water Crisis*, January 27.

Ewing, Katherine Pratt. 1997. *Arguing Sainthood: Modernity, Psychoanalysis, and Islam*. Durham NC: Duke University Press.

Faiz, Faiz Ahmed. 1995. *The Rebel's Silhouette: Selected Poems*. Translated by Agha Shahid Ali. Amherst: University of Massachusetts Press.

Fanon, Frantz. 2004. *The Wretched of the Earth*. Translated by Richard Philcox. New York: Grove Press.

Feldman, Shelley. 1999. "Feminist Interruptions: The Silence of East Bengal in the Story of Partition." *Interventions: International Journal of Postcolonial Studies* 1 (2): 167–82.

Fiskio, Janet. 2012. "Unsettling Ecocriticism: Rethinking Agrarianism, Place, and Citizenship." *American Literature* 84 (2): 301–25.

Fraser, T. G. 1984. *Partition in Ireland, India and Palestine: Theory and Practice*. New York: St. Martin's Press.

Gaard, Greta. 2010. "New Directions for Ecofeminism: Toward a More Feminist Ecocriticism." *ISLE: Interdisciplinary Studies in Literature and Environment* 17 (4): 643–65.

———. 2016. "Ecofeminism." In Adamson, Gleason, and Pellow, *Keywords for Environmental Studies*, 68–71.

Garrard, Greg. 2011. *Ecocriticism*. New York: Routledge.

———. 2016. "Ecocriticism." In Adamson, Gleason, and Pellow, *Keywords for Environmental Studies*, 61–64.

Gazdar, Mushtaq. 1997. *Pakistan Cinema, 1947–1997*. New York: Oxford University Press.

Ghosh, Amitav. 2006. *The Hungry Tide*. New York: Mariner Books.

Ghosh, Palash. 2011. "Hurricane Watch: 1970 Cyclone in Bangladesh Killed 500,000." *International Business Times*, August 22. http://www.ibtimes.com/hurricane-watch-1970-cyclone-bangladesh-killed-500000-302837.

Gilroy, Paul. 2004. *After Empire: Melancholia or Convivial Culture?* New York: Routledge.

Go, Julian. 2013. "Fanon's Postcolonial Cosmopolitanism." *European Journal of Social Theory* 16 (2): 208–25.

Gramsci, Antonio. 2008. *Selections from the Prison Notebooks of Antonio Gramsci.* Edited and translated by Quintin Hoare and Geoffrey Nowell Smith. New York: International Publishers.

Green, Matthew. 2013. "Insight: Once a Landlord's Serf, a Pakistani Woman Enters Election Fray." *Reuters*, April 14. https://www.reuters.com/article/us-pakistan-feudals-insight/insight-once-a-landlords-serf-a-pakistani-woman-enters-election-fray-idUSBRE93D01320130414.

Gronewold, Nathaniel. 2010. "What Caused the Massive Flooding in Pakistan?" *Scientific American*, October 12. http://www.scientificamerican.com/article/what-caused-the-massive-flooding-in-pakistan.

Gross, Aaron. 2012. "Introduction and Overview: Animal Others and Animal Studies." In *Animals and the Human Imagination: A Companion to Animal Studies*, edited by Aaron Gross and Anne Vallely, 1–24. New York: Columbia University Press.

Guha, Ramachandra, and Joan Martinez-Alier. 1997. *Varieties of Environmentalism: Essays North and South.* London: Earthscan.

Habib, M. A. R. 2003. Introduction. In *An Anthology of Modern Urdu Poetry: In English Translation, with Urdu Text*, edited and translated by M. A. R. Habib, xiii–xxxii. New York: Modern Language Association of America.

Hai, Ambreen. 2000. "Border Work, Border Trouble: Postcolonial Feminism and the Ayah in Bapsi Sidhwa's *Cracking India*." *Modern Fiction Studies* 46 (2) (Summer): 379–426.

Hanjra, Munir A., and M. Ejaz Qureshi. 2010. "Global Water Crisis and Future Food Security in an Era of Climate Change." *Food Policy* 35 (5): 365–77.

Haraway, Donna J. 2008. *When Species Meet.* Minneapolis: University of Minnesota Press.

Harcourt, Wendy. 2016. "Place." In Adamson, Gleason, and Pellow, *Keywords for Environmental Studies*, 161–64.

Haroon, Anis. 2001. "'They Use Us and Others Abuse Us': Women in the MQM Conflict." In *Women, War and Peace in South Asia*, edited by Rita Manchanda, 177–213. Thousand Oaks CA: Sage Publications, South Asia Forum for Human Rights.

Harvey, David. 2004. "What's Green and Makes the Environment Go Round?" In *The Cultures of Globalization*, edited by Fredric Jameson and Masao Miyoshi, 327–55. Durham NC: Duke University Press.

Hashim, Asad. 2014. "Families of Missing Baluch March for Justice." *Al Jazeera*, February 28. http://www.aljazeera.com/indepth/features/2014 /02/families-missing-baloch-march-justice-2014227101949360898.html.

Hashim, Asad, and Alia Chughtai. 2017. "Sufis Return to Sehwan Shrine in Defiance of ISIL." *Al Jazeera*, February 17. http://www.aljazeera .com/news/2017/02/sufis-return-sehwan-shrine-defiance-isil-blast -170217161946062.html.

Heise, Ursula K. 2008. *Sense of Place and Sense of Planet: The Environmental Imagination of the Global*. Oxford: Oxford University Press.

Hoodbhoy, Pervez. 2009. "Whither Pakistan? A Five-Year Forecast." *Bulletin of the Atomic Scientists*, June 3. http://www.thebulletin.org/web-edition /features/whither-pakistan-five-year-forecast.

Hoodbhoy, Pervez, and Abdul Hameed Nayyar. 1985. "Rewriting the History of Pakistan." In *Islam, Politics and the State: The Pakistan Experience*, edited by Mohammad Asghar Khan, 164–77. London: Zed Books.

Hossain, Rubaiyat, dir. 2011. *Meherjaan*. Bangladesh: Era Motion Pictures.

Huggan, Graham. 2004. "'Greening' Postcolonialism: Ecocritical Perspectives." *MFS: Modern Fiction Studies* 50 (3) (Fall): 701–33.

Huggan, Graham, and Helen Tiffin. 2015. *Postcolonial Ecocriticism: Literature, Animals, Environment*. 2nd ed. New York: Routledge.

Hussain, Delwar. 2013. *Boundaries Undermined: The Ruins of Progress on the Bangladesh-India Border*. London: Hurst.

IFAD (International Fund for Agricultural Development). 2012. "Country Technical Note on Indigenous Peoples' Issues: Islamic Republic of Pakistan." Rome: IFAD. https://www.ifad.org/documents/10180/c5ae343f -4e30-429f-958e-c34703a2e163.

ILO (International Labour Organization). 1957. "C107 — Indigenous and Tribal Populations Convention, 1957 (No. 107): Convention Concerning the Protection and Integration of Indigenous and Other Tribal and Semi-Tribal Populations in Independent Countries." Geneva: ILO. http://www.ilo.org/dyn /normlex/en/f?p=NORMLEXPUB:12100:0::NO::P12100_ILO_CODE:C107.

Imran, Rahat. 2008. "Deconstructing *Islamization* in Pakistan: Sabiha Sumar Wages Feminist *Cinematic Jihad* through a Documentary Lens." *Journal of International Women's Studies* 9 (3): 117–54.

———. 2016. *Activist Documentary Film in Pakistan: The Emergence of a Cinema of Accountability*. New York: Routledge.

International Dalit Solidarity Network (IDSN). 2014. "Working Glob-
    ally against Caste Discrimination: Annual Report 2013." Copenha-
    gen: IDSN. http://idsn.org/fileadmin/user_folder/pdf/New_files/IDSN
    /AnnualReport-2013-web.pdf.
Jabbar, Mehreen, dir. 2008. *Ramchand Pakistani*. Pakistan: Geo Films.
Jackson, John Brinckerhoff. 1984. *Discovering the Vernacular Landscape*. New
    Haven CT: Yale University Press.
Jaffrelot, Christophe. 2004. "Islamic Identity and Ethnic Tensions." In *A His-
    tory of Pakistan and Its Origins*, edited by Christophe Jaffrelot, 9–38. Lon-
    don: Anthem Press.
Jahan, Rounaq. 1997. "Genocide in Bangladesh." In *Century of Genocide: Eye-
    witness Accounts and Critical Views*, edited by Samuel Totten, William S.
    Parsons, and Israel W. Charny, 291–316. New York: Garland Publishing.
Jaikumar, Priya. 2007. "Translating Silences: A Cinematic Encounter with
    Incommensurable Difference." In *Transnational Feminism in Film and
    Media*, edited by Katarzyna Marciniak, Anikó Imre, and Aine O'Healy,
    207–25. New York: Palgrave Macmillan.
Jain, Pankaj. 2011. "From *Padosi* to *My Name is Khan*: The Portrayal of Hindu-
    Muslim Relations in South Asian Films." *Visual Anthropology* 24 (4): 345–63.
Jalais, Annu. 2010. *Forest of Tigers: People, Politics & Environment in the Sundar-
    bans*. New York: Routledge, 2010.
Jalal, Ayesha. 1995a. "Conjuring Pakistan: History as Official Imagining."
    International Journal of Middle East Studies 27 (1): 73–89.
———. 1995b. *Democracy and Authoritarianism in South Asia: A Comparative
    and Historical Perspective*. Lahore: Sang-e-Meel Publications.
———. 2014. *The Struggle for Pakistan: A Muslim Homeland and Global Poli-
    tics*. Cambridge MA: Harvard University Press.
Jalal, Ayesha, and Sugata Bose, eds. 2011. *Modern South Asia: History, Culture,
    Political Economy*. 3rd ed. New York: Routledge.
Jamal, Amina. 2005. "Transnational Feminism as Critical Practice: A Read-
    ing of Feminist Discourses in Pakistan." *Meridians: Feminism, Race, Trans-
    nationalism* 5 (2): 57–82.
———. 2014. "Feminism and 'Fundamentalism' in Pakistan." In *Dispatches
    from Pakistan*, edited by Madiha R. Tahir, Qalandar Bux Memon, and
    Vijay Prashad, 104–20. Minneapolis: University of Minnesota Press.
James, Erin. 2015. *The Storyworld Accord: Econarratology and Postcolonial Nar-
    ratives*. Lincoln: University of Nebraska Press.
Javid, Hassan. 2011. "Class, Power, and Patronage: Landowners and Politics
    in Punjab." *History and Anthropology* 22 (3): 337–69.

Kabir, Ananya Jahanara. 2009. "Hieroglyphs and Broken Links: Remediated Script and Partition Effects in Pakistan." *Cultural and Social History* 6 (4): 485–506.

———. 2011. "Deep Topographies in the Fiction of Uzma Aslam Khan." *Journal of Postcolonial Writing* 47 (2): 173–85.

———. 2013. *Partition's Post-Amnesias: 1947, 1971 and Modern South Asia*. New Delhi: Women Unlimited (an associate of Kali for Women).

Kanwal, Aroosa. 2015. *Rethinking Identities in Contemporary Pakistani Fiction: Beyond 9/11*. New York: Palgrave Macmillan.

Kaplan, Caren. 1996. *Questions of Travel: Postmodern Discourses of Displacement*. Durham NC: Duke University Press.

———. 2001. "Hillary Clinton's Orient: Cosmopolitan Travel and Global Feminist Subjects." *Meridians: Feminism, Race, Transnationalism* 2 (1): 219–40.

Kern, Robert. 2003. "Ecocriticism: What Is It Good For?" In *The ISLE Reader: Ecocriticism, 1993–2003*, edited by Michael P. Branch and Scott Slovic, 258–81. Athens: University of Georgia Press.

Khan, Ali, and Ali Nobil Ahmad, eds. 2016. *Cinema and Society: Film and Social Change in Pakistan*. New York: Oxford University Press.

Khan, Shahnaz. 2006. *Zina, Transnational Feminism, and the Moral Regulation of Pakistani Women*. Vancouver: UBC Press.

———. 2009. "Floating on Silent Waters: Religion, Nationalism, and Dislocated Women in *Khamosh Pani*." *Meridians: Feminism, Race, Transnationalism* 9 (2): 130–52.

Khan, Sorayya. 2006. *Noor*. Wilmington NC: The Publishing Laboratory.

Khan, Uzma Aslam. 2003. *Trespassing: A Novel*. London: Picador.

———. 2009a. *The Geometry of God*. Northampton MA: Clockroot.

———. 2009b. "Pakistan: Women and Fiction Today." *World Pulse: Connecting Women's Voices to Transform Our World*, August 18. http://www.worldpulse.com/en/voices-rising/stories/pakistan-women-and-fiction-today.

Khan, Yasmin. 2007. *The Great Partition: The Making of India and Pakistan*. New Haven CT: Yale University Press.

Khurshid, Muhammad. 1994. "The Role of Landlords and Pirs in the Punjab Politics and Its After-Effects." *Journal of the Research Society of Pakistan* 31 (2): 45–60.

Kirk, Gwendolyn S. 2014. "Working Class Zombies and Men in Burqas: Temporality, Trauma, and the Specter of Nostalgia in *Zibahkhana*." *BioScope* 5 (2): 141–51.

Klein, Naomi. 2014. *This Changes Everything: Capitalism vs. The Climate*. New York: Alfred A. Knopf.

Kolodny, Annette. 1975. *The Lay of the Land: Metaphor as Experience and History in American Life and Letters*. Chapel Hill: University of North Carolina Press.

Kreft, Sönke, David Eckstein, and Inga Melchior. 2016. "Global Climate Risk Index 2017: Who Suffers Most from Extreme Weather Events? Weather-Related Loss Events in 2015 and 1996 to 2015." Bonn: Germanwatch. https://germanwatch.org/sites/germanwatch.org/files/publication/16411.pdf.

Krishna, Sankaran. 1994. "Cartographic Anxiety: Mapping the Body Politic in India." *Alternatives* 19:507–21.

Krishnaswamy, Revathi, and John Hawley, eds. 2008. *The Postcolonial and the Global*. Minneapolis: University of Minnesota Press.

Langah, Nukhbah Taj. 2012. *Poetry as Resistance: Islam and Ethnicity in Postcolonial Pakistan*. New York: Routledge.

Latour, Bruno. 2004. "Whose Cosmos, Which Cosmopolitics? Comments on the Peace Terms of Ulrich Beck." *Common Knowledge* 10 (3): 450–62.

Leopold, Aldo. 1987. *A Sand County Almanac and Sketches Here and There*. Oxford: Oxford University Press.

Li, Victor. 2009. "Necroidealism, or the Subaltern's Sacrificial Death." *Interventions* 11 (3): 275–92.

Lindholdt, Paul. 2003. "Literary Activism and the Bioregional Agenda." In *The ISLE Reader: Ecocriticism, 1993-2003*, edited by Michael P. Branch and Scott Slovic, 243–57. Athens: University of Georgia Press.

Lynch, Tom, Cheryll Glotfelty, and Karla Armbruster. 2012. Introduction. In *The Bioregional Imagination: Literature, Ecology, and Place*, edited by Tom Lynch, Cheryll Glotfelty, and Karla Armbruster, 1–29. Athens: University of Georgia Press.

Malewitz, Raymond. 2014. "Narrative Disruption as Animal Agency in Cormac McCarthy's *The Crossing*." *MFS: Modern Fiction Studies* 60 (3): 544–61.

Mamdani, Mahmood. 2004. *Good Muslim, Bad Muslim: America, the Cold War, and the Roots of Terror*. New York: Pantheon Books.

Manchanda, Rita. 2001. "Where Are the Women in South Asian Conflicts?" In *Women, War and Peace in South Asia: Beyond Victimhood to Agency*, edited by Rita Manchanda, 9–41. Thousand Oaks CA: Sage Publications, South Asia Forum for Human Rights.

Mannur, Anita. 2009. *Culinary Fictions: Food in South Asian Diasporic Culture*. Philadelphia: Temple University Press.

Manto, Saadat Hasan. 1997. "Toba Tek Singh." In *Mirrorwork: 50 Years of Indian Writing, 1947-1997*, edited by Salman Rushdie and Elizabeth West, 25–31. New York: Henry Holt.

Marshall, Gene. 1993. "Step One: Mapping the Biosphere." In *Boundaries of Home: Mapping for Local Empowerment*, edited by Doug Aberley, 51–56. Gabriola Island BC: New Society Publishers.

Mascarenhas, Anthony. 1971. "Genocide." In *Bangladesh Documents*, edited by Sheelendra Kumar Singh, 358–72. Columbia MO: South Asia Books, 1999. (Reprinted from *The Times* [London], June 13, 1971.)

Massey, Doreen. 1994. *Space, Place, and Gender*. Minneapolis: University of Minnesota Press.

———. 2005. *For Space*. Thousand Oaks CA: Sage Publications.

Memon, Muhammad Umar. 1983. "Pakistani Urdu Creative Writing on National Disintegration: The Case of Bangladesh." *Journal of Asian Studies* 43 (1): 105–27.

Menon, Ritu. 2006. "No Woman's Land." In *Women Writers on Partition of Pakistan and India*, edited by Ritu Menon, 1–11. Islamabad: Vanguard Books.

Menon, Ritu, and Kamla Bhasin. 1998. *Borders & Boundaries: Women in India's Partition*. New Brunswick NJ: Rutgers University Press.

Mir, Farina. 2012. "Genre and Devotion in Punjabi Popular Narratives: Rethinking Cultural and Religious Syncretism." In *Punjab Reconsidered: History, Culture, and Practice*, edited by Anshu Malhotra and Farina Mir, 221–60. Oxford: Oxford University Press.

Mohanty, Chandra Talpade. 2003. *Feminism without Borders: Decolonizing Theory, Practicing Solidarity*. Durham NC: Duke University Press.

Monani, Salma. 2014. "Evoking Sympathy and Empathy: The Ecological Indian and Indigenous Eco-activism." In *Moving Environments: Affect, Emotion, Ecology, and Film*, edited by Alexa Weik von Mossner, 225–47. Waterloo ON: Wilfrid Laurier University Press.

Mookherjee, Nayanika. 2007. "The 'Dead and Their Double Duties': Mourning, Melancholia, and the Martyred Intellectual Memorials in Bangladesh." *Space and Culture* 10 (2): 271–91.

———. 2012. "The Absent Piece of Skin: Gendered, Racialized, and Territorial Inscriptions of Sexual Violence during the Bangladesh War." *Modern Asian Studies* 46 (6): 1572–601.

———. 2015. *The Spectral Wound: Sexual Violence, Public Memories, and the Bangladesh War of 1971*. Durham NC: Duke University Press.

Moon, Penderel. 1962. *Divide and Quit*. Oakland: University of California Press.

Morey, Peter, and Amina Yaqin. 2011. *Framing Muslims: Stereotyping and Representation after 9/11*. Cambridge MA: Harvard University Press.

Mukherjee, Upamanyu Pablo. 2010. *Postcolonial Environments: Nature, Culture and the Contemporary Indian Novel in English*. London: Palgrave Macmillan UK.

Nabhan, Gary Paul. 2016. "Agrarian Ecology." In Adamson, Gleason, and Pellow, *Keywords for Environmental Studies*, 7–9.

Naess, Arne. 1993. *Ecology, Community, and Lifestyle: Outline of an Ecosophy.* Cambridge: Cambridge University Press.

Nagappan, Ramu. 2005. *Speaking Havoc: Social Suffering & South Asian Narratives.* Seattle: University of Washington Press.

Nakachi, Sachi. 2012. "'Why a Second Bomb?': Kamila Shamsie's Challenge to American Xenophobia in *Burnt Shadows.*" *Journal of Ethnic American Literature* 2:132–41.

ND-GAIN (Notre Dame Global Adaptation Index). 2018. "Pakistan." South Bend IN: ND-GAIN, University of Notre Dame Research. https://gain.nd .edu/our-work/country-index/.

Neely, Brett. 2010. "Why We've Given Less to Pakistan's Flood Victims." *All Things Considered.* NPR. September 2. http://www.npr.org/templates /story/story.php?storyId=129605789.

Nixon, Rob. 2005. "Environmentalism and Postcolonialism." In *Postcolonial Studies and Beyond,* edited by Ania Loomba, Suvir Kaul, Matti Bunzl, Antoinette Burton, and Jed Esty, 233–51. Durham NC: Duke University Press.

———. 2011. *Slow Violence and the Environmentalism of the Poor.* Cambridge MA: Harvard University Press.

Nussbaum, Martha C. 2005. "Women's Bodies: Violence, Security, Capabilities." *Journal of Human Development* 6 (2): 167–83.

Obaid-Chinoy, Sharmeen, dir. 2015. *A Girl in the River: The Price of Forgiveness.* Pakistan: SOC Films.

O'Brien, Susie. 2001. "Articulating a World of Difference: Ecocriticism, Postcolonialism and Globalization." *Canadian Literature* 170–71 (Autumn/ Winter): 140–58.

———. 2004. "On Death and Donuts: Irony and Ecology after September 11." *Cultural Critique* 58 (Fall): 148–67.

Oldenburg, Philip. 1985. "'A Place Insufficiently Imagined': Language, Belief, and the Pakistan Crisis of 1971." *Journal of Asian Studies* 44 (4): 711–33.

Oppermann, Serpil. 2013. "Feminist Ecocriticism: A Posthumanist Direction in Ecocritical Trajectory." In *International Perspectives in Feminist Ecocriticism,* edited by Greta Gaard, Simon C. Estok, and Serpil Oppermann, 19–36. New York: Routledge.

Panuganti, Sreya. 2012. "Desert Solitaire: Why India and Pakistan Should Collaborate to Combat Desertification." Washington DC: Stimson Center. https://www.stimson.org/content/desert-solitaire-why-india-and -pakistan-should-collaborate-combat-desertification.

Pezzoli, Keith. 2016. "Bioregionalism." In Adamson, Gleason, and Pellow, *Keywords for Environmental Studies,* 25–28.

Purewal, Navtej. 2003. "The Indo-Pak Border: Displacements, Aggressions and Transgressions." *Contemporary South Asia* 12 (4): 539–56.

Qureshi, Irna. 2011. "Destigmatising Star Texts: Honour and Shame among Muslim Women in Pakistani Cinema." In *South Asian Media Cultures: Audiences, Representations, Contexts*, edited by Shakuntala Banaji, 181–200. New York: Anthem Press.

Raghavan, Srinath. 2009. "A Coercive Triangle: India, Pakistan, the United States, and the Crisis of 2001–2002." *Defence Studies* 9 (2): 242–60.

———. 2013. *1971: A Global History of the Creation of Bangladesh*. Cambridge MA: Harvard University Press.

Rahman, Hamoodur. 2013. "Hamoodur Rahman Commission Report." Pakistan People's Party (USA), May 24. https://web.archive.org/web/20120304011310/http://www.pppusa.org/Acrobat/Hamoodur%20Rahman%20Commission%20Report.pdf.

Rahman, Shazia. 2007. "Rachna Mara's Cosmopolitan (yet Partial) Feminisms." *Ariel: A Review of International English Literature* 38 (2–3): 1–17.

Rahman, Tariq. 2015. *A History of Pakistani Literature in English, 1947–1988*. Oxford: Oxford University Press.

Ramachandran, Nira. 2007. "Women and Food Security in South Asia: Current Issues and Emerging Concerns." In *Food Insecurity, Vulnerability and Human Rights Failure*, edited by Basudeb Guha-Khasnobis, Shabd S. Acharya, and Benjamin Davis, 219–40. New York: Palgrave Macmillan, United Nations University.

Rashid, Ahmed. 2009. *Descent into Chaos: The U.S. and the Disaster in Pakistan, Afghanistan, and Central Asia*. London: Penguin Books.

Riaz, Fahmida. 2004. "Mantra." In *Four Walls and a Black Veil*, 68–75. Translated by Patricia L. Sharpe. Oxford: Oxford University Press.

Rocheleau, Dianne, and Padini Nirmal. 2016. "Culture." In Adamson, Gleason, and Pellow, *Keywords for Environmental Studies*, 50–55.

Roos, Bonnie, and Alex Hunt, eds. 2010. *Postcolonial Green: Environmental Politics and World Narratives*. Charlottesville: University of Virginia Press.

Roy, Arundhati. 1999. *The Cost of Living*. New York: Modern Library.

———. 2008. *The God of Small Things*. New York: Random House.

Roy, Olivier. 2004. *Globalised Islam: The Search for a New Ummah*. Lahore: Alhamra Publishing.

Roy, Parama. 2010. *Alimentary Tracts: Appetites, Aversions, and the Postcolonial*. Durham NC: Duke University Press.

Sadaf, Shazia. 2017. "*I Am Malala*: Human Rights and the Politics of Production, Marketing and Reception of the Post-9/11 Memoir." *Interventions:*

International Journal of Postcolonial Studies 19 (6): 855–71. https://doi.org
/10.1080/1369801X.2017.1347053.

Saeed, Humaira. 2009. "*Ramchand Pakistani, Khamosh Pani* and the Traumatic Evocation of Partition." *Social Semiotics* 19 (4): 483–98.

Saikia, Yasmin. 2010. "Listening to the Enemy: The Pakistan Army, Violence and Memories of 1971." In *Beyond Crisis: Re-evaluating Pakistan*, edited by Naveeda Khan, 177–209. New York: Routledge.

———. 2011. *Women, War, and the Making of Bangladesh: Remembering 1971.* Durham NC: Duke University Press.

Sangari, Kumkum. 2008. "Gendered Violence, National Boundaries and Culture." In *Constellations of Violence: Feminist Interventions in South Asia*, edited by Radhika Coomaraswamy and Nimanthi Perera-Rajasingham, 1–33. New Delhi: Women Unlimited.

———. 2015. *Solid: Liquid: A (Trans)national Reproductive Formation.* New Delhi: Tulika Books.

Sarkar, Bhaskar. 2009. *Mourning the Nation: Indian Cinema in the Wake of Partition.* Durham NC: Duke University Press.

Schaeffer, R. K. 1999. *Severed States: Dilemmas of Democracy in a Divided World.* Lanham MD: Rowman & Littlefield.

Sen, Amartya. 2006. *Identity and Violence: The Illusion of Destiny.* London: Penguin Books.

Seshadri, Kalpana Rahita. 2012. *HumAnimal: Race, Law, Language.* Minneapolis: University of Minnesota Press.

Shah, Syed Ali. 2013. "Balochistan Unrest: 592 Mutilated Bodies Found in Last Three Years." *Dawn*, September 12. http://www.dawn.com/news /1042164.

Shahzad, Asif, and Jibran Ahmad. 2018. "Nobel Winner Malala Visits Hometown in Pakistan for First Time since Shooting." *Reuters*, March 31. https://www.reuters.com/article/us-pakistan-malala-swat/nobel-winner -malala-visits-hometown-in-pakistan-for-first-time-since-shooting -idUSKBN1H7O52.

Shaikh, Farzana. 2009. *Making Sense of Pakistan.* New York: Columbia University Press.

Shamsie, Kamila. 2009. *Burnt Shadows.* New York: Picador.

Shamsie, Muneeza. 2017. *Hybrid Tapestries: The Development of Pakistani Literature in English.* New York: Oxford University Press.

Shiva, Vandana. 2000. *Stolen Harvest: The Hijacking of the Global Food Supply.* Brooklyn NY: South End Press.

———. 2014. *Ecofeminism.* Winnipeg MB: Zed Books.

————. 2016a. *Seed Sovereignty, Food Security: Women in the Vanguard of the Fight against GMOs and Corporate Agriculture.* Berkeley CA: North Atlantic Books.

————. 2016b. *Staying Alive: Women, Ecology, Development.* Berkeley CA: North Atlantic Books.

Singh, Harleen. 2012. "Insurgent Metaphors: Decentering 9/11 in Mohsin Hamid's *The Reluctant Fundamentalist* and Kamila Shamsie's *Burnt Shadows.*" *ARIEL: A Review of International English Literature* 43 (1): 23–44.

Sisson, Richard, and Leo E. Rose. 1990. *War and Secession: Pakistan, India, and the Creation of Bangladesh.* Oakland: University of California Press.

Spivak, Gayatri Chakravorty. 1999. *A Critique of Postcolonial Reason: Toward a History of the Vanishing Present.* Cambridge: Harvard University Press.

Sturgeon, Noël. 2009. *Environmentalism in Popular Culture: Gender, Race, Sexuality, and the Politics of the Natural.* Tucson: University of Arizona Press.

Sumar, Sabiha, dir. 2003. *Khamosh Pani* (Silent waters). Performance by Kirron Kher. Pakistan: Vidhi Films.

Sundar, Pavitra. 2010. "Silence and the Uncanny: Partition in the Soundtrack of *Khamosh Pani.*" *South Asian Popular Culture* 8 (3): 277–90.

Takaki, Ronald. 1995. *Hiroshima: Why America Dropped the Atomic Bomb.* Boston: Little, Brown.

Talbot, Ian. 2005. *Pakistan: A Modern History.* New York: Palgrave Macmillan.

Thayer, Robert L., Jr. 2003. *LifePlace: Bioregional Thought and Practice.* Oakland: University of California Press.

Thomashow, Mitchell. 1999. "Toward a Cosmopolitan Bioregionalism." In *Bioregionalism,* edited by Michael Vincent McGinnis, 121–32. New York: Routledge.

Tohid, Owais. 2003. "In Pakistan, 'Slavery' Persists." *Christian Science Monitor,* December 15. http://www.csmonitor.com/2003/1215/p08s01-wosc.html.

Toor, Saadia. 2011. *The State of Islam: Culture and Cold War Politics in Pakistan.* London: Pluto Press.

UK Department for International Development. 2008. "Pakistan." December 4. London: UK Department for International Development.

UNDP (United Nations Development Programme). 2015. "Human Development Report 2015: Work for Human Development." New York: UNDP. http://hdr.undp.org/sites/default/files/2015_human_development_report.pdf.

UNIFEM (United Nations Development Fund for Women). 2010. "Women from Flood-Affected Areas of Pakistan Voice Their Concerns." New York: UNIFEM.

Walls, Laura Dassow. 2016. "Cosmos." In Adamson, Gleason, and Pellow, *Keywords for Environmental Studies,* 47–50.

Walther, Sundhya. 2014. "Fables of the Tiger Economy: Species and Subalternity in Aravind Adiga's *The White Tiger*." MFS: *Modern Fiction Studies* 60 (3): 579–98.

Waterman, David. 2015. *Where Worlds Collide: Pakistani Fiction in the New Millennium*. Oxford: Oxford University Press.

Weiner, Myron. 1978. *Sons of the Soil: Migration and Ethnic Conflict in India*. Princeton: Princeton University Press.

Westhead, Rick. 2011. "Tenant Farmers Become Unlikely Land Owners in Pakistan." *Toronto Star*, April 30. https://www.thestar.com/news/world/2011/04/29/tenant_farmers_become_unlikely_land_owners_in_pakistan.html.

Whyte, Kyle Powys. 2016. "Indigeneity." In Adamson, Gleason, and Pellow, *Keywords for Environmental Studies*, 143–46.

World Food Programme. 2014. *Pakistan Food Security Bulletin*, no. 2 (December). https://documents.wfp.org/stellent/groups/public/documents/ena/wfp271228.pdf?_ga=2.186115497.1004014934.1536103930-577149476.1536103930.

World Wildlife Fund (WWF)–Pakistan. 2015. "Annual Report 2015." Lahore: WWF-Pakistan. http://www.wwfpak.org/publication/pdf/annualreport2015.pdf.

Wright, Laura. 2010. *Wilderness into Civilized Shapes: Reading the Postcolonial Environment*. Athens: University of Georgia Press.

WWSF (Women's World Summit Foundation). 2003. "Khalida Bibi Awan." Prize for Women's Creativity in Rural Life. http://www.woman.ch/june09/women/laureates03/laureates-asia-10.php.

Yaqoob, Munazza. 2015. "Environmental Consciousness in Contemporary Pakistani Fiction." In *Ecocriticism of the Global South*, edited by Scott Slovic, Swarnalatha Rangarajan, and Vidya Sarveswaran, 249–62. New York: Lexington Books.

Yousuff, Nasiruddin, dir. 2011. *Guerrilla*. Bangladesh: Impress Telefilms.

Zaheer, Khadija, and Anna Colom. 2013. "Pakistan: How the People of Pakistan Live with Climate Change and What Communication Can Do." Climate Asia, BBC Media Action. http://downloads.bbc.co.uk/rmhttp/mediaaction/pdf/climateasia/reports/ClimateAsia_PakistanReport.pdf.

Zaidi, Syed Manzar Abbas. 2011. "Polarisation of Social Studies Textbooks in Pakistan." *International Perspectives on Curriculum and Pedagogy* 22 (1): 43–59.

Zaman, Niaz. 2001. *A Divided Legacy: The Partition in Selected Novels of India, Pakistan, and Bangladesh*. Oxford: Oxford University Press.

Zaman, Niaz, and Asif Farrukhi, eds. 2008. *Fault Lines: Stories of 1971*. Dhaka: University Press.

Zamindar, Vazira Fazila-Yacoobali. 2007. *The Long Partition and the Making of Modern South Asia*. New York: Columbia University Press.

Index

Page numbers in italics refer to illustrations.

133–34, 135; and silkworms, 120, 121–22, 128, 132–33, 134–35; spirituality of, 131–35

Didur, Jill, 12, 153, 155–56, 177n18

Dilli, 150–51, 159, 161, 164

disappearances, 110–11

displacement, 17, 20, 111, 122, 139, 141–66; Bangladesh partition and, 79; birds symbolizing, 146; from capital cities, 190n2; nuclear violence causing, 156–57; and oppositional notions of place, 141; Pakistan partition and, 114, 122, 141, 150, 177n16, 190n2; Punjab partition and, 23–28; of Raza, 161–62; "recovery" from, 158–59; resistance to, 32, 151, 153; Sindhi, 124, 127

Dooley, Patrick K., 125–26

Dowling, Sarah, 146, 149

Drèze, Jean, 176n9

dualisms. See binaries

Dwyer, Rachel, 54

East Pakistan. See Bengal

Ebrahim, Zofeen, 60

Eckstein, David, 5, 191n2

eco-cosmopolitanism, 15, 17–18, 19, 26–27, 187n1; of Ayesha, 34–35, 37, 41, 47; bioregionalism and, 56; and cosmopolitics, 187n1, 189n12; definition of, 117; of Dia, 122, 132, 133–34, 135; feminist, 17, 18, 23–50; and food security, 47; global, 130; of Heise, 26, 56, 116, 117, 122, 126; and nonhuman animals, 19–20, 120–31, 177n18; Pakistani, 114, 115, 117–18, 119, 130; religion and, 131–36; of Salaamat, 125

ecocriticism, 13–15, 16–17, 85–86; agrarianism and, 58, 70; animals in, 6, 13–15, 115, 144–45, 153, 177n18; attachment to land in, 179n24; definition of, 175n2; dualities avoided in, 9, 83–84, 86; feminism and, 12–15, 178n20; on partitions, 175n1, 179n24; pitfalls of, 154–55; postcolonialism and, 115–17, 123, 144–45, 154–55, 166, 188n3; survival as value in, 123, 124, 127; vernacular landscape and, 86, 88, 179n22; whiteness of, 115–16

ecofeminism, 12–15, 21, 175n5; definition of, 13–14; as essentialist, 13, 14, 21; in India, 173; marginalization of, 178n20; Muslim, 131–36

ecological crises. See climate change; natural disaster

ecological risk, 3

economics. See extraction economy; globalization

ekphrasis, 18–19, 86, 95–96, 97–98

empathy, 182n11

English-language literature, 176n7

environment: foregrounding, 16–17; global consciousness of, 55, 56, 155; literature and, 3–4; in postcolonial theory, 1–4, 6–7, 15, 169; and war, 121, 128–29, 141, 154

environmental humanities, 2–3, 5, 175n4

environmental justice: advocacy and, 166; vs. deep ecology, 20, 168–69; in fictions, 17; gender and, 172–73; in the global south, 3, 15, 20, 169–73; as movement, 15, 88, 126; place informing, 184n1; and social justice, 167–71, 172–73, 192nn4–5

and, 125–26, 137; positive vs. negative, 45–46; vulnerable communities and, 19

global south, 169, 173; biases against, 20, 49, 168–69; environmental justice and, 3, 15, 20, 169–73; justice movements originating in, 15; resource curse of, 96

Glotfelty, Cheryl, 56, 57

Gramsci, Antonio, 188n7

Green, Matthew, 65

Gronewald, Nathaniel, 192n3

Gross, Aaron, 145

Guattari, Félix, 190n3

Guha, Ramachandra, 169

Gujarat, 54

Habib, M. A. R., 190n13

Hai, Ambreen, 60

Haiti, 171

Hamoodur Rahman Commission Report, 91

Handley, George B., 154–55, 169

Hanjra, Munir, 42

Haraway, Donna, 20, 152, 153

Harcourt, Wendy, 26, 176n6, 184n1, 185n9

Haris, 184n2

Haroon, Anis, 114

Harvey, David, 126, 138

Hashim, Asad, 110, 183n18

healing, 82, 84, 86–87, 96, 124–25

Heise, Ursula, 18, 19, 23, 27, 114; on bioregionalism, 55–56; on deterritorialization, 157, 190n3; eco-cosmopolitan framework of, 26, 56, 116, 117, 122, 126; on globalization, 126

Hekman, Susan, 13, 14

hibakusha, 156

Hikmatyar, Gulbuddin, 162

Hindi, 78

Hindus in Pakistan, 54, 57–58, 69, 71

Hiroko (character), 20, 143, 144, 145, 164, 165–66; animalization and, 144–45, 148–50, 152–53, 156, 165; bioregion and, 157–58; deterritorialization of, 156–57; dreams of, 147–48, 149; father of, 156; Harry Burton and, 158–59; and Konrad, 149–50, 158; Nagasaki experience of, 145–47, 149–50, 152, 156, 157–58; Sajjad and, 143–44, 150, 158, 160, 164, 191n5

Holi, 71

homeland as privilege, 66

homelessness. *See* deterritorialization

homeplace, 184n3

honor killings, 18, 24, 49, 78, 182n10

Hoodbhoy, Pervez, 130

hospitality, 32, 39–40, 44

Hudood Ordinances, 12, 181n5

Huggan, Graham, 115, 116, 144–45, 166, 188n5

humanism, 143, 146, 154, 190n1, 190n13

humanity, recognizing, 156

human rights discourse, 43–44

humans as part of nature, 155, 169

Husain, Intizar, 90

Hussain, Delwar, 179n23

Hussein (character), 93, 107, 109

identities: borders nationalizing, 62, 73–74; collective, 95; defining, 11; denationalized, 177n16; food and, 183n20; place-based, 5–6, 11, 21, 22, 77, 113; religious nationalism and, 8, 10, 118, 122, 135, 178n19 imperialism, U.S., 2, 119, 128, 131, 190n13

Imran, Rahat, 176n13

India: agriculture in, 43; ecofeminism in, 173; integrationist films in, 54; nuclear tests by, 156; and Pakistan, 59, 184n5; partition films of, 179n24; spiritual nationalism of, 131; terrorist attack on, 184n5

indigeneity: Andean, 187n1, 189n12; colonialism and, 15; cosmopolitanism and, 177n17, 187n1, 189n9; definition of, 180n26; erasure of, 55; habitat loss and, 154; land attachment and, 36; of non-indigenous people, 189n9; and traditional crafts, 133, 135–36. *See also* language

indigenous languages, 122, 183n22, 189n11

indigenous Pakistanis, 123, 180n26, 183n17, 184n22; protection of, 184n2; rhetoric of, 177n17; as "tribal" people, 183n17; war between, 119. *See also* Sindhi people

Indo-Pakistani War (1971), 6

industrialization, 191n1

intellectuals, Pakistani, 11, 130–31, 178n19, 188n7, 190n13

interdependence, 153

International Crimes Tribunal, 187n8

International Dalit Solidarity Network, 54

International Labour Organization Convention 107, 184n2

Iraq, 121

Islam: Ahmadi, 71, 181n5; and economic opportunity, 40; egalitar-ianism in, 28; ethnicity and, 9, 26, 35–36, 118, 122, 130; local vs. global, 36–37, *38*, 71; and Muslim ecofeminists, 131–36; nature and, 7–12; orientalism and, 29; Shia, 71, 118; transnationalism in, 9–10, 26; and the "true Muslim," *38*, 71. *See also* fundamentalist Islam

Islamization, 12, 178n19, 181n2, 181n5; as anti-Shia, 71, 118; food prices and, 29, 47–48, 49; globalization and, 45; indigenous practices suppressed by, 36–37, 71, 183nn16–18; in *Khamosh Pani,* 17–18, 24–25, 27–32, 48

Islamophobia, 136, 146, 147, 168, 171–72

Ismail (character), 162, 163

Jabbar, Mehreen, 5, 18, 53–79, 167; Sumar and, 53–54, 57, 58, 70–71

Jackson, John Brinckerhoff, 88, 99, 179n22

Jaffrelot, Christophe, 122

Jaikumar, Priya, 28, 34–35, 182n11

Jain, Pankaj, 73

Jalais, Annu, 186n3

Jalal, Ayesha, 7, 11, 28, 87

Jama'at-i Islami, 178n19

Jamal, Amina, 12, 29

Japanese people, racism and, 152, 191n4

Jaswant (character), 31–32

Javid, Hassan, 4–5

Jinnah, Mohammad Ali, 122, 185n7

Joseph (character), 148, 149

justice, hermeneutics and, 116–17, 166. *See also* environmental justice

jute, 87–88

rejection of, 191n5; and transnationalism, 9–10, 155; undercutting narratives of, 61, 70–79. *See also* religious nationalism

natural disaster: Bhola cyclone, 83–84, 100–101; floods, 50, 169–72, 192n3; government aid for, 100, 172; preparedness for, 5, 176n11; violence worsened by, 83–84

nature: capabilities theory and, 22; as contested idea, 180n27; and culture, 6, 7–12; devaluing of, 13–14; humans as part of, 155, 169; and nature/human binary, 114, 168–69, 177n18; relationship to, 14, 20

Nazi Germany, 55–56

necroidealization, 145

Neely, Brett, 171–72

Nirmal, Padini, 6

Nixon, Rob, 115, 188n5; on bioregionalism, 55; on fast vs. slow violence, 171; on landscapes, 88; on resource-cursed societies, 96, 163

Nizam-e-Mustafa (Governance inspired by the Prophet), 48

nomadism, 141

nongovernmental organizations (NGOS), 20, 172–73, 192n5

nonhuman life: attachment to, 2, 17, 115, 121–22, 123; in *Burnt Shadows*, 144–45, 146, 149–50, 165–66; hermeneutics emphasizing, 155–56; and humans, 84, 186n3, 188n2; peaceful relations with, 120; perspective of, 115, 123; racism affecting, 168; seashells and, 120, 121, 129; suffering of, 191n1; trees, 36, 37; in *Trespassing*, 113–

14, 115, 120–24, 132–33, 134–35. *See also* animalization; animals

nonviolence, 20, 150–51

Noor, 5, 6, 18–19, 81–111; forgiveness in, 108, 109–10; light in, 97, 100, 102; nonnarrative elements of, 81–82, 86, 95–96, 97–99, 103–5; river in, 103–4, 105

Noor (character), 94, 103; art by, 95–96, 97–105, 110; empowerment of, 107–8; name of, 97, 100

nuclear tests, 156

Nussbaum, Martha, 22

Obaid-Chinoy, Sharmeen, 182n10

O'Brien, Susie, 123, 160–61

ocean, attachment to, 2

Oldenburg, Philip, 89

Operation Searchlight, 83, 89

Oppermann, Serpil, 14

orientalism, avoiding, 29

otherness, 77

"overcoming," 158–59

overfishing, 121, 137–38

Pakistan: Bengalis in, 87–89; borders of, 11; censorship in, 89, 90; climate change affecting, 5, 169–71, 191n2; corruption in, 172; ethnic conflict in, 82–83, 118–19, 120, 123; films of, since partition, 176n13; immigrants in, 143–44; intellectuals of, 11, 130–31, 178n19, 188n7, 190n13; leftist discourse in, 178n19; "low human development" of, 5, 176nn10–11; nature of, 7–8; nuclear tests by, 156; official narratives of, 70–79; Operation Searchlight and, 83, 89;

man life affected by, 168; U.S., 121, 147, 152; war and, 121, 147, 152, 191n4

Raghavan, Srinath, 83, 100–101, 184n5

Ramachandran, Nira, 4, 176n9

Ramchand (character): crossing borders, 57, 61, 69, 74, 75, 77; disappearance of, 67; dream of, 68–69; herding goats, 63, 64; Kamla and, 72, 73, 74; return of, 68, 74–75, 76, 77; Shankar and, 73, 185n10; song in, 74–75, 77

Ramchand Pakistani, 5, 18, 50–51, 53–79; border crossing in, 57, 57, 59; education in, 63–64; prison in, 72–74, 73; shifts in visuality in, 59, 68–70; synopsis of, 59

rape, 8; charges of, 187n9; as emasculation of men, 24; genocidal, 23–24, 82–83, 85, 89, 187n9, 187n11; homogenization of experience of, 105; honor killings and, 18, 24, 31, 181n4; masculinity asserted through, 102, 187n11; of men, 85; as weapon of war, 102–3, 105–6

Rashed, N. M., 190n13

Rasheed (character), 29–30, 36, 45, 48

Rashid, Ahmed, 131

Rasool, Ghulam (character), 64

Raza (character), 156, 164; Abdullah and, 143–44, 145; displacement of, 161–62; Hiroko's dream of, 148; nationalism and, 158, 191n5

Raza, Mohsin, 191n1

reconciliation, 95–96, 108

Rehana (character), 157

Rehman, Javaid, 183n22, 184n2

religion in Pakistan: barriers of, transcended, 73; caste and, 35; culturalism and, 49; ethnicity and, 35–36, 78–79, 82–83, 118, 122, 130–31; exclusivity of, 31–32, 34; and Hinduism, 54, 57–58, 69, 71; indigenous, 180n26, 183nn16–18; as political tool, 29; stereotypes of, 3; syncretism of, 54, 71

religious nationalism, 7, 8, 9, 10, 18; attachments to nonhumans and, 120–22, 132, 134–35, 168; as cosmopolitan, 26; food prices and, 44–45, 46, 48; geography undercutting, 61; identity and, 8, 10, 118, 122, 135, 178n19; intellectuals and, 2, 6, 119, 130; Islamization and, 28; religious minorities and, 53–54, 77; "sons of the soil" rhetoric of, 37; vs. U.S. imperialism, 2, 119

resilience, 144

resistance vs. accommodation, 123–24, 127

Revolutionary Association of Women of Afghanistan (RAWA), 163

Riffat (character), 135–36, 137

Rocheleau, Dianne, 6

rootedness and re-rooting, 113 14, 122–23, 125–27

Roy, Arundhati, 145, 173, 175n1, 183n21

Roy, Olivier, 9–10, 36–37

Ruffin, Kimberly, 175n3, 184n1

rural dwellers, 180n25, 192n4

Sadaf, Shazia, 1

Saeed, Humaira, 68, 74, 77, 78

Saikia, Yasmin, 81, 86, 93, 106, 187n7

space-time, 70, 84–85, 86, 97–98, 141–43, 161

spatial relations, 94, 110, 142–43

Sturgeon, Noël, 2–3, 13–14

subaltern, sacrifice of, 145

Sufism, 132, 190n14

suicide: of Ayesha, 28, 32, 33–35, 34, 40–41, 48–49; bombings, 147–48, 183n18, 190n14; Champa considering, 78; as choice, 34–35; of farmers, 43; men encouraging, 18, 24, 27, 28, 30–31, 181n4; silence around, 39

Sumar, Sabiha, 18, 23, 24–25, 27–51, 167, 183n16; documentary films of, 181n2; Mehreen Jabbar and, 53–54, 57, 58, 70–71

Sundar, Pavitra, 39, 40

the Sundarbans, 186n3

"superimposed map," 61

Suresh (character), 65, 67

survival through accommodation, 123–24, 127

Sylhet. See Bengal

sympathy, 28, 182n11

syncretism, 54, 71

Takaki, Ronald, 152, 191n4

Talbot, Ian, 87

Taliban, 50, 130, 162–63, 171

Thar, 17, 18, 53–79, 185n9; bonded labor in, 65–66; migration within, 66–67, 70; water shortages in, 78–79

Tharparkar district, 60

Thayer, Robert, Jr., 56

Thomashow, Mitchell, 66, 153–54, 159

"throwntogetherness," 142, 143

Tiffin, Helen, 144–45, 166, 188n5

Tohid, Owais, 65

Toor, Saadia, 7, 11, 89, 178n19, 190n13

transnationalism, Islamic, 9–10, 26

trees, 36, 37

Trespassing, 5, 6, 19–20, 113–39; ethnicity in, 118–19, 137; nature privileged in, 176n12; the sea in, 120–21, 123–24, 127, 129–30, 133, 137–38; sexuality in, 136–37; synopsis of, 115, 120

Turpo, Mariano, 189n12

turtles, 113, 115, 120–21, 123, 127

two-nation theory, 45

United Nations Development Fund for Women (UNIFEM), 50

United Nations Development Programme (UNDP), 5

United Nations Genocide Convention, 92

United States: bombing by, 20, 121, 128–29, 141, 145–47, 156; Daanish and, 128–29, 130; imperialism of, 119, 128, 131; Islamophobia in, 136, 147, 163, 171–72; Mexico and, 185n6; in Pakistani affairs, 190n13; post-9/11 policy of, 147, 161, 163, 188n6; racism of, 121, 152; Taliban supported by, 162–63

University of Notre Dame's Global Adaptation Index (ND-GAIN 2018), 5

Urdu language, 78, 89–90

Veero. See Ayesha/Veero (character)

violence: ethnic, in Karachi, 118–19, 120, 123; "fast" vs. "slow," 171; nuclear, 146, 152, 154, 156, 165–66; "overcoming," 158–59; separatist, 124–25;

violence (*continued*)
treated as inevitable, 84–85. *See also* animalization

violence against women, 102–6; domestic, 103, 106–7; as environmental violence, 18, 27, 30–32, 42, 82; and honor killings, 18, 24, 49, 78, 182n10; punishment for, 103; religion blamed for, 49; verbal, 106

Vishesh (character), 74, 75, 76

Voice for Baloch Missing Persons (VBMP), 111

Wahhabi fundamentalism, 190n14

Walls, Laura Dassow, 187n2

Walther, Sundhya, 144

war: deterritorialization and, 145, 154, 163; earth confused by, 148, 149; ecological effects of, 121, 128–29, 141, 154; food crises caused by, 160–61; journalism on, 128–29; racism and, 147, 152, 191n4

war crimes tribunals, 92, 110, 186n6

water: connection to, 31; in *Khamosh Pani*, 30–32, 37–42; positive portrayals of, 32; scarcity of, 42–43, 58, 65, 78–79; silence of, 37, 39, 41; utility, shut-down of, 138–39; violence against, 18, 27, 30–32; well vs. stream, 40–41

Westhead, Rick, 184n4

wholeness, 125

Whyte, Kyle Powys, 180n26

widowhood, 69

women: borders oppressing, 53, 54, 58, 78–79; climate change affecting, 20, 50, 167, 171, 172–73; clothing of, 182n12; colonialism's impact on, 15; as doubly victim-ized, 102; as farmers, 4, 37, 63–64, 64, 184n4, 192n5; food secured by, 4, 46–47, 176n9; land owned by, 173, 184n4; nature and, 13–14, 20, 21; partition affecting, 8–9, 23–24, 27–32; religious practices of, 36, 37, 38, 68–69, 71, 72; religious right mobilizing, 12; religious vs. national lens on, 7–12; restrictions on, 113; as scapegoats, 1, 28; sexuality of, 107; as symbols, 28–29; under Taliban, 162, 163

World War II: kamikaze pilots in, 148; Nagasaki bombed in, 20, 141, 145–47, 156; racism in, 147, 191n4

World Wildlife Fund–Pakistan, 172, 192n4

xenophobia, 55–56

Yaqin, Amina, 171

Yaqoob, Munazza, 176n12

Yoshi (character), 149, 156

Yousafzai, Malala, 1–2, 171

Zamindar, Vazira, 11, 190n2

Zia-ul-Haq, Muhammad, 24–25, 28, 29–30, 181n5; exclusion fostered by, 40, 118; food insecurity and, 47–48; Hudood Ordinances of, 12, 181n5; Islamization under, 9, 24–25, 28–30, 118, 181n5; U.S. support for, 119

Zina Ordinance, 12

Zubair (character), 30

Zubeida (character), 39–40, 47, 49; clothing worn by, 182n12; religious practice of, 36, 37, 38; Saleem and, 30, 40

In the Expanding Frontiers series

To order or obtain more information on
these or other University of Nebraska
Press titles, visit nebraskapress.unl.edu.